Strategic Planning for School Improvemen .

BEMAS/Pitman Publishing Titles

Managing the National Curriculum Edited by Tim Brighouse and Bob Moon

The Search for Standards Edited by Harry Tomlinson

Implementing Educational Reform Edited by Tim Simkins, Linda Ellison and Viv Garrett

Education and Training 14–19 Edited by Harry Tomlinson

Women in Education Management Edited by Janet Ouston

The Supply and Recruitment of School Teachers Edited by Brian Fidler, Barry Fugl and Derek Esp

Improving Initial Teacher Training? New Roles for Teachers, Schools and HE Edited by Myra McCullogh and Brian Fidler

The Management of Educational Policy: Scottish Perspectives Edited by Walter M. Humes and Malcolm MacKenzie

Effective Governors for Effective Schools Edited by Derek Esp and Rene Saran

Strategic Planning for School Improvement

Brian Fidler

with
Maureen Edwards, Barbara Evans,
Philip Mann and Peter Thomas

in association with
The British Educational Management and Administration Society

PITMAN PUBLISHING
128 Long Acre, London WC2E 9AN
Tel: +44(0) 171 447 2000
Fax: +44(0) 171 240 5771

A Division of Pearson Professional Limited

First published in Great Britain 1996

© British Educational Management and Administration Society, 1996

British Library Cataloguing in Publication Data
A CIP catalogue record for this book can be obtained from the British Library.

ISBN 0 273 61645 5

10 9 8 7 6 5 4 3 2 1

Typeset by Phoenix Photosetting, Chatham, Kent
Printed and bound in Great Britain by Redwood Books, Trowbridge, Wiltshire.

The Publishers' policy is to use paper manufactured from sustainable forests.

Contents

Notes on authors

Maureen Edwards is a headteacher in a primary school in Buckinghamshire. She has spent fifteen years in the teaching profession and has been in her present post for five years. She is studying for an MSc in School Management at the University of Reading.

Barbara Evans is a Head of Faculty at the Richard Aldworth Community School, Basingstoke, with responsibility for personal, social, careers and physical education. She has been a secondary-school teacher for twenty years. Her interest in the management of secondary schools through a strategic approach to planning was developed through her work for an MSc at the University of Reading. She carried out an action research project in her own school on strategic management.

Dr Brian Fidler teaches and researches at the University of Reading. He is senior lecturer and course leader for the MSc in Managing School Improvement and editor and author of a number of books on school management. He is editor of *School Organisation*, the international journal specialising in school management and school development. He is also treasurer of the British Educational Management and Administration Society.

Philip Mann, since qualifying as a teacher of physical education at Borough Road College, Isleworth in 1974, spent sixteen years teaching in the London Borough of Ealing at a number of primary schools. For the last five years he has been headteacher of a primary school in Berkshire, during which time he gained an MSc degree in School Management at the University of Reading.

Dr Peter Thomas is headteacher of Tanbridge House School, Horsham, Sussex. He trained as an English teacher and carried out research at Exeter University. He has taught in five large comprehensive schools and community colleges. Before teaching he trained in management and worked in industry. He has contributed to several books on management in schools.

Preface

This book brings together and expands previous work by me on strategy which has appeared in BEMAS publications—the chapter on strategy in schools in *Effective Local Management of Schools* and its companion workbook *ELMS Workbook: Planning Your School's Strategy*. Geoff Bowles and I worked on those two books together and I should like to acknowledge the contribution which discussion with him on the concepts, and his experience of working with schools on their practice, made to my growing understanding of strategy.

I first encountered the concept of strategy when searching for suitable material to be part of a new MSc degree in School Management in 1986 at Bulmershe College, Reading. At that stage it was a small contribution to a course on analytical methods. Subsequent groups of students on that part-time inservice course, who were all practising managers in schools, convinced me that these ideas were relevant and, after the Education Reform Act, essential to senior managers in schools. I have gained a great deal from working with students on that course and its successor, the MSc in Managing School Improvement. They have listened to the ideas, probed, contributed positively and creatively, and helped me to appreciate more fully the significance of the concepts and their operation in schools. The results of a course assignment on strategic analysis became more sophisticated as I and the course members gained experience with strategic ideas.

My co-authors, all heads or senior managers in schools, completed such an assignment and went on to apply the principles of strategic management in their schools. They come from three different local education authorities with different practice in School Development Planning, but have each discovered that strategic planning goes far beyond SDPs and tackles much more fundamental issues. In three of their case studies falling rolls played some part in an interest in strategy. This was at a time when the fall in the roll was not irreversible. This illustrates a fundamental feature of strategy. It involves looking ahead and foreseeing difficulties, rather than waiting until external forces are irresistible.

I am most grateful to my co-authors for finding the time to write their chapters and comment and add to the other sections of the book at a time when they were extremely busy managing schools. Their writing gives a true flavour of the long-term nature of implementing strategy, the strong influence of the culture of the school and of the need for the head and senior managers to take a long view. They tried to press on when possible, to recognise when time was needed for staff to become acquainted with and contribute to the ideas and, finally, gained acceptance for the need for strategic plans.

We all hope that this convinces heads and senior managers of other schools of the importance of strategy and provides evidence of how to go about it successfully.

I should like to acknowledge the support of the BEMAS Publications Committee and particularly its chair, Tim Simkins, in the publication of this book.

Brian Fidler
The University of Reading
September 1995

Terms and abbreviations

Below is a list of terms and abbreviations used in this book. They are collected together and very briefly explained here in order to facilitate continuous reading of the text. The descriptions should not be taken as full explanations of the terms. Further details can be found in the appropriate sections indicated by the index.

Administration   The steady-state process of ensuring that an organisation performs smoothly and efficiently to achieve predetermined goals.

AWPU   Age-weighted pupil unit: the income brought in by each pupil is dependent on the age of the pupil.

Base budget or standstill budget   The resources required to carry out existing commitments but not improve or otherwise augment provision at constant prices.

BPR   Basic Process Re-engineering.

BTEC   Business and Technology Education Council.

Budget   A spending plan indicating organisational priorities.

Cost-benefit analysis   A technique for weighing the total cost of an activity against the perceived advantages resulting from that activity.

DES   Department of Education and Science (1964–92).

DFE   Department for Education (1992–95).

DFEE   Department for Education and Employment (1995–   ).

DVE   Diploma in Vocational Education.

Earmarked expenditure (or budget)   If a particular budget is only permitted to be spent on one type of activity (even though it is a delegated budget) then it is described as earmarked. Inservice training expenditure is one example of this kind. Even though delegated to schools, the total sum may only be spent on inservice training.

Effectiveness   This is the process of ensuring that organisational goals are pursued.

Efficiency   This is the process of ensuring that operations are carried out at least cost. It makes no assumptions about the value of the operations.

ERA   Education Reform Act 1988.

External relations   The process of two-way communication with the world outside the school.

FAS   Funding Agency for Schools: a body administering and funding grant-maintained schools.

Formula funding   ERA has indicated that all primary and secondary schools are to be formula-funded. This means that they will receive funds according to a predetermined set of rules (or formulae). At least 85 per cent of funds will depend on pupil numbers.

FTE (Full-time equivalent)   Where there are part-time pupils or staff the fractions of a full-time person can be aggregated to produce the full-time equivalent persons.

GEST   Grants for Education, Support and Training: grants approved and partly funded by central government which are distributed by LEAs. There are equivalent grants which go directly to GM schools.

GMS   Grant-maintained school (qv).

GNVQ   General National Vocational Qualification.

Grant-maintained school   A school which has been through voting procedures and received the approval of the Secretary of State to cease to be maintained by an LEA will receive similar funding directly from the DFEE.

GRIDS   Guidelines for Review and Internal Development in Schools.

HEADLAMP   Headteachers' Leadership and Management Programme: a scheme for providing training resources for those in their first headship.

HoD   Head of Department.

HRM   Human Resource Management.

IIP   Investors in People.

Incremental budgeting   Devising next year's budget by reference to this year's budget and making small variations, but leaving the general pattern of expenditure unchanged.

Inset   Inservice Education and Training (of teachers).

IT   Information Technology.

LMS   Local Management of Schools.

Management   The proactive process of defining a strategy and goals for an organisation and ensuring that an organisation works towards these goals efficiently and effectively. Goals and strategy will need to be periodically reassessed to ensure that they remain appropriate.

Management information system   A systematic way of generating, manipulating and displaying data to make them useful for assisting management decision-making.

Marginal cost   The cost of providing an extra unit of output (generally assumed to require no extra capital expenditure). This is generally produced at lower cost than the average cost as capital expenditure is spread over more units.

Marketing   For commercial organisations this covers the processes of market research, product/service design, promotion of the product or service and sales.

NFP   Not-for-profit organisations.

NVQ   National Vocational Qualification.

OD   Organisation Development.

OFSTED   Office for Standards in Education: a body responsible for organising school inspections and giving advice to government.

OL   Organisational Learning.

Open enrolment   Parents can express a preference for the school they wish their child to attend. Where the school has spare places the child will be admitted. Where the school is oversubscribed the school has to operate systematic admission procedures to admit children by following predetermined rules.

Opportunity cost   This is the cost of the lost opportunity. It is the value of the best alternative way of deploying the same resources.

Opting-out   The process by which a school may vote to cease to be maintained by its LEA and instead receive equivalent funding directly from the DFEE via the FAS. It thereby becomes a grant-maintained school after approval by the Secretary of State.

Organisational culture   The organisation's shared set of values and procedures that are regarded as organisational norms or 'the way we do things here'.

Organisational strategy   The plan of action for the organisation which affects the whole organisation in the long term and which takes full account of the organisation's environment, including its clients.

Performance indicator   A measure which indicates the level of results being achieved or the operation of a process.

PPBS (Planning Programming Budgeting System)   A process for systematically considering alternative ways of achieving the desired results and identifying the least costly means of achieving the chosen results or outputs.

Promotion   The process of making the activities of an organisation known to the wider community.

PTA   Parent Teacher Association.

SBR   School-based Review.

SCAA   Schools Curriculum and Assessment Authority.

SDP   School Development Plan.

SMT   Senior Management Team.

Standard Admission Number   This is the number of children who may be admitted to a school each year in line with its capacity. This is based upon the amount of space in the school.

STRB   School Teacher Review Body: A statutory body giving advice to government on teachers' pay and conditions of service (1992–   ).

SWOT   Strengths, Weaknesses, Opportunities and Threats.

Top-slicing   The removal of a sum of money from an overall budget before the remainder is then apportioned. In effect this becomes the first priority for spending.

TQM   Total Quality Management.

TSI   Technology Schools Initiative.

TTA   Teacher Training Agency: a statutory body giving advice to Government on initial teacher training and Inset (1993–   ).

TVEE   TVEI Extension: a generalisation of TVEI (qv) to all schools, but with lower funding.

TVEI   Technical and Vocational Education Initiative: extra finance given to selected secondary schools from the Employment Department for agreed additions to the 14–18 curriculum from 1983. These generally involved co-operation between neighbouring schools.

Value-added   An assessment of progress made by children in a school. It is based on the difference between the measured attainment of each child on entering and leaving that phase of education. Recently it has been suggested that positive and negative value-added should relate to the expected progress a child would make in a typical school.

Zero-based budgeting   The taking of spending decisions by re-considering from first principles the justification of every item of expenditure and its contribution to objectives (also called output budgeting or programme budgeting.

Introduction

Purpose of the book

In *Effective Local Management of Schools* (Fidler and Bowles, 1989) we said that we saw 'the need for a strategic plan for the school as of the most over-riding importance' (p. 6). This was because such a plan provided the co-ordination between all other management processes. A chapter introduced the idea of strategy and gave a brief description of the strategic management process. These ideas were further developed in *ELMS Workbook: Planning Your School's Strategy* (Fidler *et al.*, 1991) together with some 60 exercises to help prepare a strategy. The present book presents a synthesis and further development of those ideas, with four examples of strategic management in action. Its purpose is to explain and exemplify the concepts of strategy, strategic planning and strategic management and to help headteachers and other senior staff in schools to develop their strategic thinking and to provide a systematic approach to strategic management.

Since the publication of *Effective Local Management of Schools* the word strategy has begun to be used in education management. However, its meaning is generally assumed to be self-evident but seldom seems to mean anything more than long-term. There is thus an urgent need to try to clarify the concept and introduce some of its complexities. Like staff appraisal, performance-related pay and many other topics, the same word can be taken to mean very different things. This is the source of much needless confusion. There are very different approaches to strategy.

The variety of approaches is instanced by Mintzberg's (1990) ten uses of strategy, Toft's (1989) seven 'one-best ways' of forming strategy and the four-fold typology of approaches to strategy by Whittington (1993). As we make clear, our approach assumes that school aims are pluralist, that strategy is formulated at the school level, and that strategy should be used for planning purposes. However, we follow Mintzberg (1994) in arguing that in strategic planning the accent should be on 'strategic' and not on 'planning', because of the excessively rational and deterministic connotations which this word has for some readers. Thus our approach is different to the rationalist, predictive, top-down approach which characterises the small amount of literature on strategy in school systems in the USA.

Perhaps the most important part of strategy is the attitude of mind by which it is formulated: *strategic thinking*. This is the mode of thinking which encompasses the long term, is constantly researching the external factors which may influence the school in the future, thinks in whole-organisation terms and is aware of, and tries to fully use, organisational capabilities. This is an attitude of mind and many headteachers will intuitively have developed their capacity for forward thinking in this way. Both strategic thinking and strategic management processes are necessary. Just as carrying out the processes in a mechanical way without engaging in strategic thinking would be a waste of time, so strategic thinking inside the head of only one person has its limitations.

The strategic management models provide a way of engaging in strategic thinking in a more systematic way and also provide a way of sharing the process and the results, and their implications, with other people. We believe that this is a vital strength of a systematic approach to strategy.

An important idea related to strategy is that of a strategic decision. A knowledge of strategic management should provide help in recognising such decisions. They are decisions which have strategic implications once they are made. For example, almost any decision concerned with buildings is likely to be strategic. The location of a new school and the positioning and design of new buildings have long-term implications for future pupil numbers and teaching arrangements. These range from the number and size of teaching groups which can be formed, to the kind of activities which can be carried out. A decision to build or extend an 'open-plan' school is such a strategic decision. Many other areas also contain strategic decisions; for example staffing appointments and taking part in externally funded initiatives.

Such opportunities to make strategic decisions often come up at short notice (though the time-scale for their implementation may be long-term) and so it is important to have a strategy in mind such that when such opportunities come along there is a basis for evaluating their implications. Without a broadly conceived strategy there are no opportunities (or threats). Only if there are intentions can opportunities and hindrances be recognised. The first imperative is to recognise a strategic decision. Often it may seem at first sight to be insignificant, and only with further examination do some of the long-term possibilities show up. Having recognised a decision as strategic, its seriousness and importance can be appreciated.

Although this book is intended to be of practical help to those in schools who are engaged in, or wish to engage in, strategic planning, its style is primarily to contribute to an understanding of how the process can be carried out. The models need to be adapted to the circumstances of each school. Practical exercises to help devise and implement strategy are available in *ELMS Workbook: Planning Your School's Strategy.*

The explanation of strategic management and the copious references to other sources to follow up will, we hope, make this a suitable course reader for those engaged in courses of study for masters' degrees and other courses in school management.

Theory, models and conceptual frameworks

We echo the plea in *Effective Local Management of Schools* for an appreciation of the value of conceptual frameworks, models and theories as an aid to management understanding and practice.

What we have in mind for useful theory is that elements of it should:

- provide a shorthand for describing events
- summarise much empirical evidence
- provide concepts of some explanatory power
- use models to demonstrate inter-relationships
- use models and theories to provide a language to exchange ideas with other people

To do these things we have in mind not one great theory, but a series of models and inter-relationships which provide a framework for thinking about a particular aspect of management. This will involve the creation and adaptation of concepts and the linking of ideas together for particular purposes.

Models and theories should provide an aid to understanding. But models and theories cannot give a best course of action. They can, at the most, give a conditional best course of action. The successful manager is the one who can match the model or theory to the appropriate conditions and use it to understand the situation, discuss it with others and move on to appropriate action, whilst storing away the learning experiences from having managed the course of action.

All managers have their **implicit theories of action**:

Introduction

> *To paraphrase John Maynard Keynes, the great economist, 'Practical men, who believe themselves to be quite exempt from any intellectual influences, are usually the slaves of some defunct theorist'.* (Quinn et al., 1988, p. xviii)

Or as Anne Jones puts it in *Leadership for Tomorrow's Schools*, when talking of the spider's-web model of leadership:

> *. . . we see that it was the Headteachers with this invisible role model in their heads who felt the greatest sense of failure.* (Jones, 1987, p. 128)

Schon's work (1983; 1987) suggests that professionals need to be exposed to formal theoretical knowledge so that they can combine this with their own particular abstraction of theory-from-experience, in order to engage in refection-in-action when carrying out their professional work (Fidler, 1994).

The intimate connection between theory and practice is well expressed in this quotation:

> *There is nothing impractical about good theory . . . Action divorced from theory is the random scurrying of a rat in a new maze. Good theory is the power to find the way to the goal with a minimum of lost motion and electric shock.* (Mort and Ross, 1957, p. 4)

Finally,

> *Theory presents an integrating and common framework for the development of knowledge . . . theory guides action, for it should provide the basis for making decisions about practical everyday questions. Concepts and theories enable the practitioner to 'make sense' out of the complexities of reality and thus provide for strategic and rational action. Without useful concepts and theories, both researchers and practitioners flounder aimlessly on a random tide of events.* (Hoy and Miskel, 1978, p. 23)

A good test of theoretical ideas is that proposed by Edgar Schein:

> *For me a theory is no good if I cannot find illustrations in everyday life of the phenomenon with which the theory deals and if I cannot observe and feel the impact of what the theory or model purports to explain.* (Schein, 1985, p. xii)

It is our intention that the theoretical material in this book should meet this test. We have sought theoretical ideas from a diversity of sources, particularly the literature on strategic management in non-educational organisations. But it has been chosen for its relevance to strategic management in schools.

Managing school improvement

The whole basis of strategic management is that each school decides on its own strategy. This takes account of its present strategic position, present and future external influences and what its stakeholders expect of it. The effects of stakeholder expectations are an integral part of the calculus of formulating an acceptable strategy. An integral part of strategy is a reconsideration of the aims of each school. Thus the concept of school effectiveness relates to each school rather than being absolute, since the aims of schools are not universalistic.

Similarly, the improvements which the strategy incorporates will relate to the needs of the individual school at this point in time and for the medium-term future (five years or more). Again there can be no universalities about what improvements are needed. Some will involve remedying deficiencies and others will involve a creative vision of a better future. This all puts into context the value of the school effectiveness and school improvement movements. Evidence from research from these two areas should be critically appraised for its value for the task of each individual school as it plans its own strategy. These issues are pursued in more detail in Chapter 2.

Again we return to *Effective Local Management of Schools* for the basis of the assumptions on which we offer any guidance given in this book:

1 whilst there is considerable professional agreement about what characterises an effective school, it remains for each school to articulate in its own terms what will constitute an effective school;

2 we believe effective schools, if they come about in an intentional way, come about through the action of effective leadership and management at all levels;

3 we believe effective management consists of deploying resources efficiently and working with and through people in order to achieve desired results;

4 we believe what constitutes an effective school can only really be articulated in terms of its outcomes for pupils and staff;

5 outcomes include cognitive and behavioural learning and the development of positive attitudes;

6 we believe each school should develop its own strategy for improvement which meets needs that have been identified in the strategic analysis process.

Thus, effective schools have to articulate the sorts of outcomes that they wish pupils leaving that school to attain. Managers then have to articulate the means by which these outcomes will be achieved. The fundamental point is that schools primarily exist to facilitate students' learning. Thus, the strategic management process is an enabling process for that fundamental purpose. School management is about facilitating and ensuring effective education. There should be no ducking the issue that what constitutes an effective school and what constitutes improvement are value-judgements.

We believe the challenge for school managers is to identify indicators of what both they and their clients believe to represent an effective school, and thereby demonstrate the increasing success of their school based on these criteria.

Plan of the book

Chapters 1, 3, 4, 5 and 6 present theoretical work on strategy. The practical implications of the theory are indicated. Chapter 2 critically examines school effectiveness research and some approaches to school improvement. It also outlines an approach to the management of planned change, and briefly describes some current management approaches to improvement. Chapters 7 and 8 describe the approach of two primary schools to strategic management for school improvement, whilst Chapters 9 and 10 describe two secondary schools' approaches. A final chapter briefly examines the features that emerge from the case studies and examines four factors that might be used to aid strategic planning in schools.

Chapter 1 investigates strategy and approaches to strategy in not-for-profit organisations and schools. It introduces the concept of strategy and identifies a number of issues on which writers about strategy differ. It examines the difficulties and the advantages which schools have in engaging in strategic planning. Some examples of school strategies are presented and school improvement is defined. Finally, a warning to beware of fads is given.

Strategic management is not an easy process to envisage and so in Chapter 3, three complementary approaches are modelled. Each highlights certain features of the process and, taken together, they should help illuminate the techniques of analysis, choice and implementation. The final model considers the effects of strategy formation under conditions of severe competition and unpredictable and rapidly changing environmental conditions. Whilst these conditions may not be prevalent in most schools, the conditions which give rise to the failures of the strategic planning process are worth considering, since these are always potential weaknesses of the strategic planning process.

Chapter 4 begins by rehearsing some models for thinking about the working of schools as organisations. Any choice of model should be based on which one is helpful for thinking and planning for any particular issue in a particular school. Leadership actions will be different, depending on which model is selected. The value of models is both for the individual, and his or her thinking, and also for groups. A model can be discussed and tested in a group in order to validate its appropriateness. It also provides a common framework for discussion between group members about a situation.

Leadership is a major topic discussed in Chapter 4. Increasingly, leadership is taken to mean those processes of bringing about change by inspiring others to follow. Management is reserved for the processes of implementing the changes. Clearly both are vitally important. The four styles of leadership of Bolman and Deal (1991) indicate four components which may be needed within leadership. Although an individual headteacher will have a personal preference for a style, there may be others in the senior team who can complement the strengths of the headteacher. The crucial questions concern—for the model of organisation which we consider our school to be—which style(s) of leadership will be required to go through the strategy formation process successfully. Compared to many other management processes, strategy will place a higher emphasis on symbolic leadership. There are two aspects to symbolism. One is carrying out actions for their symbolic value, the other is considering how others may imbue primarily rational actions with unintended symbolic significance.

The details of the strategic management process are considered in Chapters 5 and 6. Chapter 5 considers the processes of strategic analysis and strategic choice. Environmental scanning is one of the components of strategic analysis and is, perhaps, the principal instrument of strategic orientation and strategic thinking. It is the process of sensing and analysing external influences on the school which may be important to its future. At this level, it could be taken to mean a static process of auditing the present; however, the essence of strategy is to be forward-thinking and to try to foresee which influences may be important in the future. These need to be tracked, as time goes by, for their rising or falling influence. Many of these influences will be political as they would be in many organisations, particularly public-sector organisations; but an additional source for schools with curricular responsibilities is the diagnosing of trends that have curricular implications. What may be important to introduce into the curriculum to prepare children for the future?

A further element of some significance in the analysis process is an assessment of the culture and values of the school. This is important for two reasons. First, unless the prevailing assumptions in the organisation are brought to the surface, these will unwittingly condition the results of the whole analysis process. The culture is the repository of the perspective through which facts, and more importantly prospects, are viewed. Thus an unconsciously biased view of the future would emerge. Second, any large change will involve a change to the culture. Some assessment of how difficult this will be is needed before any decision is taken. At any point in time some strategies may be ruled out because the change in the culture of the school is too great.

As Mintzberg (1994) has pointed out, one of the least remarked processes in strategy formation is how a creative plan emerges from a largely reactive, analytical process. Three techniques for aiding this process are presented in Chapter 5—vision formation, strategic issues identification and goal setting.

Chapter 6 covers the process of strategic change and the implementation of strategy. Influences on school culture are examined in some detail. We take the view that in ordinary conditions only restricted changes can be made to the culture at any time. More may be possible in adverse circumstances (such as falling rolls), but in more normal circumstances there are limits to the changes that people make in their deeper levels of basic assumptions about the purpose and operation of an institution like a school. The long history of changes never institutionalised is testimony to this view. With good planning, change is possible, but there are limits. The means of bringing about change in school culture is discussed. A most significant means is the employment of new staff—such staff need to be selected on this basis, and great trouble taken with their induction.

Strategy is only a means to an end and not an end in its own right. Implicitly, strategy is concerned with improvement, although in some cases it will be survival that is the major spur. In this latter case it may still represent an improvement compared to the situation of no new strategy or strategic drift. We take a very neutral view of school improvement. However, we do assume that the improvement is chosen by the school, it is implemented by the school and it is consonant with the operation of the school. At first sight the findings of school effectiveness research would appear to be a fruitful place to search for ideas.

Chapter 2 critically appraises literature on school effectiveness and school improvement. School effectiveness correlates (Edmonds, 1979), such as:

- strong leadership

- concentration on basics

- orderly atmosphere

- high expectations

- frequent monitoring of progress

are recognised as correlates with elementary school education in inner-city schools concerned with basic skills in the USA, and hence are of restricted value for schools in the UK. They and other correlates based on work in the UK are seen as of limited value as regards the process of school improvement and to have other conceptual and methodological weaknesses. For example, where is any empirical evidence on the value of strategy, management development or school-based review?

School effectiveness, like value-added, is an appealing concept which has huge methodological difficulties when empirical research is contemplated. Initial efforts look to produce interesting results, but more effort and critical scrutiny of the methodology show up inadequacies which subsequent effort is not able to put right. Such work needs informed scrutiny rather than uncritical acceptance. So far, only cognitive results (which most readily lend themselves to quantitative work) have been the main focus for school effectiveness and value-added research, but the outcomes of schooling cover much else in addition to exam results.

As we said in 1989 it is for schools to decide what is effective in terms of what they and their clients expect of the school. Although the OFSTED framework for school inspections has appeared subsequently, it too should be treated as a general guide. The particular priorities in terms of the various outcome measures and process measures on which OFSTED inspectors report should be regarded as management information for the school, to be assessed in its planning processes, rather than slavishly followed.

The management of planned change is thought to offer a different and worthwhile approach to improving schools compared to the findings of school improvement researchers. Most such work has consisted of external attempts to improve schools rather than internal attempts. The over-riding conundrum for such attempts is how to get commitment from schools for top-down improvement schemes, since all the evidence points to the essential need for commitment from head and staff. This book is written for those inside schools who wish to take the initiative to improve. They may use external help, but as consultants to the school, and not as purveyors of school improvement. It is for each school to decide what, how and when to improve.

Introduction

A range of possible management and other innovations and aids to improvement are briefly described and further reading cited. Some of these could be strategies, and others could be parts of strategies. The range is:

- Organisational Learning (OL)

- Organisation Development (OD)

- Quality initiatives

- Basic Process Re-engineering (BPR)

- School-based Review (SBR)

- School inspections

- Human Resource Management initiatives (HRM)

- Consultancy

The four case studies in Chapters 7 to 10 show strategy in action in two primary and two secondary schools. In three schools it is the formulation of a strategy for the whole school which is described; in the other it is a strategic decision to broaden the scope of sixth-form provision. The authors describe at first hand their experience of beginning a strategic approach. They give the context of their schools to allow the reader to appreciate similarities with and differences from their own context, and give the previous history of school development planning in their school. They give their reasons for engaging in strategic management and then relate their experience of strategic analysis. In each case, data were collected from a number of stakeholders—parents, children, governors and staff. The value of this, in terms of changing the orientation of the school to be more outward-looking rather than predominantly inward-looking, is clear. Following analysis, choices were formulated and courses of action for the medium term (five years and over) planned in greater detail for the early stages than the later ones. The confidence which comes from the clarification of the purpose of each school and plans to make improvements is clearly evident.

These case studies are enormously valuable. They give credibility to the process and illustrate the ways in which the participants have learned about strategy in schools and from which the reader can learn too. It is important to start by creating a plan of how the process of strategic planning will be conducted. This is the guide from which departures can be noted and adjustments made.

The final chapter examines the lessons from the case studies and proposes ways in which strategic planning for school improvement could be encouraged.

As we warned in the *ELMS Workbook,* the ideas may seen daunting. However, it is possible to select from the strategy process that which seems achievable in the first instance, with the expectation that in future a more comprehensive approach can be carried out. There will inevitably be learning from practice which will inform future actions.

1

What is strategy?

Introduction

This chapter examines the concepts of strategy and strategic planning. It identifies a number of distinctly different approaches to strategic planning. Whilst these were developed for the business world, they have increasingly been taken up by public and not-for-profit organisations. Their applicability to schools is considered and some examples of strategies in schools are given. Finally, the definition of school improvement used in this book is given with a warning of the need to differentiate improvements from mere fads.

The concept

Strategy is concerned with the long-term future of an organisation—that which makes it distinctive, the broad direction it takes.

Quinn (1980, p. 7) describes strategy thus: 'A strategy is the pattern or plan that integrates an organisation's major goals, policies, and action sequences into a cohesive whole.'

Drawing on Olsen and Eadie (1982), Bryson (1988, p. 5) identifies the essence of strategic planning for the non-profit sector as: 'a disciplined effort to produce fundamental decisions and actions that shape and guide what an organisation . . . is, what it does, and why it does it'.

It is the plan which integrates all the actions of the school, as shown in Figure 1.1.

Based upon the definition of strategy used by Johnson and Scholes (1993) we shall take the distinguishing features of the strategic plan to involve:

1 the long term

2 the future of the whole school in an integrated way

Strategic Planning for School Improvement

Figure 1.1   Strategic plan as an integrating element
Source: Fidler and Bowles, 1989, p. 273

3 taking account of future trends in the world outside the school, and

4 taking account of its present, and likely future, resources

The advantages of a systematic approach to strategy as proposed in this book are:

(a) important factors are less likely to be neglected

(b) information and reactions can come from a wider group

(c) others in the organisation develop a whole-organisation view

(d) the opportunities and constraints are known to everyone and others can propose developments which take advantage of opportunities

(e) other decisions can be made in the knowledge of the strategy

(f) implicit strategy can be tested and improved by the constructive criticism of others

(g) strategic decisions can be more easily recognised

Strategic decisions are those decisions which when taken have strategic implications. Those decisions which have long-term consequences are most likely to be strategic. Thus decisions concerning buildings and staffing are likely to be strategic.

Often 'opportunities' come along and relatively quick decisions are required to take advantage of them. However, what may be an opportunity to one school may not be to another. It is only when a school has a strategy that opportunities can be recognised.

From the foregoing, it can be seen that in some senses strategy is a way of thinking and that perhaps the most important attribute is to be able to think strategically.

Strategy is a difficult concept, and some popular writing and prescription have suggested new ways of devising strategy without fully understanding the original ideas. Thus there is a great tendency to pronounce that processes don't work, and to offer a 'gee whiz' quick-fix alternative, without ever having fully understood the concepts. Snakeoil salespeople abound!

Development of strategic ideas

In the business sector there has been increasing interest in strategic management for more than thirty years, with an explosion of publications in the last fifteen. Influential writers include Quinn and Porter in the USA and Mintzberg in Canada. A very valuable synthesis and development of this work appeared in this country in 1984 by Johnson and Scholes and was revised extensively in 1993. Strategy in business organisations has two facets:

1 deciding on what business to be in (usually called corporate strategy), and

2 deciding how best to conduct that business

Clearly for schools the first question is already largely decided and only the second question remains.

Some of the recent literature has acknowledged that strategic management should go on in all sectors, whether commercial or not. Thus there has been adaptation of the ideas from the business world to the *not-for-profit sector* (Bryson, 1988), where it is recognised that political considerations are likely to play a much larger part than in commercial organisations. Some of these sources attempt to add a management dimension to previous work on policy-making in public-sector organisations.

As the concept of strategy has developed, differences have emerged in views about whether strategy should be:

- explicit or implicit

- prospective or emergent

- carried out by planners or managers

Explicit or implicit

The debate concerns whether strategic plans exist only in the minds of individuals (but nevertheless affect their actions) or whether they are set down in writing.

The contribution of the two approaches is described by Steiner (1979, p. 10) thus:

> It is not at all unusual to find in organisations a clash between these two approaches to strategic decision-making ... They can and should complement one another. A formal system can and should help managers sharpen their intuitive–anticipatory inputs into the planning process.

Barry (1986, p. 14), after considerable work with small non-profit-making organisations in the USA, gives this advice:

> In one sense strategic planning can be viewed as an effort to duplicate what goes on in the mind of a gifted intuitive leader. Such leaders know well the strengths and weaknesses of their organisations; they see opportunities and threats before others do; they know instinctively the best way to proceed—sometimes without formal planning ... If your organisation has such a leader, you may not need to develop a formal strategic plan. Strategic planning, however, is sometimes used by such leaders as a way of sharing their vision—of bringing others along for the ride.
>
> Other organisations prefer to muddle along without formal planning. In its best form, muddling is jumping in and responding quickly to new opportunities as they emerge ... Done well, creative muddling can be an effective form of operating. Done poorly, it can kill an organisation. If your organisation is an effective muddler, you may want to consider whether formal strategic planning is the best way to go.

Prospective or emergent

This debate concerns whether strategy is formulated before action, or whether it is only apparent in retrospect after a series of decisions have been made:

> Strategies may be looked at as either a priori statements to guide action or a posteriori results of actual decision behaviour. One, therefore, must look at the actual emerging pattern of the enterprise's operant goals, policies and major programmes to see what its true strategy is. (Mintzberg, 1972, quoted in Quinn et al., 1988, p. 4)

Mintzberg uses the term 'emergent strategy' for that which is evident after the event and 'intended strategy' for that which was planned. The difference reflects the observation that change generally produces some unexpected results. It is not intended that there should be any inconsistency between what is announced as the strategy and subsequent actions. Cynicism can be expected if this is the case.

Figure 1.2 (from Mintzberg, 1994) shows the process of changing from an emergent (current strategy) to a new strategy (realised strategy). Deliberations in the planning process produce an intended strategy. As this is put into effect, the deliberate strategy is that part which is implemented, but the combination of the existing strategy and the deliberate strategy produces a realised strategy, which is a combination of the two. This is a change from the present, but not wholly what was intended.

Clearly, in this diagrammatic representation, it is the angle between the realised strategy and the intended strategy which is an indication of the extent to which it is sensible to talk about using strategy for planning purposes in anything more than an indicative way. If there is a large angle between the two, then the planned strategy was not a good indication of the final outcome.

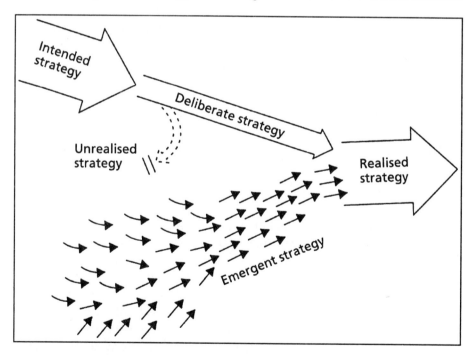

Figure 1.2   Intended, emergent and realised strategies
Source: reproduced from Mintzberg, 1994, p. 24, by permission of the publisher, Prentice Hall International, Hemel Hempstead

Some writers have pointed out the unpredictable environment in which schools and other organisations find themselves and have concluded that such long term planning as strategy requires is not possible. They point to recent work on the study of chaos (Gleick, 1988) and how final outcomes are very sensitive to initial conditions. Any mis-diagnosis of these will lead to large errors within a short space of time. However, we believe that such conclusions are not generally valid because:

1 They postulate a precise, rigid strategy which operates unchanged in the long term rather than one which can be modified under adverse circumstances.

2 A cardinal feature of the strategic model proposed here is the detection, monitoring and anticipation of changes in the environment.

3 Detecting trends in the environment is a skill which improves with practice.

Mintzberg (1994), however, warns against too free a use of the concept of 'flexible planning', a term which he regards as an oxymoron. Planning has value precisely because it gives predictability to actions and so if plans are changed the value of planning is undermined. This must be a matter of degree rather than an absolute, but he is quite right; there are limits to the flexibility which can be claimed whilst retaining the major value of plans.

We follow Mintzberg in recognising that in strategic planning the accent should be on strategy rather than planning.

Mintzberg (1994) has also pointed out, with a series of examples, that every decade seems turbulent to writers who experience it whilst the previous decade, by comparison, seems to have been relatively placid and predictable. This would suggest that few contemporary writers have any sense of history and that environmental trends are easier to distinguish in retrospect than prospect.

However, such criticisms do point out the need for continuous monitoring of the external world so that large influences are detected as they grow, rather than a once-and-for-all assessment being made at one point in time and this assessment forming the basis for planning which is both inflexible and insensitive to changing conditions. Hargreaves (1995) has pointed out the importance of 'feedback' within the monitoring process to take action if new influences come along or if implementation does not proceed as expected. However, as Stacey (1993) warns, in complicated systems, feedback itself can be a cause of instability and the political nature of many organisations means that all feedback is not necessarily of the negative kind which leads to stability.

Four approaches to strategy

As strategy has become more important in commercial organisations the number of approaches to strategy has increased. Thus to talk of strategic management as a monolithic entity is rather wide of the mark. Toft (1989) has analysed seven 'one-best ways' to generate strategy; Bryson and Roering (1987) identified nine private-sector approaches to strategic planning and assessed their applicability to public and non-profit organisations; Mintzberg (1990) has classified ten schools of thought on strategy formation; and Whittington (1993) has produced a four-fold typology to group different approaches.

In addition to the differences of purpose between profit-making organisations and the more pluralistic purposes of not-for-profits, there is a further distinction concerned with the two alternative theoretical approaches to strategy identified above—whether strategy is deliberate or emergent. Whittington (1993) has helpfully classified different approaches to strategy based on their differences on these two dimensions—the purposes of the organisation and the view of strategy (see Figure 1.3).

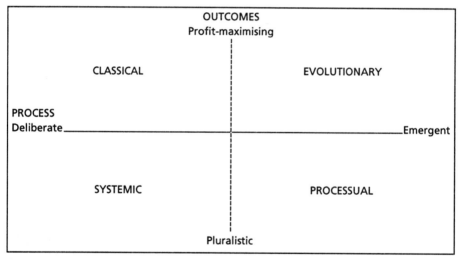

Figure 1.3 Four approaches to strategy
Source: reproduced from Whittington, 1993, p. 3, by permission of the publisher, Routledge, London

View of the process

There are those who propose the purposeful creation and management of strategy—directing strategy—and at the other end of the continuum there are those who maintain that strategy is only visible in retrospect—emerging strategy.

Clarity of outcomes

The extent to which the outcomes of strategy are few and clear compared to many-faceted, ambiguous and value-laden is also a dimension which divides those who have studied strategy.

Thus Whittington (1993) divides approaches to strategy into four quadrants with the above two dimensions as axes. From this it is clear that only those approaches which are at the pluralistic end of the clarity spectrum are likely to be of value to schools. This, however, still leaves competing approaches as to how far strategy can be a positive planning tool, as opposed to a process which involves taking strategic decisions, many of which are only acknowledged as such in retrospect. It is clear that either of these views in pure form is likely to be untenable. In practice both views will have some validity, and it must be a matter of judgement as to which is the best descriptor of the process in particular circumstances.

Needless to say, the approach proposed here lies in the bottom left quadrant. Outcomes are regarded as problematic, value-laden and likely to be different in different schools. However, we believe that strategy can be a useful planning tool, not in a deterministic sense but more in a probabilistic sense. The approach deals in probabilities of likely effects and outcomes rather than accurate predictions.

Carried out by planners or managers

As we have indicated earlier, there is a good deal of confusion between strategy and long-term planning. Indeed, as we have seen above, in the rational quadrant they have much in common. Much of the long-term planning literature consists of quantitative forecasting. Not surprisingly, in rapidly changing conditions, such long-term forecasts soon become inaccurate and out-of-date. They have generally not tried to take environmental, resource and cultural influences into account and thus do not merit the title strategic.

Such planners have also played a part in strategic planning and in Mintzberg's (1994) view have played an over-dominant role. From the title of his recent book, *The Rise and Fall of Strategic Planning*, it might be thought that the present book is redundant, but fortunately, even following Mintzberg's thesis, this isn't so. His argument is that in large corporations strategic planning has been left to corporate planners and this has led to an over-emphasis on rational long-term plans. After illustrating the results of this in detail it is clear that he is calling for managers to play a larger part in formulating strategy and it is the 'rise and fall of strategic planners' that is his real target. Thus when it is reported that large corporations are abandoning strategic planning, this is a misunderstanding. They are downgrading their strategic planning departments, but strategic planning remains an essential function for managers.

Mintzberg draws attention to the planning dilemma: planners have time but not power or the necessary soft information about the environment, whilst managers don't have time but do have the power and information. At the limit this involves a choice between 'extinction by instinct' if strategy is left to managers and 'paralysis by analysis' if it is left to planners (Kast and Rosenweig, 1970, p. 390). Thus Mintzberg proposes complementary roles for planners and managers, both in terms of what information they bring to the process, and also in terms of their abilities and interests.

In schools, of course, there are no specialist planners, only managers. However, many of the attributes contributed by planners can be substituted by adopting a systematic process as we have proposed earlier, in order for managers and others in schools to plan strategy. Time, however, will remain a problem.

Strategy in business

Not surprisingly, strategy in business thinking is very bound up with competition: 'The fundamental basis of above-average performance in the long run is *sustainable competitive advantage*' (Porter, 1985, p. 11).

In commercial organisations Porter believes that there are two types of competitive advantage: low cost or differentiation. For non-commercial organisations, where there is no direct cost to the client, clearly this would reduce to differentiation from the client's point of view (the funder, however, may be interested in low cost). Differentiation could be achieved either across the whole range of an organisation's activities or in a narrow segment (some of these activities). This latter is called differentiation focus or niche differentiation.

There are a number of means of differentiation 'if there are a number of attributes that are widely valued by buyers' (p. 12). These may go beyond just carrying out the basic organisational task better. They may be achieved by the way that the organisation goes about the task, or by its marketing approach.

Porter's basic thesis is that organisations must choose which is their basic strategy and then follow it. He believes that those who try to follow more than one generic strategy become 'stuck in the middle' and this is 'a recipe for below-average performance' (p. 16) because the different strategies generally require inconsistent actions and none are then successful:

> *Being 'all things to all people' is a recipe for strategic mediocrity and below average performance because it often means that a firm has no competitive advantage at all.* (p. 12)

Once achieved, the generic strategy has to be sustained. This requires constant effort in a competitive world. Competitors may imitate or the advantage may fade in the eyes of the consumers. Thus it is usually necessary for a firm 'to offer a moving target' to its competitors (p. 20).

Even for public-sector organisations, which do not basically see themselves as competitive, this concept of differentiation may be a useful one. It can encourage them to tease out what their basic strengths are, both to inform their clients and also to give a sense of pride to the organisation.

Not-for-profit organisations and strategy

The spur to commercial organisations to engage in strategy has largely been competition from other organisations and a need to anticipate trends in the environment in which they operate. For many not-for-profit organisations the attraction of devising a strategy has been even more basic. Where their funding has been discretionary, they have recognised that to survive they need to ensure that they offer a desirable, credible and fundable service (Hatten, 1982; Barry, 1986; Bryson and Roering, 1987; Bryson, 1988; Wheelan and Hunger, 1990).

Not-for-profit organisations have a number of distinctive features compared to most commercial organisations. They generally have more diffuse aims and have a strong service ethic. They are generally judged and are influenced to a greater extent by political considerations. Finally, and perhaps most critically, their clients do not usually fund the service directly.

This last feature, which is shared with publicly funded schools, means that income and client satisfaction are not directly related. Whilst there may be high client satisfaction, funding may go down for quite unconnected reasons. This also means that greater income cannot be raised by increasing the client satisfaction of existing clients, because they are not in a position to pay more for the service provided. Thus there may be two different agendas: one concerned with providing a good service and the other concerned with pleasing paymasters who may have a rather different political set of criteria for judgement.

Although there are these and other differences compared to commercial organisations, there are a number of trends which have gone right across the public sector and other organisations—delegation of authority and finance to lower levels; pressure on quality of client service; concentration on outcomes and cost. Perhaps because of these trends and the attraction of strategic planning in its own right, there has been increasing interest in approaches to strategic planning in the public and not-for-profit sector.

Strategy and schools

The Education Reform Act and LMS have attempted, in part, to make a connection between a school's income and the service it provides. The clear connection is to the number of children in the school, but it is still not directly related to client satisfaction or quality of service. The effects that competition between schools may have on these latter two factors will both depend on geography (with least effect on a rural school), and in any case will be two of many influences on choice of school. Strategically, however, pupil numbers now exert a strong influence on the future of a school.

In addition to sharing the features of other not-for-profit organisations, state schools in England and Wales also have additional distinctive features. These are:

1 *Value laden*: unlike most services offered, there are large differences of opinion about the purposes of schools which depend on value positions.

2 *Majority of professional workers*: the majority of full-time members of staff are highly educated and share professional assumptions.

3 *Combination of professional and managerial work by most workers*: most organisations have a group that manages and a larger group that provides the service.

4 *Dual client*: parents and children are the primary clients, in addition to others who the school serves.

5 *Professional standards set by national inspection*: there are standards which will be inspected, and published, by other professionals who are neither funders nor clients.

6 *Legal requirements to follow a curriculum*: the school is not free to offer its own curriculum, which reduces the extent to which a school can make itself distinctive.

7 *Difficulty in measuring outcomes*: there are difficulties in assessing professional outcomes and these may, or may not, be the basis on which clients make their choice of school and express their satisfaction.

8 *Ambiguous employer for LEA schools*: personnel responsibilities are shared between the LEA and the school.

Before the Education Reform Act, state schools could reasonably suppose that they were part of a managed system; that their need for planning was restricted to internal school developments; and that their future survival and general position in the sector were in the hands of the LEA.

As a result of research in twenty schools and questioning many heads on training courses, Everard (1986, p. 57) observed:

> *My impression is that school managers are weak in . . . the ability to sense what is going to happen and then to get ready to meet the future head-on—forward planning, in fact.*

In a book in the late 1980s Anne Jones, a former headteacher, recognised the need for a strategic view including:

> *the ability to articulate a coherent framework or philosophy, a set of over-arching goals which mean something to the members of the whole school community.* (Jones, 1987, p. 9)

Thus there has been an embryonic realisation of the importance of some explicit overall direction for the school that now assumes increasing importance in an era of choice and diversity. Since 1985 the process of school development planning has been increasingly used (Fidler, 1996a) by schools to plan their curriculum and staff development. However, the survival of the school is rather more fundamental than envisaged by school development planning, and the National Audit Office (1994) has reported the need for a more encompassing plan for grant-maintained schools. The principal differences between school development planning and strategic planning (Fidler, 1996a) are that strategy:

- questions the aims of the school

- investigates the strategic standing of the school

- takes account of present and future environmental influences

- incorporates a vision of what the school should be like

- plans for the longer term

- is holistic

- is proactive or initiative-taking

Strategy is not, however, in the forefront of heads' thinking. Neither recent accounts of the management experiences of secondary heads, nor a recent book for primary heads looking forward to the next century, contained any mention of strategy. Strategy is, however, beginning to appear in the education management literature, but often as a word which is not clearly defined and appears to mean little more than a general reference to the longer term. However, there is some literature from the USA containing strategic ideas for those in schools (McCane, 1986; Patterson *et al.*, 1986; Kaufman and Herman, 1991; Kaufman, 1995). These envisage a very restricted role for schools in strategies set by school districts. Even worse, Mintzberg (1994, p. 405), commenting on literature such as Kaufman and Herman (1991), regards the machine-bureaucratic and rationalistic planning, of such a top-down kind, as entirely inappropriate for professional organisations. He describes this as 'trying to fit square pegs of planning, into the round holes of organisation'.

A paper by Warner (1994) from Israel compares two approaches to strategy for a religious school in France. One is described as a 'values-based cultural approach' attributed to Sergiovanni (1990; 1991), and the other a classical rational approach. He sees these as complementary approaches which a principal should use. Other work is forthcoming (Giles, 1995a; 1995b; Glover *et al.*, 1996).

These are in addition to the chapter entitled 'Strategic Planning in Schools' (Fidler, 1989) and the *ELMS Workbook: Planning Your School's Strategy* (Fidler *et al.*, 1991).

Advantages schools have in planning strategy

Schools have many advantages as regards strategy and strategic management.

1 Purpose

Schools have as their prime purpose the education of children and young people. They don't have the difficult task of deciding which business to be in. They are in the education business, although they may be able to:

- opt out of LEA control

- merge infant and junior schools

- select their entry

- extend their age range
  11–16 to 11–18
  11–18 to 7–18 (London Oratory School has been given permission to take a small number of junior pupils with musical ability (Scott-Clark and Hymas, 1995))

- offer a curriculum emphasis (e.g. technology college and language college initiatives)

- offer after-school and holiday activities

However, within a general educational remit, the precise purposes of schools, as voiced by stakeholders, are very diffuse and difficult to prioritise.

2 Size

All the staff of a school can be collected together in one hall and can participate in strategy formation, compared to a multinational company where all the workforce are not even on the same continent. This is not to say that all staff should be involved in all stages, but that communication and involvement are smaller problems in smaller organisations.

3 Largely professional workforce

Teachers and most people connected with schools have many shared assumptions about how schools should operate. Teachers, through their professional training, have acquired experience and been inducted into the values of educators. By their education they have acquired the powers of critical, open-minded and constructive thought. On the other hand, this shared culture can be an impediment to radical thinking.

4 Behavioural skills

Teachers, by the nature of their work, are good at acquiring and explaining ideas to others. They are used to discussing, synthesising ideas and working together. Whilst teachers have these natural advantages compared to many organisations, there is still a need to consider and develop these behavioural skills and to manage the processes of consultation and participation.

5 Decision-makers

For most schools the decision-making body for strategy will be the governing body. This has the advantage of having members from a number of constituencies, including a majority from outside the school, and includes representatives of the parents of children in the school. However, since the members of the governing body are part-time and unpaid, most of the work involved in devising strategy will be the responsibility of those inside the school. Involving some governors in this process has the advantage of retaining an outside perspective and of ensuring a nucleus of support from the governing body, who are able to explain and defend the proposals.

As we have indicated earlier, strategy is not an easy concept. Those who have studied strategy in other organisations are not in agreement about appropriate conceptualisations, nor whether strategy can be used prospectively or only identified with any certainty in hindsight. Needless to say, we believe that it can be used for future planning and that a suitably eclectic approach is worthwhile.

However, it is worth subjecting the work of others to a critical appraisal so that the limitations of the approach to be proposed are clear. In this way, hopes will not be raised too high and realistic expectations can be satisfied.

Examples of school strategies

Some further examples of strategies in addition to the more obvious structural ones given above may be helpful to illustrate the variety of possibilities.

It is reported that some independent schools, former direct-grant grammar schools, may be interested in rejoining the state system (Hugill, 1995).

Earlier, the generic strategies of differentiation and niche differentiation were mentioned. In a school context, differentiation would most obviously apply to the curriculum. Thus whilst offering the National Curriculum, a school could plan to achieve a higher reputation for innovation or high standards in a particular subject or range of subjects, e.g. music, technology or sport. A niche strategy would involve offering this curriculum only to selected children, either by having a generally selective entry or selection on the basis of a special aptitude and interest in the school specialism. Murgatroyd and Morgan (1992) offer examples of schools from the UK and North America which illustrate these possibilities.

Where a comprehensive school with a balanced curriculum considers becoming a technology college (DFEE, 1995c), or other specialist school (DFEE, 1996), it needs to foresee the associated decisions which will be required to make a success of such a change, and whether these are possible and desirable, before making the decision and committing itself to this course of action.

Where a school has a falling roll a strategy will be needed to address this situation. This may range from, on the one hand, reversing the fall in numbers to, on the other, identifying and facilitating a merger with another school if it is not possible for demographic reasons to prevent the fall in numbers in the school. Where the fall in pupil numbers can be reversed, then that should form the strategy and it will take concerted action from a number of people on a number of fronts to achieve this. It is the appropriate choice of strategy and the co-ordination of efforts of numbers of people to achieve the strategy which is the essence of strategic management. It should be noted that falling rolls were a factor in the decision of three of the case-study examples in this book to engage in strategic planning.

Denominational schools, particularly Catholic schools, may have an admissions policy that requires children to be baptised, and may have further requirements such as regular church attendance. In an area with a falling birth-rate such a school has a strategic problem. If there are no further Catholic children who can be admitted there are only two choices. The school can reduce in size with the fall in numbers of Catholic children, or the school can consider admitting non-Catholics. This is a major decision. How far and by what means can the school retain its distinctive ethos if it widens its admissions policy? What is the limit to such a policy once started?

To take a more proactive example. If a multi-racial school contemplates the future and considers the possibilities of seeking to achieve a more balanced intake of pupils from different ethnic groups, on the one hand, or considers aspiring to be an excellent school of its type, on the other, then this is a strategic decision. What follows will depends on which of these two choices are made. Once the major decision is made, other smaller decisions are contingent on, and need to be consistent with, this larger decision.

Raising pupil achievement is a possible strategy as it requires many consistent actions in order to be successful. There are a number of possible choices of action that could be made, but the guiding principles are that they should be consistent, mutually reinforcing and all play a part in facilitating the total enterprise of raising pupil achievement.

Improvement

The title of this book includes the word 'improvement'. By that, we do not mean as a response to the prescriptions of others, but as a result of internal decisions made after professional judgement.

Definition of school improvement

Some writers assume that school improvement involves implementing the results of school effectiveness research. Others have a particular value stance which requires certain changes to be regarded as improvement. Here we take a quite neutral view following the definition given in the International School Improvement Programme (Miles and Ekholm, 1985, p. 48):

> *a systematic, sustained effort aimed at change in learning conditions and other related internal conditions in one or more schools, with the ultimate aim of accomplishing educational goals more effectively.*

It is not concerned with changes that are 'individually-focused, unimplemented, unsystematic, or limited to minor innovations' (p. 34).

We assume that the impetus for change is manifested at the school level. The need for change may lie outside the school, but it is the realisation of a need to change and a commitment to change which we assume comes from the school. Depending on how the school is managed, such decisions may be taken by small or large groups of people inside the school, although change of the magnitude envisaged here will need to be formally ratified by the board of governors, whether or not they play any more active a role.

Thus it is an axiom of our approach that the focus is on the school. Each individual school is assumed to follow its own approach to the strategic planning process outlined here and to decide for itself the areas for improvement that it wishes to tackle. It doesn't follow that it need complete any of these processes without assistance, but it is assumed that it is the school which decides when, from whom and how it will seek external assistance. Such assistance could be in the form of a consultant, an adviser or other person knowledgeable about change in schools.

Fads and silver bullets

Those who have surveyed the failure of past innovations in education have been able cynically to content themselves that since these may have been passing fads or even wrong-headed, their failure is no great loss (Fullan, 1992). Unfortunately, there is too great a degree of truth in this assertion for comfort. Fads abound in education. Slavin (1989) takes one particular teaching scheme in the USA as an example to show that by the time the scheme was widely adopted, evaluation reports were beginning to show its futility. He identifies the combination of an identified need, a ready-made innovation and a few 'gee whiz' stories at the right time about the success of the innovation, to launch it into the big time. He bemoans the lack of evaluation of innovations before they are widely promoted.

Such fads are easier to recognise in retrospect than in prospect, but anyone with a sense of history in education should be in a position to be more discriminating about what are genuine and long-lasting improvements and what are mere passing fads. The aim of strategic management is to allow such discriminating choices rather than to encourage an uncritical adoption of external initiatives. It is also important to question the extent to which presumed mandatory requirements have an element of choice about them.

Fads, however, are not confined to education. Management is also prey to them, where they are known as silver bullets. There is a constant search for the next competitive advantage. However, if the pace of change is slow, then the next panacea overtakes the previous one and even those which might work are never properly tried and only a series of half-implemented and often contradictory changes take place. Watson (1994) charts the confusion and cynicism in one telecommunications organisation over a number of years as seemingly sensible changes are half-understood and half-implemented, leaving those in middle management trying to make sense of it all and largely carrying on despite the 'improvements'.

One might surmise that any field where the organisational technology (teaching) is not theoretically well understood; where cause and effect are not clearly related; and where the pressure to perform is very great, might be subject to a regular flow of new panaceas. Thus, it is not the prevalence of panaceas which is surprising but the lack of a critical appreciation of them as potentially mere passing fads that is of concern. This is not a plea for conservatism, but rather an appeal for a critical appraisal of new ideas. Particularly, this critical appraisal might start by identifying which problem any new proposal might solve and any unintended consequences if it were adopted.

2

Improving schools

Introduction

Strategy is concerned with planning a successful future for a school. For some schools this will involve starting from a strategic problem such as falling rolls, but for many others the plan will be concerned with improving an already successful school. The strategic management models which will be introduced in subsequent chapters provide a process for analysing the current state of the school, the influences upon it, and choosing a strategy; but they do not suggest educational or other outcomes. Nor do they give detailed guidance on how to implement the strategy beyond a general series of issues which need to be addressed. In some ways both these characteristics are great strengths, since the models are very generic and flexible and not inextricably linked with some form of development which may only have a passing appeal. However, they do assume that their readers are familiar with approaches to school improvement which they could contemplate incorporating, in whole or part, into their strategy. This chapter presents such a background.

Improvement approaches

There are a number of possible topics which could be included in this section and thus the selection has involved making judgements about the most appropriate. Two prime candidates are:

1 'school effectiveness'

2 'school improvement'

It has been remarked many times that these two areas of research activity have developed relatively independently in Britain and could productively come together. Each has a number of sub-strands which will be explained in this chapter, but there are other areas of relevant knowledge which are equally vital, the most important of which is:

3 'the management of planned change'

There are a number of other management and educational developments which all have their place in a chapter such as this as possible developmental vehicles for school improvement:

- Organisational Learning (OL)
- Organisation Development (OD)
- Quality initiatives
- Basic Process Re-engineering (BPR)
- School-based Review (SBR)
- School inspections
- Human Resource Management initiatives (HRM)
- Consultancy

Some of these initiatives could be strategies in their own right and some could be components of strategies.

School effectiveness research

Lists of factors associated with 'effective schools' have appeared and continue to appear. It should be noted that such lists do not generally include any discussion of their validity beyond the almost universal statement that they have been identified by 'research'. That such lists are not all identical could imply that work is continuing and that later more comprehensive lists represent more refined findings. It is the purpose of this section to issue a 'health warning' about these findings and to suggest that they are critically appraised and subjected to experienced professional scrutiny.

There are in fact two distinct strands of research on effective schools:

1 a search for internal factors associated with schools that have high pupil achievements when some, more or less sophisticated, allowance is made for the ability of their pupils on intake (school effectiveness correlates);

2 a more sophisticated search for schools with high 'value-added' (or measure of pupil progress) and an attempt to identify a 'school effect', or the extent of the difference which an effective school makes compared to an average school.

Search for school factors

Both types of research have been carried out mainly by academic researchers who have studied schools and their results. Broadly, the first strand has been carried out in the USA and the second in the UK. The work of Rutter *et al.* (1979) and Mortimore *et al.* (1988), both carried out in London, are significant exceptions. These studies are also exceptional in interpreting effectiveness more widely than basic cognitive skills.

Work on school effectiveness started in the late 1960s and early 1970s in the USA as a response to the findings of Coleman *et al.* (1966) and Jencks *et al.* (1972), who were dismissive of the effects of schools on pupil achievement when compared to the effects of home background (Firestone, 1991a). Thus the search began to find schools that were succeeding against the odds. This means that the results are predominantly for:

(a) inner-city elementary schools in the USA

(b) achievements in test scores in basic language and maths

(c) exceptional or 'outlier' schools

How far there are similarities between schools in the USA and the UK is an empirical question which seems never to have been asked by those who commend the results to schools in the UK. Similarly, how far the results apply to typical suburban and rural elementary schools for high-level skills is a matter of conjecture. For secondary schools in the UK the comparison is obviously being overstretched. These are the problems involved in identifying and matching the schools, but there are other problems.

First, the factors associated with effectiveness are only correlations. The research designs are cross-sectional and not longitudinal, so they are not able to give evidence on whether these factors were responsible for an effective school; only that they are associated in some way. Second, the factors will only be discovered if data have been collected on them. This means particularly that factors such as school-based review will not appear, because they are not features of American schools. In that sense the list is arbitrary. Third, the strength of the factor is unknown. The methodology identifies individual factors which are unlikely to have occurred by chance, but not how important they are. Fourth, the correlates are with past measures of effectiveness and are therefore backward-looking, rather than identifying correlates which will be associated with successful schools in the future. Fifth, the research gives no guidance on how to change an ineffective school into an effective one. Finally, from a practical point of view, the factors are so imprecise (and not operationalised in similar ways in different research studies)—strong leadership, for example—as to give very little guidance even to pragmatic action.

Levine and Lezotte (1990), in a review of the work in the USA, recognise that context makes a difference and that what factors have emerged for inner-city working-class schools show signs of being different for those from more middle-class suburban ones. They also acknowledge that little work has been done on American secondary schools. Bliss (1991) identifies two distinct images of effectiveness emerging from the effective schools research covering curriculum, teaching methods and leadership. One is fairly directive and covers basic skills in inner-city areas and the other is more holistic, emphasising student-centred curricula, varied teaching methods and teacher autonomy. It also appeared to be more in evidence in middle-class schools.

Work in the UK has mainly come from two areas—schools in London and Scotland. Work in twelve London secondary schools was done in the 1970s, in fifty London primary schools in the late 1970s and early 1980s, and in Scotland in the mid-1980s. Thus the results are not widely representative nor current. The methodology had fewer shortcomings than most work in the USA (but was not without its critics—see the following on the research of Rutter et al., 1979; Acton, 1980; Heath and Clifford, 1980; Maughan et al., 1980; Bennett and Rutter, 1980), but the final six criticisms will still apply.

Given this long catalogue of reservations about the results and their usefulness, what is the value of the findings? As commentators have noted, what is impressive about the findings is that they are remarkably consistent. Thus although there may be doubts about any individual piece of research, the combined weight of evidence has to be taken more seriously, although the six criticisms above are still valid. Perhaps it is not surprising that the factors have a ring of truth about them for they are in accord with management principles and their converse has little face validity. For example, a nonfunctioning deputy head would hardly be a likely finding in an effective school (Mortimore *et al.*, 1988); nor would weak leadership.

The following is a list of factors from the Rutter study associated with twelve secondary schools obtaining (a) good pupil progress to GCSE; (b) high attendance; (c) good behaviour; and (d) low levels of delinquency, in inner London in the 1970s (Reynolds, 1992):

- balance of pupil ability (prevented sub-group anti-school cultures)
- rewards and punishments
- good working conditions
- children taking responsibility
- homework and clear academic goals
- good teacher models—timekeeping, dealing with problems
- good teaching—preparation, praise, attention, dealing with disruption
- firm leadership with consultation

The following is a list of factors from the Mortimore study associated with junior schools obtaining good progress in (a) language skills and verbal reasoning; (b) maths skills; (c) behaviour; (d) attitudes; (e) perceptions; and (f) attendance, in 50 junior schools in London in the early 1980s (Mortimore, 1991):

- *Leadership*
  Purposeful head and functioning deputy with involvement of other teachers.

- *Management of pupils*
  Sessions structured, work-centred and challenging, whilst behaviour is controlled by rewards.

- *Management of teachers*
  Involving and obtaining consistency from teachers. Good role models of work and communicating with pupils. Broad, balanced curriculum, with structured sessions allowing pupils to focus.

- *Pupil care*
  Encouraging participation of pupils and parents. Valuing pupils. Systematic record-keeping.

- *School environment*
  Attractive and stimulating.

- *School climate*
  Engendering positive attitudes to learning and behaviour.

Search for value-added and a school effect

Rather more British work has been carried out on school effectiveness of the value-added type. Children's progress has been investigated by testing at entry to the particular phase of schooling and testing at the end. Thus the progress achieved by schools and groups of children can be compared. This provides a much fairer way of comparing schools than the raw league tables which are currently published. SCAA (1994) is currently investigating the feasibility of publishing value-added information for parents alongside raw examination data. So schools should be investigating their own value-added results, both to check their own performance and also to see how they will come out on these new comparison statistics.

Without data from all other schools, an individual school can only look at its performance at a particular time and compare with an earlier year. Where data are available for a large number of schools, plotting prior attainment against outcomes allows a regression line to be drawn which is the best predictor of individual scores. A school's position above or below this line indicates its effectiveness (see Figure 2.1).

A serious disadvantage with this methodology is that it is norm-referenced in the sense that the line dividing ineffective schools from effective ones is the 'average' line, and there will always be approximately as many schools deemed ineffective as there are effective. Even if all schools were to improve,

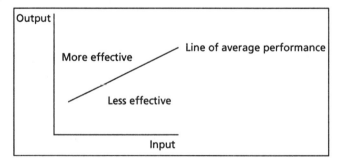

Figure 2.1   Line of best fit and effective schools

there would be just as many ineffective schools. This is contrary to any functional ideas about effectiveness and improvement.

A further problem with comparisons of this kind is that factors contribute to outcome performance of pupils and the school, over which the school has no control. As Willms (1992) has argued, there are two types of comparison which can be made, and a school's position can be very different depending on whether the comparison is a crude one or whether it tries to eliminate those effects which the school cannot alter. Figure 2.2, which arises from work in Scottish secondary schools, shows the effects of gender, prior ability, home background, and social status of the school on school comparisons. Data are unlikely to be available for most schools to provide this more sophisticated comparison and thus schools should be aware of the potential unfairness of the value-added comparisons which are likely to be made.

The diagram (McPherson, 1992) shows the relative positions of six schools. The position is based on their examination results as children leave at 16.

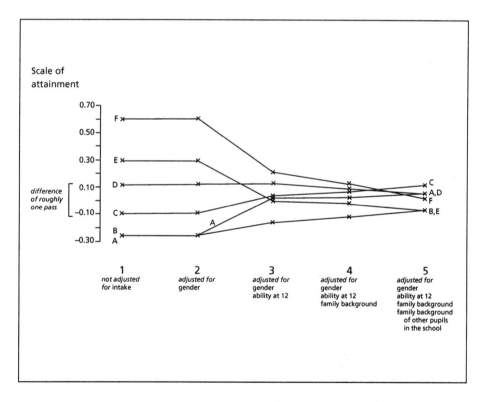

Figure 2.2 Average pupil attainment in six schools unadjusted for pupil intake, and with four adjustments

Source: based on Paterson (1991), in McPherson, 1992, p. 3, by permission of the author

The horizontal lines are to allow the relative positions of each school to be determined as various allowances are made for the pupils in each school. First, an allowance is made for gender, since girls are shown to perform better than boys of similar ability at this examination stage. Then an allowance is also made for measured ability of pupils at entry to the school. This changes the relative positions of the schools, particularly schools A and E. Adjusting for family background and the social mix of the schools produces the final school rankings. Now school C is the best performer and none of the factors which have been adjusted were within the control of the school.

More recent work on value-added has drawn attention to the need to collect and analyse data on each individual pupil in calculating a school effect, and not just to calculate average input and output scores for a school. Multi-level modelling has been suggested as a more appropriate technique to use than simple linear regression to analyse the results at different levels in a system, but others point to some disadvantages of this.

The most readily calculated are the value-added scores for sixth formers since GCSE and A level grades are available (Audit Commission, 1991b; Audit Commission, 1993). These techniques were used in the school cited in Chapter 9.

One criterion suggested for an effective school in the early school effectiveness research in the USA was a school which was improving its exam results (Richards, 1991). This has recently been suggested in the UK (SCAA, 1994); however, it should be recognised that although data to calculate improvement are readily available, these may be very misleading without any measure of the change in the ability of the pupils (Glogg and Fidler, 1990).

School improvement

In the USA, the early school effectiveness findings were soon taken up in school improvement schemes often called 'effective schools programs'. These frequently drew pragmatically on the results from 'school effectiveness' research and supplemented them with what were judged to be improvements from a professional stand-point (Firestone, 1991b).

In contrast to work on school effectiveness, school improvement work has generally been qualitative and has been carried out by practitioners and developers from a variety of backgrounds, including some from universities. Again, in contrast to the two clear strands in school effectiveness research, school improvement has been much more diffuse. There is no clear framework within which different approaches can be compared. It should be said that there are few examples of schools taking the initiative to improve, and countless instances where a local authority or similar local or regional educational administration either mandated schools to take part or invited schools to take part.

A framework

Hopkins *et al.* (1994) have suggested one four-fold framework which differentiates improvement efforts on the basis of whether the school is provided with a series of possibilities (or ingredients), or a process (or recipe). A further sub-division is between those approaches which have a predetermined mix of activities (*table d'hôte*) or whether the school is left to make its own selection (*à la carte*). The sub-division of the process approach is between following a rigid process (mechanical), compared to a flexible process which can be adapted to the particular context. This is in analogy with the Burns and Stalker's (1961) dichotomy of management structures (see Table 2.1).

Approach	Strategy	Example
Ingredients	*Table d'hôte*	Improving the urban high school (Louis and Miles, 1992)
	A la carte	The doors to school improvement (Joyce, 1991)
Recipe	Mechanistic	The self-managing school (Caldwell and Spinks, 1988)
	Organic	School development planning

Table 2.1   The Hopkins *et al.* (1994) classification of school improvement efforts
Source: Hopkins et al., 1994, p. 70

Table d'hôte

In the early 1980s, states and school districts in the USA took up the correlates emerging from the effective schools movement and instituted programmes to implement them in schools. Thus these improvement schemes took the menu to be fixed (though different) in each programme. Experience showed the need to tailor implementation to each school, at least in the initial stages.

As Cuban (1984) and others pointed out, there were worries about the effective schools correlates, and it was not clear how they could help to improve schools. In particular, the position of the individual school was ambiguous. Effective schools research had taken the individual school as the unit of analysis in quantitative and case-study research, and in improvement efforts there was a general recognition that what happened at building level was crucial. However, in the highly bureaucratic educational system of the USA at the time, any large-scale change had to start at least at the district level if not higher, for both political and financial reasons.

That a school improving on its own was unusual is illustrated by Levine and Lezotte's (1990) use of 'maverick' to describe principals who protected their staff from unwarranted district-level intrusions. It was also used more generally as a term to describe those few and exceptional principals who made an institutional-level decision to change, rather than being drafted by higher levels in the system.

Thus the *table d'hôte* above represents a commitment to implement the school effectiveness correlates. Later work in school effectiveness research increasingly called into question whether it was defensible to have one list of effective schools correlates or whether they were much more context-specific and contingent. Levine and Lezotte (1990) tried to amalgamate results to produce an ever longer list of correlates, but with increasing recognition that the support for each came from different contexts. In terms of leadership, there was already the recognition that 'successful leadership in one type of organisation may be ineffectual in another' (Hallinger and Murphy, 1985, p. 3).

Louis and Miles (1992) is rather an atypical example to take for this kind of research, since it deals with secondary schools. It is a relatively positive account of at least two of five inner-city schools studied making substantial progress, and two more making some progress (Louis and Miles, 1991).

A la carte

Although some effective schools programmes have a single innovation at their core, they are unusual and run counter to the series of linked changes which the correlates have thrown up. Joyce's (1991) list of doors to school improvement was brought together from eight contributions by well-known school improvement authors from 1980 to 1990. These authors opened different doors to schools improvement. Each door is a pathway into the culture of the school:

1 *Collegiality*: this is using the problem-solving techniques of OD. This may lead on to other data collection and problem-solving.

2 *Research*: particularly effective schools research.

3 *Collecting data*: this can be relevant to everyday concerns of teachers and can lead into formal evaluation.

4 *Curriculum initiatives*: this has a fairly depressing history if the initiative required anything more than new materials. Usually the aim is to start with one subject, hoping that this will encourage others.

5 *Instructional initiatives*: staff development which focuses on teaching methods. The history of this is that it doesn't seem to take off.

Recipes

The effective schools programmes prescribed what should be the end result of the changes, but did not give guidance on how the change should be accomplished. The recipes, on the other hand, have a process but not necessarily any content. The first recipe is the model of Caldwell and Spinks (1988), operating a modified form of management by objectives and programme budgeting, and which has been used in one school in Tasmania. Hopkins *et al.* (1994) see this as mechanistic when compared to the organic approach of school development planning, which provides a framework but calls for adaptation by its users.

From the foregoing, the reader will recognise that strategic planning is of this second kind.

In fact effective schools programmes are beginning to erect an orthodoxy for their improvement programmes in the sense that there is a diagnosis; an organisational phase; and a general 'climate' setting with a recommendation to move on to changes in teaching methods at an early stage. Technical help of various kinds is used and the likely types and stages of such help, including staff development, are emerging (Levine and Lezotte, 1990).

Although helpful, the framework has its limitations. It does not include the:

■ locus of action—inside or outside the school

■ prime mover—head, staff, external change agent

■ starting point—evaluation, staff development, problem, external innovation, mandate

- comprehensiveness—new philosophy of management, or new teaching scheme in one subject
- subject of the improvement

School improvement starts in the school

For a book such as this, which takes the locus of action to be within the school and centred on the headteacher, there is an obvious problem in that there are varying states of readiness and capability of heads and schools. They could be:

1 keen to improve

2 needing encouragement to improve

3 reluctant to change

4 unable to change

These groups require different treatment. The first group needs to acquire knowledge about ways of improving that will enhance its capability and harness its basic proactivity. The second group, in addition to aids to capability, also needs motivation. This book is written for these first two groups.

Experience of school improvement suggests that schools which are complacent and those which are crisis-ridden are the least ready to embark on change (Miles and Ekholm, 1985). External initiatives will be needed to mobilise the third group, and the final group needs help to survive its crisis. There is abundant evidence showing the relative ineffectiveness of external innovation and so this would be inappropriate for the first two groups, but unavoidable for the second two.

These considerations cover both attitudes to improvement and capability of improvement. Figure 2.3 indicates the needs of different groups.

The challenge for a book such as this is to demonstrate models of operation for schools to follow that are in the first two groups. This needs to be done in such a way that they are able to develop their capability of improving and demonstrate the attributes of a self-renewing organisation which does not need external imposition of improvement strategies.

Attitude to improvement

		Positive	Negative
	High	knowledge	external stimulation
Capacity to improve	*Low*	knowledge staff development some help	major help

Figure 2.3   Capacity and attitudes to improvement

Management of planned change

School improvement research generally reads as if the writers are outsiders looking in. Such work has usually been based on case studies and the general advice based on them suffers from amalgamating the results of studies of individually successful changes into some requirement for leadership which would be daunting to all (Huberman, 1992).

The management of planned change takes a different perspective. It takes as an axiom that the managers of an organisation are charged with managing change and innovation, i.e. ensuring that change is accomplished successfully. It does *not* follow that all ideas have to come from managers, that all decisions are made by managers or that change is forced on an unwilling staff. But it does however follow that these decisions are made, and that someone is responsible for ensuring that planning, implementation and evaluation all take place successfully. Thus far more worthwhile than research findings out of context are a conceptual overview and planning tools to aid the leadership of schools in making decisions about:

(a) whether to consider an innovation

(b) assessing the current state of readiness of the organisation

(c) preparatory steps which may be needed to increase the state of readiness

(d) planning the future state

31

(e) mobilising support

(f) planning the transition

(g) implementing the transition

(h) ensuring innovation is supported

(i) evaluating the innovation

Beckhard and Harris (1987) caution against accepting even externally imposed change without question. They suggest techniques for assessing whether change is:

- inevitable and without choice of time-scale, e.g. National Curriculum

- inevitable but with some choice of timing, e.g. staff appraisal

- desirable, e.g. curriculum review

- entirely at the choice of the institution, e.g. greater involvement of governors

Some further factors to be considered for each change are: the degree to which the change is embraced in terms of the number of people affected (all the school or only part); and whether it will need a fundamental review, or whether it is merely an addition or replacement for an aspect of current operations. Operating in this more discriminating way it follows that changes may be prioritised and sequenced in time, rather than all being taken on because they all happened to come to the attention of the school at the same time.

Beckhard and Harris (1987) suggest a grid for assessing the sources of change and potency of changes to help sort out priorities. Whether other influences are for or against each change can also be indicated and may provide further information to assess institutional priorities. However, they caution that the information must be accurate and complete; and the manager's own blind spots and biases must be recognised and overcome.

Kurt Lewin (1947) has contributed a number of techniques to analyse and conceptualise change. His basic assumption was that an organisation was at equilibrium with its surroundings when forces for change balanced forces resisting change. His force-field analysis diagram allows the relevant forces to be identified. By decreasing the resisting forces and increasing the driving forces, change can be accomplished. The analysis helps choose the appropriate forces to work on.

He also conceptualised the change process in three stages. These are compared with those used later by Fullan (1989):

Lewin	Fullan
unfreezing	initiation
moving	implementation
refreezing	institutionalisation

Lewin's terms are particularly helpful in terms of diagnosing readiness for change. In his terms, unless the present state is sufficiently 'unfrozen', change will not take place. This means that people have to begin to feel uncomfortable with the present state before they will readily contemplate moving. Schein (1992) has elaborated three steps within the unfreezing process:

1 presence of evidence of a problem

2 connection of this problem with the organisation's purpose causing anxiety and/or guilt

3 a possible solution which is not so unsettling as to cause a denial of the problem

If all three steps have been completed to some degree, the unfreezing has begun to take place and the change can be planned.

Beckhard and Harris (1987) have suggested the use of readiness and capability charts to examine whether key organisation members are ready for the change and also, and quite separately, whether they have the skills and attitude to deal with the change. Action to unfreeze and/or develop skills and provide support can then be planned. They have also designed a simple commitment chart to analyse the present and desired positions of key people concerned with the change (Everard and Morris, 1990; Fidler et al., 1991).

Chin and Benne (1976) have devised three approaches to change. The first is the *power/coercive*. In this approach, organisation members are compelled or put under great psychological or other pressure to change. The second is the *rational-empirical* approach, where the logical advantages of the proposed change are set out. Finally, the *normative/re-educative* approach uses more emotional and interpersonal means to persuade people to accept the change. These are not necessarily alternatives, but rather should be seen as an armoury of approaches from which to select or use in combination at appropriate points in the change process.

Training and support will almost certainly be needed in order to increase individual and collective capability. Whilst pre-training was thought to be the most effective preparation, trials which have used training at different stages, depending on the nature of the change, have shown that providing on-going support of a more advisory and counselling kind increased the effectiveness of change.

The final stage of the Lewin three-stage process is refreezing. This involves changing organisational norms—policies and procedures—such that the change represents the accepted way of operating from now on rather than being only a temporary measure.

A range of improvement strategies

The following are possible improvement vehicles. The phase of improvement (preparation, analysis, process, outcome) to which they relate is indicated.

- Organisation Development (OD)
    process

- Organisational Learning (OL)
    process

- Quality Assurance initiatives (QA)
    analysis, process, outcomes

- Basic Process Re-engineering (BPR)
    analysis, process, outcomes

- School-based Review (SBR)
    analysis

- School inspections
    analysis

- Human Resource Management initiatives (HRM)
    preparation, analysis, process, outcomes

- Consultancy
    analysis, process, outcomes

Organisation Development (OD)

OD from the 1960s onwards has offered a means of organisations becoming 'problem solving' or 'self-renewing' organisations, using techniques from the behavioural sciences and an external consultant. Many of the ideas in school improvement draw their ideas loosely from OD, although there is little general awareness of OD as such (Gray, 1993).

Schmuck and Runkel (1985, p. 20) identify organisational adaptability or the capacity of the organisation to solve its own problems as a key feature of the concept of OD. It is composed of four metaskills, the ability to:

1 diagnose the functioning of groups in the school;

2 gather information and other resources from within and outside the school;

3 mobilise synergistic action in the schools; and

4 monitor the other three metaskills.

They recognise that 'improving subsystem effectiveness, coupled with efforts to improve interpersonal skill and satisfy human motives, constitutes the core of organisation development' (p. 23).

The following list gives seven highly interdependent capabilities in an effective subsystem. When one capability is increased, it is easier to increase others:

1 clarifying communication

2 improving group procedures in meetings

3 establishing goals

4 uncovering and working with conflict

5 solving problems

6 making decisions

7 assessing changes

There are four types of OD activities:

1 training

2 survey-data-feedback

3 constructive confrontation

4 process observation and feedback

OD consultants work with the school on one or more of these designs. The amount of time needed to complete one of the designs is quite extensive. The intention is that the school should gradually move to being self-sufficient at solving its own problems. It is somewhat difficult to tell the success of OD initiatives, since many very different programmes in the USA have all been loosely called OD (Fullan *et al.*, 1981).

An example of an OD approach in school improvement in England is given by Pocklington and Weindling (1996).

Organisational Learning (OL)

Those who espouse OL, which is a specific approach to OD, point out that since the nature of future changes is unknown, the best way of preparing for the future is to develop organisational capabilities which will increase the organisation's ability to deal with the future. By analogy with individual learning, organisations too are assumed to have the capacity to learn.

In a recent review of school effectiveness research findings, Sammons *et al.* (1995) included organisational learning in a list of eleven characteristics of effective schools, despite the lack of empirical support for the concept or its relationship to effectiveness. The arguments advanced in its favour relied on professional judgement.

Argyris and Schon (1978) posited single loop and double loop learning, and recently Swieringa and Wierdsma (1992) have added triple loop learning. Single loop learning consists of detecting errors in performance and correcting them. There is a single feedback loop which connects detected errors in outcomes of action to organisational processes so as to keep organisational performance within set norms. This is incremental learning.

Double loop learning is more complex and requires a change in organisational norms. When a conflict is detected between a new problem and what can be solved by improving current operations, this calls for double loop learning. One loop of learning concerns the detection of the error and the recognition that this does not fit the pattern of single loop learning. The second loop of learning concerns the process of feedback about organisational norms.

> *Double loop learning consists not only of a change in organisational norms but of the*
> *particular sort of inquiry into norms which is appropriately described as learning.*
> (Swieringa and Wierdsma, 1992, p. 22)

The authors refer to these as *why* questions rather than *how* questions. They then go on to differentiate triple loop learning as the learning which goes on when 'the essential principles on which the organisation is founded come into discussion' (p. 41). In other words, the basic corporate strategy is questioned.

The emphasis in organisational learning is on the organisation's ability to carry out these processes and on its learning as a result how to carry them out again in the future when needed. Leithwood *et al.* (1995) have proposed a model for organisational learning in schools and obtained data from six schools in Canada which show some evidence of the process in action.

Quality Assurance initiatives

Various quality initiatives have come to prominence in industry and commerce—Total Quality Management (TQM), Deming's ideas, BS 5750 etc. These have received some attention in the educational world. They basically consist of a process (and a philosophy) by which the organisation can produce quality goods and services. They have the distinction of being concerned with outcomes in a generic sense.

Quality Assurance and Quality Control

The customary process of ensuring a quality output is quality control. This involves inspecting the output of a process and rejecting anything that fails to achieve the required level of quality. School self-evaluation is a form of Quality Control. It takes place *after the event*. The alternative form of ensuring quality is Quality Assurance (Tovey, 1994). This involves designing systems to deliver quality *before the event*. The professional training of teachers is one aspect of a quality assurance process. A quality assurance approach to teaching would work backwards from the teacher in the classroom to ask what are the prerequisites to ensure that:

(a) an appropriately knowledgeable teacher

(b) teaches appropriate material

(c) to an appropriate group

(d) at the appropriate time

(e) in the appropriate place.

Each of these requirements would be traced back to ensure what conditions were necessary for there to be a high expectation that they would be fulfilled. As little as possible would be left to chance. The watchword is 'right first time'. Further and higher education have been working on these ideas for some time (Sallis and Hingley, 1991), and they may be equally worthwhile for schools.

BS 5750 is a particular set of Quality Assurance procedures which has been taken up in a wide variety of organisations. Healy (1994) describes the application of BS 5750 to a secondary school.

Total Quality Management (TQM)

Sallis (1993, p. 13) asks whether quality in the guise of TQM is just another fad, and decides that it is different:

> It is a philosophy and a methodology which assists institutions to manage change, and to set their own agendas for dealing with the plethora of new external pressures.

The distinctiveness of TQM lies in two major features—a commitment to continuous improvement, and the involvement of all members of the organisation (Oakland, 1993). In terms of cultural change, TQM is massive.

TQM defines quality in relative terms (Sallis, 1993) as:

1 measuring up to specification

2 meeting the needs of the customer or client

The customers and clients are seen as both internal (within the same organisation) and external. In that sense, TQM is little different to conventional marketing approaches. However, it also proposes process approaches and a philosophy for defining quality and for the process of producing quality services. Such factors as building quality assurance into the production process, rather than putting defects right later, emphasise what might be implicit and lesser priorities in normal operations. Individual quality initiatives emphasise particular factors.

The approach based on Deming places emphasis on the importance of structures and systems rather than individual effort and competence in terms of ensuring a quality output. If basic structures and processes are not designed appropriately, a lot of time and individual effort is spent fruitlessly trying to compensate for basic design errors. This is not to say that individuals do not matter, but rather that they should be used productively and not used to patch up basic design flaws (Horine and Lingren, 1995).

Although the quality initiatives have the appearance of clarifying the goals of the organisation, they are better suited to commercial operations than to schools or other NFPs. The multiplicity of clients and the ambiguity of their expectations are polarised but not resolved by the quality analysis (West-Burnham, 1992a). Some approaches speak of negotiating client requirements for quality, and this is likely to be a particular feature of quality in schools where the teacher with professional knowledge is negotiating with parents on behalf of their children. Where wider social goals are also included in the service this is going to be particularly problematic.

Murgatroyd and Morgan (1992) identify steps that need to be taken to introduce TQM to a school. They recognise the cynicism of yet another initiative and try to make clear the exceptional commitment required of all organisation members by TQM. Where TQM has taken off successfully it has to be seen as the 'central platform for all the work of the organisation' (p. 189). An example of the Deming approach to school improvement is given by Hinkley and Seddon (1996).

Murgatroyd and Morgan (1992) present an example of a fishbone diagram (Ishikawa, 1990), a technique useful for discovering and investigating the causes of problems in a school. They give an example of acceptance letters sent to new parents which arrived late. The possible causes are located and the most potent ones to work on circled, in order to prevent the problem occurring again.

Murgatroyd (1993) examines some causes as to why TQM fails and tries to give pointers to prevent failure. There are already indications that many business organisations find TQM disappointing. How far this is because it has not been implemented appropriately, and how far it is because only some organisations are at a suitable state of readiness to contemplate the change to TQM, is conjectural. A major incentive to use such methods is that they were seen as a contribution to the success of Japanese manufacturing. However, the slow incremental improvement of TQM does not seem to offer any hope of moving ahead of the Japanese, who have been practising such techniques for a long time. Basic Process Re-engineering has been devised as a way of leap-frogging and jumping ahead of competitors based upon quality ideas.

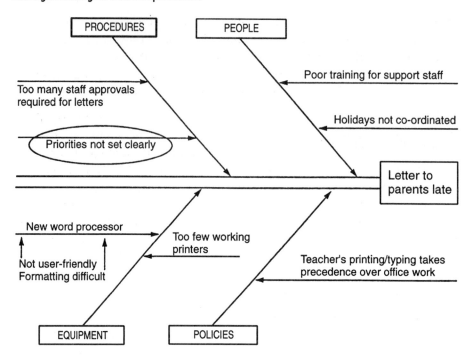

Figure 2.4　Fishbone diagram—letter to parents sent late

Source: reproduced from Murgatroyd and Morgan, 1992, p. 170, by permission of the publisher, Open University Press, Buckingham

Basic Process Re-engineering (BPR)

Recently, books have begun to appear on aspects of BPR. In addition, examples of business organisations which have taken this up as a further development of quality initiatives (Hammer and Champy, 1993) have been reported. BPR covers three distinct approaches—process improvement, process redesign and process re-engineering (Macdonald, 1995).

These represent increasing levels of radical change. TQM emphasises process improvement. This is single loop learning. Much of what is described as BPR is process redesign and involves double loop learning. Improvements which go beyond the incremental are investigated, particularly from a customer's point of view, and often make use of improved information technology. The most radical option is process re-engineering. The aim is to obtain superior operations at less cost.

This is the organisational equivalent of zero-based budgeting in finance. It has much in common with strategic management, in that it questions the basic rationale of the organisation. Many companies have moved on to the next two

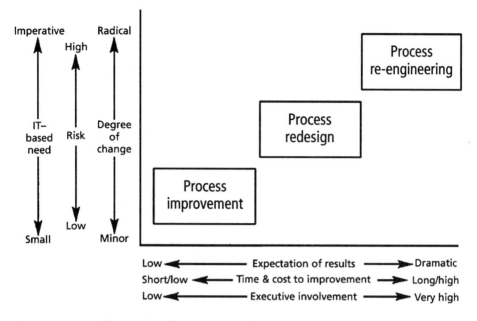

Figure 2.5   Quality approaches
Source: Macdonald, 1995, p. 7

processes having tried TQM, and some see TQM as a natural first step to further quality initiatives. All of these approaches will involve increasing degrees of cultural change. The process starts from the needs of clients, takes account of the views of stakeholders and considers the potential of new technology to transform work practices. However, the process concentrates on outcomes rather than tasks. The essential techniques are process-mapping, simulation, statistical and other measurement methods and team decision techniques.

For a school, BPR would involve rethinking the education of children. Fletcher (1994) suggests considering the role of IT in classrooms as a source of fresh ideas. Undoubtedly there is some potential to use IT to store and process data directly accessible by the teacher, but the only way to achieve radical change would be to examine the replacement of the teaching task by computers. Schools are already rather lean organisations; they are heavily labour-intensive in providing personal service to each client. So the prospects of the efficiency gains which a small number of well-publicised companies with heavy paper-pushing bureaucracies have made seem somewhat illusory for schools.

O'Looney (1993), using the following eight principles, reflects on restructuring American schools:

41

1 Develop a cross-functional perspective

2 Organise around outcomes not tasks

3 Have those who use the output of the process perform the process

4 Subsume information-processing work into the real work that produced the information

5 Treat geographically dispersed resources as though they were centralised

6 Link parallel activities instead of integrating their results

7 Put the decision point where the work is performed, and build control into the process

8 Capture information once and at source

Whilst these principles might help to design a strategy for making maximum use of IT within a school, they hardly seem to have the potential to change schools radically.

School-Based Review (SBR)

SBR can contribute to the analysis phase of school improvement. It is a way of involving teachers in examining their own practice and the working of parts of the institution. GRIDS (McMahon *et al.*, 1984) for primary and secondary schools has been widely used and is process-oriented. It needs instruments and ideas on how to undertake individual areas of investigation.

School inspections

A new system of school inspections began in England and Wales in 1993. This system of inspections organised by OFSTED (1992) involves the production of a report on a school's operation and identifies areas which the school should improve. This can provide a systematic and independent assessment of a number of aspects of a school's operations. OFSTED's intention is that the results of inspection should aid improvement (Matthews and Smith, 1995).

An action plan is required after the inspection and this needs to be incorporated into the school's improvement strategies. There is evidence that schools find the process helpful for their own development (Fidler *et al.*, 1994; 1995; Ouston *et al.*, 1996).

The inspection will be of most value if it is used positively by a school to steer the process towards areas of its work on which it would find an external view helpful. The framework for inspection (OFSTED, 1995a; 1995b) can inform the school's own internal review processes, but needs to be treated as a guide rather than a 'bible'. A consideration of the value of OFSTED inspections for school improvement is given by Earley *et al.* (1996). The value of previous LEA inspections operating a trial of the OFSTED framework has been studied by Gray and Wilcox (1995).

Human Resource Management initiatives

There are a range of human resource management initiatives—competences, Investors In People, management development, staff development—which differ in their comprehensiveness and hence their ability to contribute to small or large parts of the process of school improvement.

Staff Development

One way of getting started on improvement is to concentrate on Staff Development as a way of developing staff skills and beginning to change the climate and culture for improvement. This is a preparatory measure before the start of a school improvement initiative *per se*. This could be targeted towards those skills which were expected to be important in strategic processes and general research methods for collecting data and developing a spirit of enquiry.

The greatest role for Staff Development is likely to be in connection with the particular innovation that is to be implemented. Experience of managing change indicates that the form and timing of staff development are what counts (Fullan, 1986). Continuing follow-up in the form of coaching (Joyce and Showers, 1988) is important rather than relying only on courses to learn new skills.

Management Competences

Competences represent an attempt to analyse the skills needed in job performance and to assess whether these are being demonstrated in practice by job holders (Esp, 1992). There are different approaches to Management Competences: looking at superior performance (Boyatzsis, 1982) or looking at satisfactory performance. Within education in the UK there are approaches by the Management Charter Initiative (MCI) (Esp, 1992); School Management South (Earley 1992a; 1992b; 1992c); Oxford Educational Assessment Centre (Esp, 1992); and the University of East London (Jirasinghe and Lyons, 1995).

Essentially, competences devised as a result of functional analysis of jobs are static views of the competences needed to perform the work of the organisation, in that they involve the current work of the organisation, rather than its future. Those involving personal competences in addition to functional competences may use skills which are forward-looking in a more generic sense. An example of using MCI competences in school improvement is given by Cleland (1996).

MCI (1995) has recently issued competences for senior managers which include strategic competences in four main groups:

1 Understanding and influencing the environment
>external trends
>internal strengths and weaknesses
>stakeholders

2 Setting the strategy and gaining commitment

3 Planning, implementing and monitoring
>programmes, projects and plans
>delegation and action
>culture
>monitoring

4 Evaluating and improving performance

The personal competences needed are:

- judgement

- self-confidence

- strategic perspective

- achievement focus

- communication

- information search

- building teams

- influencing others

Investors in People

Investors in People offers a framework for ensuring that all members of the organisation are familiar with its goals, know their part in achieving them and have appropriate means of development in order to enhance their ability to achieve the organisation's goals. The particular initiative can lead to accreditation for the institution which may be seen as a development in its own right, and will be useful in contributing to institutional differentiation and distinctiveness. Investors in People is one of the few initiatives which directly involve non-teaching staff.

Recent examples of the use of Investors in People in school improvement are given by Brown *et al.* (1996), Thomas (1996) and Zienau (1996). Zienau gives the view of a consultant on the process.

Consultancy

Although in a slightly different vein from the other material in this chapter, it is worth raising the issue of consultancy at this point. Consultants can help in a number of ways. In particular they can:

- provide an outsider's view
- act as an informed sounding board
- bring a knowledge of how other schools operate
- bring process skills and understanding of how to facilitate change
- bring training techniques to develop people's behavioural skills
- provide training in functional management skills

There are a number of instances in the literature where practice in the USA has shown the value of consultant help and other forms of technical assistance in school improvement (Huberman and Miles, 1984; Loucks-Horsley and Mundry, 1991). However, as Louis (1981) points out, consultants can come in a number of guises ranging from:

(a) those who connect schools with sources of innovation (linking agent). These may be able to link into a number of innovations or be an agent of only one, e.g. in the UK, IIP agents funded by local Training and Enterprise Councils, to

(b) those who respond to school problems or who are audience-oriented or client-oriented.

Lippitt and Lippitt (1978, p. 31) offer a range of directive/non-directive roles which a consultant might take, as illustrated in Figure 2.6.

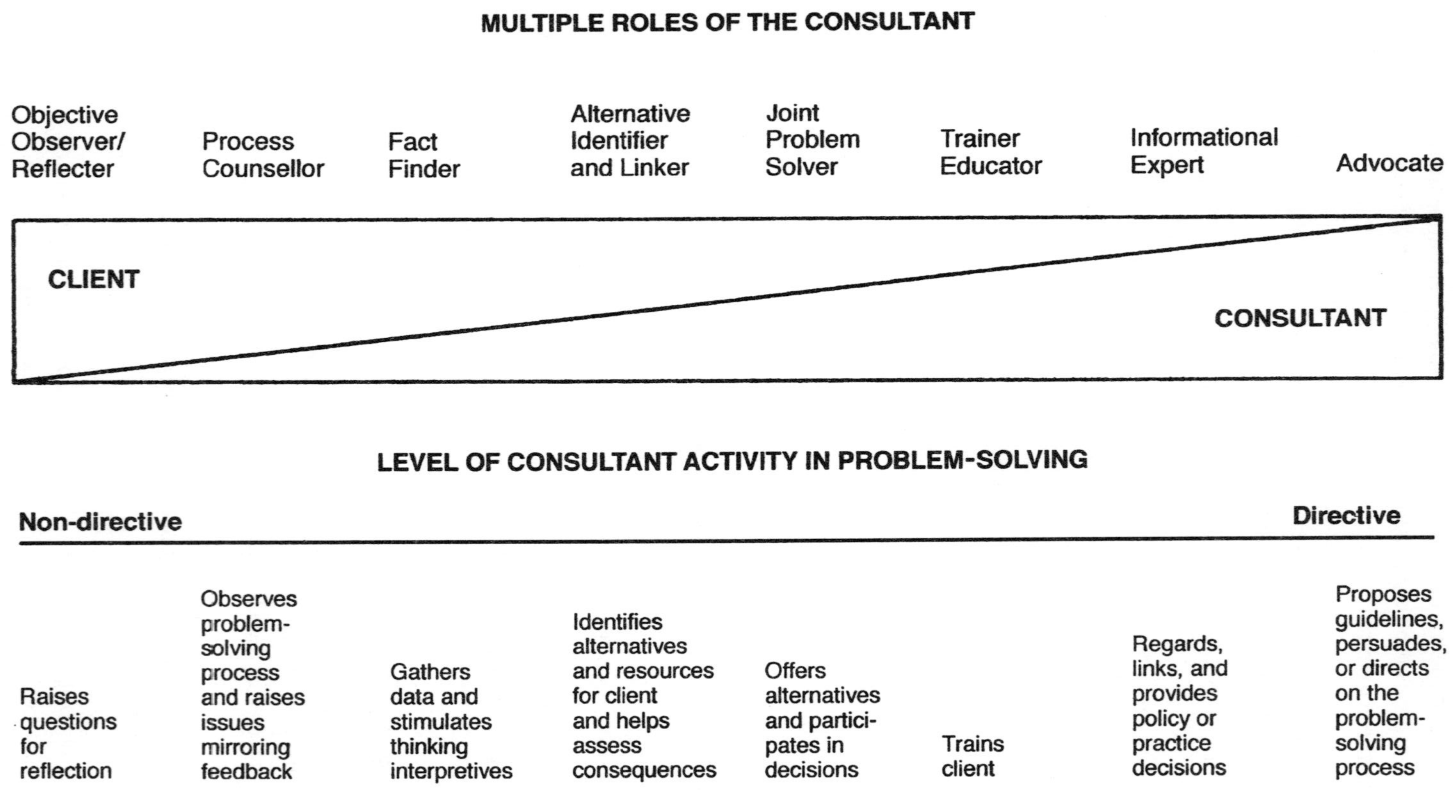

MULTIPLE ROLES OF THE CONSULTANT

Objective Observer/ Reflecter	Process Counsellor	Fact Finder	Alternative Identifier and Linker	Joint Problem Solver	Trainer Educator	Informational Expert	Advocate

CLIENT

CONSULTANT

LEVEL OF CONSULTANT ACTIVITY IN PROBLEM-SOLVING

Non-directive   Directive

Raises questions for reflection	Observes problem-solving process and raises issues mirroring feedback	Gathers data and stimulates thinking interpretives	Identifies alternatives and resources for client and helps assess consequences	Offers alternatives and partici-pates in decisions	Trains client	Regards, links, and provides policy or practice decisions	Proposes guidelines, persuades, or directs on the problem-solving process

Figure 2.6 Consultant roles on a directive/non-directive continuum

Source: Lippitt and Lippitt, 1978, p. 31

Morris (1988) adapts the managerial grid, showing concern for relationships and results to show different approaches to consultancy. This process identifies three extreme types:

- *Directive*: the consultant will focus on the organisation's measures of success; identify reasons for shortcomings and recommend changes in personnel, structure and methods to improve. The consultant may be further commissioned to implement the suggestions.

- *Behavioural*: the consultant's role is to develop the people in the organisation to handle their relationships and conflicts. There will normally be training in group dynamics and other behavioural techniques.

- *Catalytic*: the consultant helps the people to focus on organisational performance and assists them to identify and put into practice ways of improving performance. There will be some training in behavioural techniques and in management skills training in functional areas, in addition to workshops where people work directly on the organisation's problems and formulate action plans.

Both the behavioural and the catalytic are 'capacity-building functions' (Louis, 1981). Those with a concern for relationships may be termed *process* consultants. Everard (1988) offers a flavour of the role of a process consultant as someone who is:

- outside the management of the school

- in the workplace but not of it (that is, intentionally marginal)

- politically neutral (though not unaware)

- facilitating and educating about the process of organisational problem-solving

- client-oriented

- problem-oriented (rather than activity-oriented)

As Murgatroyd (1988) points out, any consultant needs a theory of organisations rather than just experience if they are to be able to compare the working of one school with another in a meaningful way.

Jamieson (1988) sees the following as precepts for curriculum consultants:

- the relationship between the consultant and client must be *voluntary*

- the relationship between the consultant and client must be *temporary*

- the relationship between the consultant and the client must be *advisory*

- the consultant is assumed to be *'expert'* in some aspects of the 'problem' under discussion

From these criteria he concluded that it is difficult to see LEA advisers, who might otherwise have been assumed to fulfil such a role, as consultants, as they had at least an implicit power relationship. He was writing before the Education Reform Act of 1988 and the situation in some cases may have changed since then. Where LEA services are offered for hire and a school can choose who to engage and for what purposes in return for payment, LEA advisers could provide a source of possible consultants in addition to universities and colleges, industry and independent consultants.

The process of engaging consultants consists of the following stages (Gray, 1988):

- Choosing a potential consultant—this will depend on the reasons for engaging a consultant and knowledge of who has the appropriate skills; reputation is a good pointer.

- Negotiation of contract—in face-to-face discussions in addition to formal matters, a decision can be made about the suitability of the consultant in terms of an appropriate personal relationship. The formal agreement should cover what is to be done, costs and time-scale. The client should be specified—the head, the school, the governors, the staff, etc.

- Agreement on ethics—confidentiality and anonymity of sources of information should be agreed.

- Outcomes—a report or other outcome should be specified.

Beginning work in an organisation is always a problem (Gray, 1988). Entry may have been granted by one person but others need to co-operate and may be suspicious. Getting to know and working with the senior team first is usually preferable, but it is then important to avoid being introduced to other members of the organisation afterwards as if the consultant is 'on side'. Murgatroyd (1988) offers some advice about ways of beginning working in a school:

- *tracking*—a manager or other person

- *mimesis*—adopt language and style of school

- *multiaccess*—talk to anyone

- *positive connotation*—be seen to look favourably on school activities

Although some of these skills and techniques should come from the consultant, a school needs to think through how it intends to use the consultant and to facilitate the work of the consultant accordingly.

3

Strategic management

Introduction

In this chapter the importance of strategic management and strategic change is explained. Four models are offered to help demonstrate strategic management processes in schools. Three of these are complementary. They describe the same process from different perspectives and highlight different aspects. This should help clarify the difference between organisational aspects of planning how to carry out the process and the process itself. The final model addresses the issue of transformational change when a turbulent environment requires a radical change of the organisation.

What is strategic management?

Strategic management is the creation and implementation of strategy in response to and in anticipation of future events and trends in the outside world. We believe that this process is as applicable to a school as to any other organisation.

Strategic management is concerned with deciding on strategy and planning how to implement it. It consists of analysis, decision-making, implementation and evaluation.

Strategic decisions are concerned with:

1 the whole scope of an organisation's activities

2 an organisation's long-term direction

3 matching of an organisation's activities to the environment

4 devising activities which are sustainable given the level of organisational resources

50

A key concept in organisation theory is for an organisation to be constantly adapting to its environment to find the best fit. The assumption is that the organisation depends on its environment for survival. Thus if it is in equilibrium and there is a change in the environment, the organisation will need to respond in some way to maintain equilibrium.

The environment means all those influences from outside the school which may affect its future. Thus the environment covers more than the local physical and social environment. It includes the framework of law which affects educational institutions and includes political, economic, social and technological pressures (PEST). Schools need to adapt not only to national legal requirements (e.g. ERA), but also to the demands of the local community. For schools, educational influences will be particularly important.

Importance of strategic management

In almost all organisations long-term survival is the most important consideration, with short and long-term success following some way behind. Anne Jones (1987, p. 62) puts the need rather graphically:

> *Without having learnt the skills of strategic management and operational planning, heads are liable to find themselves involved in nothing but crisis-management.*

In the past, most public-sector schools could have expected such long-term and wide-scale planning to have been carried out primarily at LEA level and not at institutional level. LEAs still have a strategic planning function with respect to special needs provision and the provision of adequate numbers of school places, although in some cases this may be shared with the Funding Agency for Schools (FAS). Although there has been a great deal of variation amongst LEAs in how they have reacted to the devolution of powers to schools after 1988, the threat of schools opting out of their control has tempered the degree to which they have tried to impose major changes on schools. In a great many cases LEAs have become major service providers to schools.

The whole thrust of the Education Reform Act was to make schools responsive to their parents and prospective parents by coupling their resourcing to pupil numbers. Now in a very clear way income depends on pupil numbers. Thus there is a very urgent need to monitor pupil numbers because they have implications for next year's budget income. Although this could be done as a purely reactive monitoring exercise, most schools will wish to influence pupil numbers. Schools now more than ever will be in a position where they will be largely responsible for their own destiny.

Strategy, however, is not only concerned with survival. Whilst this is a first concern, once this has been secured strategy is concerned with ensuring success for the organisation. Since success can come in many forms, strategy involves examining the possibilities and choosing which is the most likely to succeed given current and predicted future circumstances.

As Cyert and March's (1963) historic study of business organisations showed, organisations tend to reduce complexity and the accompanying uncertainty by reacting to events rather than trying to anticipate them. Since then strategic management in business has mushroomed and extensive efforts have been made to anticipate and influence the future. Schools may be in a similar position to business organisations in the late 1950s. In a small-scale study of secondary schools before the Education Reform Act, Everard (1986, p. 76) noted:

> *Few heads mentioned activities aimed at changing the environment within which the school operated, yet they reported many problems whose source lay in the LEA or the Education Committee. It was as though there was passive acceptance of situations that were decided at County Hall, and a feeling not only of powerlessness in relation to these, but of acceptance of an immutable subordinate relationship of obedience.*

Thus strategic management at school level will require new ways of thinking and acting. Since that time schools generally have engaged in development planning following the advice provided to schools by DES (1989; 1991). Thus they have gained experience of audit, constructing plans, implementing developments and evaluation if they have followed the advice in *The Empowered School* (Hargreaves and Hopkins, 1991). The research evidence on development planning (Fidler, 1996a) is rather more mixed. In some cases development planning has been imposed by LEAs to serve their purposes and has as a result been taken less seriously by schools.

However, there are many differences between school development planning and strategic planning (Fidler *at al.*, 1991, p. 27). The most fundamental features that distinguish strategic planning from school development planning are that it:

- questions the aims of the school
- investigates the strategic standing of the school
- takes account of present and future environmental influences
- incorporates a vision of what the school should be like
- plans for the longer term
- is holistic

Whilst these are substantial individual differences, perhaps the biggest difference is that strategic management is proactive. This is demonstrated in two senses. First, a strategic approach doesn't wait for change to be externally imposed, and second, it doesn't take the external world to be immutable but seeks to influence and educate it. Interaction with the external world is two-way rather than one-way.

Strategic management is important for ensuring success because it is also the key to all other school management processes. It is the blueprint which informs and co-ordinates other decisions on:

- curriculum
- staffing—appointments and development
- resourcing
- marketing/public relations

Strategy and strategic change

The rapid pace of change in the environment may require an organisation to make more than small changes in order to keep in step. Mintzberg, in a historical study of organisational strategy, identified four types of strategic change—continuity, incremental, flux and global or transformational change. Global change was infrequent but was necessary when the organisation and its environment had fallen badly out of step.

It may well be that the nature of the changes ushered in by the ERA and attendant political and social expectations may mean for many schools that a form of global change in strategic direction may be necessary. The regular inspections of schools conducted under the OFSTED framework (OFSTED, 1994a) are identifying schools in need of special measures and schools that are in danger of failing to give their pupils an adequate education. Such schools in particular could be expected to require transformational change.

There are two basic approaches to strategic change:

1 incremental change

2 radical change or global change

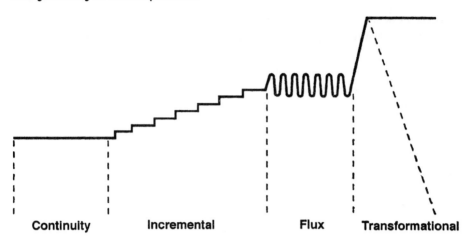

Figure 3.1 Patterns of strategic change

Source: reproduced from Johnson and Scholes, 1993, p. 35, by permission of the publisher, Prentice Hall International, Hemel Hempstead

Logical incrementalism

Changes can be more readily planned and implemented if they are small and not too rapid. This may be appropriate where the environment is changing slowly and there is a small response from the organisation with each change from the environment. Large changes can also be accomplished in this way over a longer time-scale. In this case, if there were a larger and more abrupt change in the environment, this would need to be anticipated by changes beginning in the organisation in advance of overt manifestations of change in the environment.

Quinn (1980) has identified an incremental change process in organisations, which he calls logical incrementalism. This is the process by which an organisation makes a number of small exploratory changes with a view to assessing their effects. Some will be successful and will grow and expand in scope and others will not be repeated because they are less successful. This has two advantages. The first is that if environmental trends have been spotted accurately these changes will be mainly successful. The second is that if the environmental trends have been spotted less accurately, there will be a range of internal changes whose effects can be assessed with a view to expanding the more successful and knowing more about their likely effects, rather than starting from scratch. In order to reap the benefits of logical incrementalism a high degree of planning and evaluation are needed. Johnson (1987) has provided an account of logical incrementalism in action in a UK business organisation.

Radical change

Radical change is not only more difficult in practice than incremental change but it is also more difficult to conceptualise and offer suitable mechanisms to steer the process. There is abundant evidence to show that managers in commercial organisations are not good at picking up the signs that changes of this magnitude are required. The analogy of boiling a frog slowly is a good illustration. The frog would jump out of hot water if it were suddenly immersed but no such instantaneous decision is possible if each increase in temperature is very slight and it is only the cumulative effects of all such increases which is overwhelming.

In this case radical change, when the need is manifest, could have been avoided by a series of prior incremental changes if the need for them had been recognised in advance. Thus a counsel of perfection would point out that one shouldn't be starting by having to contemplate a radical change. A harder case to suggest an alternative is when there is a sudden and unpredictable change in the environment, e.g. the Greenwich judgment about priority school places being offered to children from inside the LEA being overturned at a stroke by a court judgment (Morris, 1995).

Radical change, whether it could have been predicted earlier or whether it couldn't, presents a challenge as to how it should be accomplished. This is precisely the situation that Stacey (1993) has recognised and elaborated. The last of the four models of strategic management described in the next section deals with the formation of radical strategy.

Models of strategic management

Four models of strategic management are given in this section. The first is a basic model comprising three organising decisions and three substantive stages. The second is a model derived from that devised for the *ELMS Workbook* (Fidler *et al.*, 1991). It is a cyclic model which clearly illustrates differences compared to school development planning.

The third model which is most helpful for analysing each of the three major stages involved in strategic management, and which provides the structure for Chapters 5 and 6, is based upon that of Johnson and Scholes (1993), first formulated in 1984. A fourth model briefly examines means of responding to a rapidly changing and unpredictable environment (Stacey, 1993).

The first three models present different ways of trying to envisage and represent the same process. In that sense they are complementary, but differ in various different aspects of the process. They offer different perspectives on the process of strategic management. Greater detail on any part of the process in a particular model can be gained by reading the equivalent section on the other models in this and the next three chapters.

Basic model of strategic management

This is based upon the ideas of Barry (1986) after substantial experience with small non-profit organisations in the USA. He lists the following steps:

1 get organised

2 take stock

3 develop a strategy

4 draft and refine the plan

5 implement the plan

We have adapted this to pick out three organising decisions about how to carry out the strategy process and have separated these from the three substantive parts—analysis (2), choice (3) and implementation (5). A diagram incorporating decisions on process and decisions on substantive content based on this model is shown in Figure 3.2. In addition to the five stages described above, a sixth has been added—making decisions about how to choose strategy. In Barry's five steps this was treated as part of developing strategy, but seems more appropriately treated as the third organising decision. The organising decisions A, C, E and the strategy processes B, D and F are described below.

A. Decide how to organise

■ decide whether to develop a strategic plan

■ obtain commitment

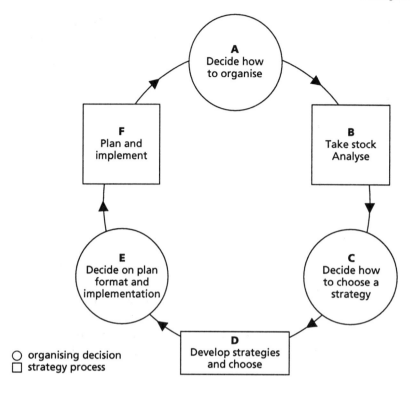

○ organising decision
□ strategy process

Figure 3.2   A basic model of strategic management

- determine if outside help is needed
- outline a formal planning process that fits
- form a planning team

This is the stage at which decisions about the planning process itself are made. Having decided to engage in strategic planning, all those involved need to be convinced that this is a process on which it is worth spending time and effort. External help can be of benefit both to those schools that lack confidence in their ability to engage in the process unaided, and also to those more confident schools that recognise the value of a 'critical friend' (and particularly a knowledgeable and experienced one) to assist and flag up issues in danger of being overlooked by those inside the school. Problems are likely to concern the availability of a suitable consultant and finance to employ such external help. A basic planning process needs to be decided that is suitable for the particular school and its staff. Questions such as the following need to be answered. Who is going to take part? From whom is evidence to be collected? Who is to be consulted? How are decisions to be made? Finally, the group who are going to carry out most of the work need to be formed on an appropriate basis.

B. Take stock—analyse

- past and present situation
- mission
- opportunities and threats
- strengths and weaknesses
- critical issues for the future

Any plan has to begin where the school is now, so the present situation must be reviewed and the historical reasons for its position assessed. The school's purpose, including the groups it serves and its broad aims, should be reviewed. A SWOT analysis will reveal Strengths and Weaknesses inside the school and Opportunities and Threats from outside the school. From this analysis some issues which are crucial for the future of the school should emerge.

C. Decide how to choose

- select a planning approach
- who should be involved and how

Having completed the analysis phase, a planning approach or combination of approaches should be selected to help create alternative strategies for the future. The approaches are:

- developing a vision
- identifying and resolving strategic issues (Bryson, 1988)
- setting goals
- a cost-benefit approach

These are described in more detail in Chapter 5. Decisions are also needed about how this should be organised. Do all participants use all the approaches, or do groups each use one approach and compare results?

D. Develop strategies and choose

- identify and evaluate alternatives

- develop strategy

- adopt strategy

The techniques and ways of working which have been selected should be used to clarify aims and outcomes and develop alternative means of achieving these ends. The means should be grouped and evaluated in order to choose a strategy.

E. Decide on plan format and implementation

- agree on plan format

- decide how it is to be implemented

A strategic plan is a complex document and the form in which it is to be produced and used needs forethought. With some agreement on format all contributors know what the document should look like and a first draft can be produced. How the plan will be used in implementation and who will be involved in implementation needs discussion.

F. Plan and implement

- develop a first draft

- refine the plan

- adopt the plan

- implement the plan

- monitor performance

- take corrective action

- update the plan

The plan needs refining through discussion and the final plan needs to be formally agreed and adopted. The plan should have actions, time-scales, resources required, staff development needs, and responsibilities incorporated, so that a schedule of action is clear. As these actions are implemented they should be monitored and compared with the plan so that any corrective action can be taken. Periodically, the plan should be updated.

Fidler and Bowles model

A model to indicate stages of strategic management in schools which supplements the Johnson and Scholes (1993) model is shown in Figure 3.3. This model is based on that devised by Fidler and Bowles (Fidler *et al.*, 1991). It shows the cyclic nature of strategic management with the evaluation process at the end of one cycle feeding into the analysis stage of the next cycle. This model brings out two important differences from school development planning which might have a similar cycle. At the analysis stage there are inputs from outside the school. These are illustrated in the model as market research, by which the views of parents and potential parents about the school's operations are sought, and environmental scanning. This is the process by which influences outside the school which might affect its future are identified and assessed, particularly those that are growing in importance. This includes such influences as new requirements from DFEE and other statutory bodies, and also includes more pervasive influences such as the possibilities of an increased use of information technology.

The second major difference compared to school development planning shown in this diagram is the presence of a creative vision of the future in addition to the results of the analysis of the present, such that both inform possible choices for the future. From these a strategy is chosen to begin the transformation towards the vision.

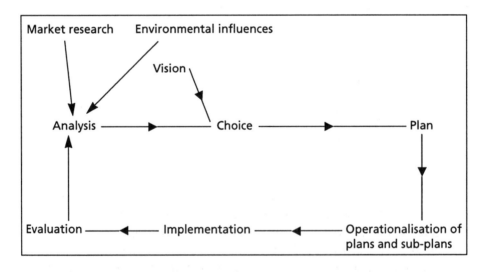

Figure 3.3   Fidler and Bowles model of strategic management in schools
Source: Fidler *et al.*, 1991, p. 25

In particular, this model elaborates the planning process to show the need to have broad plans containing long-term trends and also to operationalise and produce more precise operating or action plans.

The school will have a mission statement which gives its long-term purpose and the groups it intends to serve, and which has been questioned as part of the strategic analysis. In addition, the strategic plan will involve the creation of a short, compact, memorable, meaningful focus statement outlining the specific development of the school which this strategy encapsulates. The wording of this statement should have been refined so as to be very concise, while retaining as many of the nuances as possible that are the keys to the direction of many other aspects of the school's work. It should be capable of being 'unpacked' to yield the core values of the school and its vision of the future. The most basic feature of the statement is that it should be a guide to action.

The importance of this process is described in Chapter 10. It corresponds to the situation described by HMI at Newall Green High School (OFSTED, 1994b), where everyone in the school knew where the school was going. This is the situation which Harvey-Jones (1988) describes at ICI when major change was contemplated.

The strategic plan should have implications for each of a series of more detailed sub-plans. It should include implications both for what to do and also what not to do. In short, it should indicate (implicit) priorities.

The focus statement may be amplified by lists of long-term objectives indicating intended progress on a range of fronts. These should be consistent with each other and, where there are potential internal inconsistencies, the means by which these are to be resolved should be indicated.

The first level of detail of the strategic plan is the plan of the organisational structure and decision-making machinery of the school, including the involvement of governors. The strategic plan will have implications for the structure of responsibilities in the school which, combined with the culture of the school, will have implications for how decisions are made and the involvement of governors. Where this implies a change in the culture of the school, this should have been recognised at the choice stage and the extent of the implications of the change recognised.

The detailed sub-plans for the four main areas of decision-making in the school are:

■ curriculum (and pupil outcomes) plan
    (what we intend to contribute to children's learning)

- staffing plan
  (how we intend to recruit and develop people with the skills to do it)

- financial (and material resources and premises) plan
  (how we intend to spend the money to help us achieve it)

- marketing plan
  (how we intend to obtain the resources, support and commitment of others to enable us to do it)

Each of these plans will be inter-related and consistent with the overall strategic plan.

In each of these plans there will be long-term and short-term objectives. For example, in the staffing plan there might be a long-term aim to move to a more balanced age-profile of staff, to take on more classroom assistants and to take on more part-time teaching staff. This would provide a means of giving enhanced flexibility in the future and would be part of a longer-term plan to make full-time teachers curriculum managers, changing their role to planners and managers of learning.

Depending on finances, some limited progress on some of these may be possible, but until some full-time teachers leave by promotion, retirement or other reason no major progress may be feasible. However, the purpose of this aspect of the plan is to keep these issues in mind for the occasion when a full-time teacher leaves. Such a situation represents a strategic decision as we mentioned in Chapter 1. 'Fortune favours the prepared mind' (Louis Pasteur).

The shorter-term objectives will find their expression in action plans including plans for parts of the school such as departments or teams. Thus there is a hierarchy of plans as set out in Figure 3.4.

Johnson and Scholes model

There are many formulations of how to develop and implement strategy both in the commercial world and in NFPs. However, the deliberate approaches operating in Whittington's (1993) systemic quadrant have much in common and can generally be equated with the composite model developed by Johnson and Scholes (see Figure 3.5). This model has many advantages, including an easily memorable visual representation, and incorporates elements of the micro-politics of organisations which are helpful in planning strategy.

The model consists of three stages, each of which has three major parts. These are:

Figure 3.4   Hierarchy of plans
Source: Fidler *et al.*, 1991, p. 23

- strategic analysis

- strategic choice

- strategic implementation

This offers a model for both working on and thinking about strategic management. Although these stages might logically be seen as being sequential, in practice each is not carried out in isolation. Each will interact with the others. There is an inevitable tension between a holistic view of strategy formation and an analysis of the individual parts. The analysis both gives conceptual clarity to each process and also ensures that no part is forgotten. Although the use of the individual parts of the analysis suggests that the process is a rational one, nevertheless Johnson and Scholes have as one of their fundamental precepts of the process, that it is not only a rational analysis but also a substantial political and micro-political process.

The analysis stage represents a systematic way of taking stock of the present. It involves scanning the environment, assessing current resources and their usage and assessing the current culture and values of the school.

The choice stage represents the devising of alternative courses of action, their assessment and the choice of one or a combination of them as the strategy. These two stages are elaborated in Chapter 5.

Figure 3.5   The Johnson and Scholes summary model of strategic management
Source: reproduced from Johnson and Scholes, 1993, p. 23, by permission of the publisher, Prentice Hall International, Hemel Hempstead

The implementation stage gives three areas to consider in implementing a strategy. The strategy should have been chosen on the basis that resources would be available if they were properly planned. There may need to be changes to the organisational structure, including roles and responsibilities, decision-making structures, policies and systems. The final element is a summary one—managing strategic change. This is the organising structure, which includes the other two elements and in addition considers the people in the organisation and its culture. This will involve a consideration of the approaches in Chapter 2 on managing planned change. In particular, the people designated to make the strategy work need detailed attention. New staff may be required, either as additions or as replacements for current staff as they leave. Current staff may need development and support in the implementation phase. More importantly, modifications to the organisation's culture may be required. These issues are discussed more thoroughly in Chapter 6.

The process is an iterative one by which implementation is considered at the choice stage and choice is considered at the analysis stage. Each stage needs to use data generated by the preceding stage, and also needs to consider the implications of possible outcomes of the present stage for the next stage.

There are clearly differences of approach in thinking about who should take part in strategy formulation. It is possible that in a highly autocratic organisation members of the most senior management would be the ones to analyse, choose and implement the strategy. However, it is the contention of Johnson and Scholes that it is the responsibility of every manager to consider strategy. Each manager should have some inputs to make to the process, since each must play their part in implementation and may have unique insights into the effects of the strategy in action.

The managerial process by which all these efforts are co-ordinated is clearly a massive one and one in which individual differences between organisations will show up. It is likely that a consultative or participative mode by which all managers play a part in the formation of strategy, fully understand the strategy when it is finally chosen, and then play their part in implementing it in an appropriate way, will yield the greatest overall success.

At all stages of the process judgements are required, for example, about what environmental influences to investigate and about what importance they warrant. Thus power and influence can be expected to play a part in the process and affect the choice of strategy. This may be a clearly political process at the choice stage, but the micro-politics which are likely at all the other stages should also be recognised. Providing these differences of emphasis are within an overall shared culture, the sharing of political power may be a positive advantage as external conditions become more unstable.

Strategy far from equilibrium

Stacey (1993) has extended conventional strategic management to situations which are far from stable. He points out that there are some features of strategy which do not conveniently fit into the models we have examined so far. These are where:

1 Competitor organisations are a major feature of the environment.

In this case there will be a more dynamic interaction between the organisation and its environment than conventionally envisaged. As the organisation changes its strategy, there will be a reaction from competitor organisations which in turn will provoke a reaction from the original organisation and so on. This will be a factor where schools are in close competition with each other.

2 Cause and effect are not clearly related (and in most complex organisational processes they aren't).

The effects of change may be slow in being fed back so that attempts to apply corrections to the process of implementation may be either too slow or too uncertain. Thus the organisation moves further away from being in equilibrium with its surroundings.

3 Weak signals in the environment may grow non-linearly and require a change in the paradigm by which the organisation operates rather than a step-by-step response.

The previous point shows the potential ineffectiveness of a step-by-step response to situations of this kind. However, the major challenge of this situation is of the need for transformational change or a change of paradigm.

4 In implementing change of this paradigm-changing nature, which does not have a historical precedent, rational analysis has its limitations for planning the future of a complex organisation.

The degree of predictability which is inherent in most rationally planned processes may simply not be present. This degree of uncertainty does not fit easily with the rational long-term planning process.

Stacey is mainly concerned with business organisations in a highly competitive environment. However, some of the factors above will be true of some schools at some times. Some of his other warnings may also be true of schools. He points out that a number of empirical studies (for example Miller, 1990; Pascale, 1991) of the demise of successful companies show that this was because they got stuck in a rut, albeit an initially successful rut. They had such a strong self-reinforcing culture that they continued and exaggerated a strategy long after it had ceased to be successful. This is one of a series of paradoxes which he uncovers. Others have pondered the question, 'what does an excellent company do in the future?'.

This is an equally relevant question for schools. How do successful schools avoid either becoming complacent or continuing to work hard at the factors which made them successful long after these have ceased to be criteria that represent the forefront of development? In other words, how do successful schools innovate?

Stacey (1993) examines various prescriptions which have been offered for dealing with a rapidly changing environment. He examines the idea of a strong culture which underlies the prescription of Peters and Waterman (1982) and concludes that control by a strong shared culture is inflexible. On the other hand, the institutionalisation of a flexible structure suggested over the years by a series of writers from Burns and Stalker (1961) to Kanter (1989) emphasises self-managing groups rather than short-term control. He concludes in this case that there is simply no means of instituting short-term control in such organisations in periods of external turbulence and, more importantly, deciding what to do in the longer term.

Thus he proposes resolving the paradox of control and innovation by supplementing the formal hierarchy, which gives short-term control, by a stronger informal structure of self-organising groups operating by political interaction. Whilst such groups can only be encouraged rather than institutionalised, he identifies conditions that are conducive to such groups. Power in the hierarchy should be neither too concentrated, nor too diffuse, so that any solutions to strategic issues have to amass political support within the organisation, rather than being able to be imposed or being unimplementable. The organisational culture should not be very strong nor very weak, so that there are sufficient shared assumptions but enough differences to make their interaction productive.

In these conditions Stacey envisages informal *ad hoc* groups composed of people from different levels and different functions and representing different strands of culture within the organisation. They would be given open-ended issues to discuss and asked to formulate a response. Work in such groups should be non-hierarchical and micro-political, whereby ideas have to amass support to be pursued.

The hierarchy provides not only short-term planning and control of current operations, but also a structure to approve and resource the proposals from the self-organising group for the new long-term strategy of the organisation.

> New knowledge comes from tapping the tacit, subjective insights, intuitions and hunches of individuals and making them available for testing and use by the organisation as a whole.
> (Stacey, 1993, p. 365)

This will involve organisation members operating in a spirit of openness while tolerating conflict and uncertainty as the norms of the organisation are tested and a new strategy is created.

Those who advocate for schools:

- a strongly shared culture
- collegiality

should recognise the weaknesses of these prescriptions for innovation and long-term success, particularly in difficult conditions. As Stacey points out: 'Differences in culture are essential to change . . . difference in power distribution is also essential to change' (Stacey, 1993, p. 360).

4

Managing strategy

Introduction

This chapter is concerned with organising the strategy-making process. It begins with a consideration of different models of how organisations operate. Managers need to be able to model how their organisation, or parts of it, work. Inevitably any model will be an oversimplification, but it should provide a framework for thinking and allow discussion with others and joint planning.

Secondly, there is a discussion of leadership and styles of leadership. It is important to be aware of one's own style of leadership and also to envisage what might be required to lead the strategy-making process. No single leader will have the range of attributes and skills for every occasion, but within a senior management team there are many more possibilities.

Finally, organisational arrangements for producing strategy are considered. These cover the role of the governing body, the involvement of staff and managing change. There are models showing different aspects of the process: (a) time-scale; (b) involvement; and (c) centralisation. There is also a brief review of methods of data collection.

Models of organisation

There have been many attempts to summarise and categorise the various theoretical accounts of how organisations do, or should, work (Hughes, 1985; Ribbins, 1985; Hoyle, 1986; Hoy and Miskel, 1991; Bush, 1995). However, as always, attempts to model run into the 'dilemma of choosing between the Scylla of theoretical parsimony and the Charybdis of messy reality' (Louis, 1981, p. 192). The range of models offered here should be seen as distinctly Scyllian.

We offer two approaches to how organisations operate—the rational and the political—and a useful analytic device—the Getzels and Guba model.

A view of how a rational organisation operates assumes that rational principles apply, that decisions are made on the basis of evidence presented, and that those decisions are made to further the ends of the organisation. The alternative is to assume that rather than operating by consensus, organisations are factional and operate on the basis of a distribution of power which is highly influential in the decision-making process. In this case, personalities and interests are important considerations.

Managers need to have flexible models in their heads so as to be able to select an appropriate model for their context at a particular point in time, both to analyse what is going on and to plan effective action. Different models may be required for different parts of the same organisation and different models at different times in the same organisation. Thus managers need to build up flexibility of modelling.

Rational model

This model emphasises aims and objectives and rational means of working to achieve these aims. The aims may be generated and imposed by one person or devised and implemented in a participative way. The guiding principle for action is the achievement of the aims of the whole organisation, whether they are imposed or shared.

Bureaucracy

Most schools are likely to operate with a number of characteristics of a bureaucracy. Key decisions are made at the top of the organisation, even if there is a great deal of consultation beforehand. Individual responsibilities are delegated and the school may have a number of policies which are formulated to give a degree of consistency and impartiality to its actions. There is no suggestion here that schools operate as ideal bureaucracies, but rather that this is the best of the limited number of descriptions of organisations that are readily available.

Collegiality

Collegiality, as participative self-government is called, is rather different in operation to a bureaucracy, but has the essential feature of working towards common goals. In this case, however, those goals have been formally agreed by the organisation members, and power is distributed in a much more even way than in a bureaucracy. Such a participatory mode of working has much to recommend it and is highly commended by writers on school organisation. The research evidence fails to show these advantages in practice (Conway, 1984). We raise below what we see as some potential disadvantages from the point of view of generating strategy.

Collegiality is most in evidence in higher education institutions and here it is not without its drawbacks. Accountability and power are both problems in a collegial organisation. As Noble and Pym (1970) identified, once a committee makes a decision everybody is responsible and nobody is responsible. However, not only is there a problem of accountability, there are more insidious problems. The more power is dispersed, the more everybody feels powerless in the face of adversity, rather than empowered. Perhaps there is a critical mass of power which once diluted makes everyone unable to function. Even worse, power may be usurped by those who are unethical, politically astute or personally domineering.

The proponents of collegiality take it as self-evident that if teachers are given the freedom to operate, they will operate in the best interests of the school. The effects on children, parents and the community are never adequately considered. The discussion is entirely in terms of what might be best from the point of view of the staff (and generally, only the teaching staff). Whilst conscientious teachers will have the interests of children to guide their actions, what about those who lose sight of children's interests or who are not competent? The headteacher is in a position to safeguard the interests of children and parents where they are in conflict with the self-interest of teachers. Since such an institution is self-regulating, it is very difficult to arrest any decline that might occur. It is no accident that the self-governing universities of Oxford and Cambridge had to be reformed by Act of Parliament in the nineteenth century (Curtis, 1948). They had fallen into lethargy and corruption and operated in their own self-interests rather than those of the students they were ostensibly meant to serve.

It is because there is no one with superordinate power that it is so difficult to improve a situation of true collegiate decision-making. This could only be accomplished by a universal uprising. Given the diffuse accountability, apportioning lack of competence to individual members of a committee is extraordinarily difficult.

Political model

The alternative model is of organisations as political systems (Hoyle, 1986). Here, there are multiple and ambiguous aims and much jockeying for power and influence within the organisation. Decisions are influenced by the case and the persuasiveness and influence of the person making the case. A particular version of the political model which has been detected in higher education is the 'garbage can' model (Cohen *et al.*, 1972), in which solutions hunt for problems to fit rather than the reverse. Ideas are taken up because they happen to be around and have their proponents who are influential.

Getzels and Guba social systems model

This model is a useful analytical device for disentangling the effects of two components of behaviour in organisations. One component is the organisational dimension composed of roles and expectations and is essentially structural. The other is the personal or human dimension. This focuses on the individual people who hold the positions or roles and how their personality affects their behaviour (Hughes, 1985).

Whilst organisational structures may have one effect if they are assumed to be operated neutrally, their purpose may be subverted if operated by a particular individual. This emphasises that the holder of an office can have an effect which would not be expected in a bureaucracy. The influence of the office-holder will be stronger in an ambiguous or weak structure than in a bureaucratic one where power and procedures are highly prescribed. Similarly, collecting individuals together in groups may yield effects different to each of them operating individually.

This is a useful analytic device for rationally predicting the workings of a political system and planning how to operate it to achieve desired results.

An illustration of the effect can be envisaged by comparing the actions of the last few Secretaries of State for Education. Although they have held the same office with similar powers and expectations, within a short period it has been possible to predict how they would interpret that office and how their individual personalities would affect their actions—for better or worse. A similar effect can be observed for the holders of offices within schools.

Leadership

For all aspects of school management, leadership is a crucial ingredient (Fidler, 1996b) and this is particularly true of strategic management. It has become fashionable to differentiate conceptually between leadership and management. Leadership is particularly reserved for those proactive actions which are concerned with changing the course of organisations. This is the realm of strategy. Such leadership may need explicitly to encompass more than the rational execution of an effective task and to incorporate symbolic aspects. This section discusses these issues, and although it concentrates on leadership, good management is also required to carry out the strategic management process.

In the few instances where the work of headteachers has been analysed, the findings show that it consists of multiple short reactive tasks and is very fragmented. This is also found in the work of managers in other organisations (Stewart, 1976; 1982), although these results don't have a simple interpretation (Hales, 1986; Stewart, 1989). However, it is middle managers in other organisations who have similar working days, not chief executives. As Jenkins (1985) points out, the contrast between chief executives in industry and headteachers in schools is the lack of time which heads set aside for long-term strategic planning.

This does suggest that the leadership demonstrated in schools is largely reactive rather than part of an overall strategy and that headteachers have, in general, not examined and thought deeply about this aspect of their leadership behaviour. This reinforces the view that not all those in leadership positions can be expected to show appropriate leadership without some form of preparation and development.

Hersey and Blanchard's (1988) situational leadership model is a useful heuristic device. They maintain that a leadership style should be contingent on a number of factors:

- nature of the task
- maturity of the group
- nature of the individual leader

The two components of leadership style are task orientation (concern with outcomes) and relationship orientation (concern for people). The basic judgements are about (1) the extent to which the task is clear or problematic, with more relationship-oriented behaviour being more appropriate for ambiguous tasks, and (2) the maturity of the group being led, with a more task-oriented approach being suitable for a less mature group.

Whilst this model has a great deal of face validity, those who have critically examined the evidence supporting the theory point out that little independent empirical research has been attempted as the theory is somewhat tautological.

Relationship between leadership and management

The terms used to describe many concepts vary internationally and they also vary over time. If we take proactive and reactive modes of operation as opposite ends of a continuum, the terms administration, management and leadership can then be arranged, as shown in Figure 4.1.

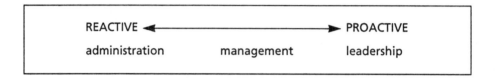

Figure 4.1 Proactive and reactive elements of management

Here, administration is seen as a maintenance function. It is concerned with the smooth and efficient operation of processes which are already established. At the opposite end of the spectrum leadership is concerned with personal initiative and new activities, and may take on a symbolic and inspirational role at its extreme. This is not to suggest that all leaders need to be of the charismatic kind, far from it; but all leaders could, and probably should, consider the symbolic aspects of their actions. In this way they can seek to portray the appropriate messages for those seeking meaning in their actions. Whilst management has both proactive and reactive aspects, current usage is tending to reduce it to the more reactive whilst still seeing it as an essential vehicle for implementing the changes which leadership has proposed and won acceptance for.

A number of writers on leadership in the USA (Bennis, 1984) have taken this latter view and this has been echoed in the educational leadership literature following reports bemoaning the need for leadership in America's schools (Bolman and Deal, 1994). Undoubtedly, there is a tension between the needs of good administration and the needs of proactive change which this formulation exposes.

Even where charismatic leadership exists, in order to accomplish tasks successfully the processes of management have to be used—planning, organising, staffing, controlling and evaluating. In this sense leadership and management are complementary. Equally, when juxtaposing innovation and routine, innovation is more likely to be successfully accomplished when systematic management processes are applied to it.

All the leadership in an organisation should not be embodied in one person. Others should exhibit leadership within their sphere of influence. Thus a head of department might be expected to exhibit leadership within a department and, possibly, in some whole-school functions. This is related to the issue of whether leadership is part of management or not. As numerous writers point out (Schon, 1984), whilst managers are in a position to exercise leadership, not all managers will exhibit leadership and some non-managers may exhibit leadership. It follows from this that most people in management positions within an organisation should be showing leadership in their area of work. There will in addition be others on particular occasions and on particular issues who should also display leadership. It follows that there should be delegated leadership in schools.

A leader within an organisation also has to be able to manage. The definition of management which is used here is 'the art of achieving results, using resources efficiently, by working with and through people' (Fidler and Bowles, 1989). Management functions include managing finance, managing staff and managing the process which achieves results. The management processes of planning, organising, and evaluating also need to be employed. Thus whatever leadership style is used, the more routine competences of management need also to be present to ensure that aims are translated into results (see Figure 4.2).

Bolman and Deal (1991) offer a four-fold typology of leadership:

- structural
- human relations
- political
- symbolic

The authors recognise that appropriate leadership needs to be situational, but they also recognise that individual leaders will have a preferred if not dominant style which reflects their own personality. Each style has advantages but should not be regarded as exclusive. They identify successful combinations where a particular style of a chief executive is complemented by a different style from another senior manager in the organisation. The result of analysing the leader's style and comparing this with the needs of the organisation at that particular time may throw up additional requirements in order for the organisation to be successful.

The structural framework is largely focused on a rational view of management. Leadership concentrates on rational analysis and operating the

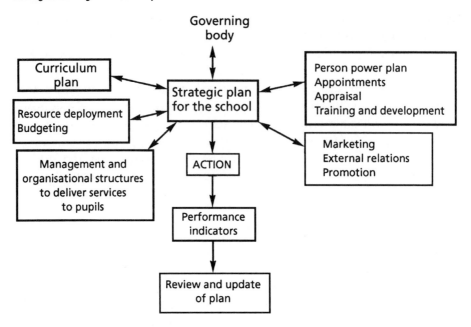

Figure 4.2   A summary model showing the relationship between strategy and other management functions
Source: Fidler and Bowles, 1989, p. 21

formal mechanism through a hierarchy of control. The human relations framework concentrates on the behavioural aspects of management and on harnessing the motivation and commitment of employees. Individuals are delegated substantial tasks and allowed the freedom to perform them in their own ways by taking initiative. Much of management training has emphasised these human relations skills.

The political framework recognises that individuals both within and without an organisation have their own private agendas of interests. Thus there will be seats of power which may lead to conflicts if skilful political arts of forming coalitions, bargaining and negotiation are not used.

The symbolic framework is also referred to as visionary leadership, and Burns (1978) used the term transformational leadership for a similar activity. Each of these terms helps to sketch the facets of this most recent of frameworks. Transformational leadership is contrasted with steady-state or transactional leadership. Transactional leadership is concerned with carrying out routine tasks rather than taking on new challenges. Visionary leadership is concerned with providing followers with insights into the nature of new challenges and what is to be achieved. This goes beyond the immediate task and reflects a distant improved future. It provides followers with a rationale for their work. The vision of the future may be drawn up collaboratively, but the leader has the task of articulating it in a compelling way. Finally, the symbolism comes in to give meaning to the task and to formulate acts which demonstrate the new approach and inspire and give confidence to organisation members. Clearly, much of this kind of activity is related to strategy.

Leadership in schools

Leading professional/chief executive

Leadership in professionally staffed organisations poses additional complications compared to leadership in other organisations (Hughes, 1985). All the foregoing requirements of leadership apply. The leader needs to act as chief executive in a managerial capacity and as a leader in the symbolic and political senses. However, the leader of a professionally staffed organisation also needs to be the leading professional, or at least a leading professional. He or she must espouse professional values and possess appropriate professional knowledge and judgement. Duignan and Macpherson (1992), in their theory of educative leadership, ascribe a 'realm of ideas' to judgements about what is of value and what is significant in the education of children. They see this as a third component, in addition to management and leadership, which is required of an educational leader.

Following LMS, many heads have realised that they have a role of chief executive or manager of managers. Many, however, have not come to terms with the additional need either to remain the leading professional or to ensure that another senior manager in the school clearly performs this function and that educational values, not financial ones, are seen to predominate.

Instructional leadership

School leaders in the UK have no framework for 'instructional leadership', to use terminology from the USA, or the management of learning or management of the curriculum as we should probably call it here. In our literature there is a dearth of writing on how to manage the curriculum. Whilst policy-making on the curriculum, usually in a consultative or participative manner, is discussed in our literature, there are no 'frameworks for thinking' with which to plan to influence what teachers actually do in classrooms. The assumption is that all teachers go into their classrooms, close the door and implement the agreed policy. We don't actually have the evidence about whether they do or they don't, but evidence from other countries is that they don't. Much more effort is required to influence classroom processes.

Work from the USA which proposes structural, cultural and interpersonal linkages to influence teachers' classroom actions seems to offer a fruitful approach to conceptualising the ways in which headteachers could influence what teachers do in classrooms (Firestone and Wilson, 1985). The structural dimension consists of all the systems and processes which the organisational structure of the school provides as formal influence processes on teachers, e.g. policies, rules, resources etc. The cultural dimension is that subtle and ever-present set of expectations about 'the way we do things here'; the taken-for-granted assumptions about institutional norms of behaviour and value, which are discussed in Chapter 5. The interpersonal dimension is the one-to-one direct influence of working together.

Strategy planning process

Our general assumption is that a relatively small strategy planning group is formed on some appropriate basis, and includes the headteacher. This group needs to plan the strategy formation process and it may also play a leading part in the process. Although related, these two aspects are conceptually separate. In most schools the group will perform both functions and one of their tasks will be to decide how others within and outside the school should be involved.

In a highly participatory school, however, the function of the group could be to deal solely with devising a process which is approved by the whole staff and within which the members of the planning group play no greater role than any other member of staff. Although this might seem somewhat contrived, it is intended to demonstrate that strategic planning need not be top-down. However, in most schools it will probably be a combination of a clear steer from the top whilst ensuring that everyone feels that they have been adequately consulted and that the process has produced an appropriate outcome.

In all cases we assume that, regardless of any more active role which it or its members may play, the strategy will be formally approved by the governing body.

The governing body

The role that the governing body expects to play and the role that it would be desirable for it to play in strategy formation both need to be considered. To an extent, the precedent may be set by the governing body's relationship to the current school development plan and financial plan. Here, practices appear to vary greatly.

Finance

The governing body is required to approve the school's budget, but this may involve only formal approval of a document in the form of a balance sheet. It is the extent to which governors participate in discussions that precede this document that is the better guide to involvement. There is often a finance committee which plays a part in building up the budget and has an understanding of the inter-relationships between the different budget heads. Members of this group might be expected to be involved in developing strategy, since ultimately the strategy will have implications for, and be a major influence on, the shape of the budget plan in future years.

School development plan

Some school governing bodies approve the school development plan, some may play a part in drawing it up, but few appear to have a committee structure which readily relates to such holistic policies. Instead there is generally a number of specialist committees—finance, staffing and curriculum—and the whole governing body. A few schools have a specialist committee that deals with long-term planning including the school development plan, and which has representatives from the other specialist committees. GM schools are required to have a finance and general purposes committee which could perform this function. Where such a specialist committee exists it would seem a natural progression for such a group to take part in, or at least receive notice of, strategic planning, and discuss and critically appraise the resulting proposals.

If there is to be realistic governor involvement then if such a specialist grouping does not exist as a standing committee of the governing body, an *ad hoc* working party involving representation from committees should be set up. This is because strategy, when formed, will have implications, if not explicit requirements, for the long-term work of each of the specialist committees and, of course, the whole school.

Specialist input to the process

In addition to their formal role as members of the governing body, it might be expected that governors might contribute because of their specialist expertise with respect to processes involved in the formation of strategy and/or have access to privileged knowledge of local conditions and other schools. Any 'outsider's' view of the school and possession of 'soft' information about local plans and expectations is an invaluable asset to the strategic planning process. Depending on the personal attributes of such people it may be advantageous to involve some of them at a core level in the process, whilst others may play a more limited role and contribute their specialist information and give feedback on plans as they are formed, in a more specific way.

Staff working together

Involvement

This is the general term which we use to describe both consultation and participation (Fidler *et al.*, 1991). It is essential that all staff are involved in the formation of strategy in some way. However, the details of who should be involved, in what way, and for what purpose need detailed consideration. In addition to the principles on which such decisions are made, there needs to be a consideration of the numbers and types of people involved and the associated logistics.

Fidler *et al.* (1991) in the *ELMS Workbook: Planning Your School's Strategy* differentiate between consultation and participation and give some guidance on how to choose appropriate forms of involvement. The initial step is to make known the basis of decision-making. If staff are being consulted then this needs to be made clear and what this entails explained. On the other hand, where staff are being invited to participate in a decision which is to be ratified by the governing body, this also needs to be made clear. Disillusionment follows when there is misunderstanding about what is to happen.

All staff need to be able to contribute both hard and soft data at the analysis stage. Staff members may have access to information which senior managers don't have and which might be crucial. There is an example from an infants' school where the early years co-ordinator knew of the importance for admissions of the recommendation from the local playgroup. Other teachers and the senior management didn't know this, yet it was a vital piece of strategic information. In a secondary school there may be an examinations board chief examiner or other person who has high-level outside knowledge.

Conflict

Most accounts of organisations assume that there is a large degree of consensus and few serious disagreements among organisation members. For many organisations, including schools, this is true for much of the time. However, in some schools for some of the time and in a small number of schools for a large portion of time, conflict, either open or hidden, is present. In order to give a complete and relatively realistic account of organisation working we need to acknowledge the possibilities of conflict and offer sources of advice.

Turning to the literature on organisational development in schools we find that conflicts are not uncommon:

> ... *Conflicts are ubiquitous in complex organisations, the best strategy for dealing with them differs from case to case. The most effective strategy depends on the severity of the disagreement, who the adversaries are, whether the conflict is potentially constructive (i.e. will produce creative tensions) or destructive, and on the authority, resources, and knowledge the administrator or teacher possesses.* (Schmuck et al., 1972, p. 136)

Working together more closely provides precisely the circumstances in which conflict is likely to emerge. Conflicts are minimised when each teacher is left to work in their own way in their own classroom. It is when they meet, discuss and are required to co-operate that conflict may arise.

> *Collaboration unavoidably brings conflict ... Conflict is normal and unavoidable in complex organisations that are moving to multifaceted goals ... the seminal point is that conflicts should be brought into the open and managed without expecting them to disappear of their own accord.* (Schmuck et al., 1972, p. 136)

Whether to resolve conflict and to what extent

Conflict resolution is not easy and if not successful may make the situation worse, so a great deal of preparatory work needs to go into deciding whether this is an issue which should be tackled.

> *Some conflicts are natural and inevitable; they even provide a creative tension which can help improve performance. Other conflicts while not directly helpful to the organisation, are not so destructive as to require the efforts of a specialist.* (Schmuck et al., 1972, p. 142)

Do the individuals need to work together closely? The closer they have to work, the more important it is to take action on problem-solving. Everard and Morris (1990) offer general advice on preventing and managing conflicts as part of the management of schools. Managers should attempt to manage any conflicts between those whom they manage. The more intractable case is when senior managers are involved in the conflicts. More specialist advice is offered by Schmuck and Runkel (1985), but for more difficult cases they assume that an OD specialist, or other external specialist, will be needed to help.

Managing change

Change can just happen or it can be managed. The approach adopted in this book assumes that change will be managed using the range of ideas and techniques included under 'Management of planned change' (pp. 31–4) in Chapter 2. The strategy planning group needs to consider the history (or not) of change in the institution. Previous experience may not have been positive and there may be a legacy to undo. Or there may have been little previous change. Whilst one may think that schools have had change imposed for quite a long time, there are still examples which come to light (generally when a new head is appointed) which show that most change has been ignored, some resisted and a little cosmetic change or rhetorical change has taken place.

Strategy, however, is rather different to planning the implementation of something imposed from outside the school and this dimension and its implications need adequate consideration. In schools which have become excessively reactive, some effort will be needed to change expectations if the liberating possibilities of strategy are to be realised.

This analysis should extend to groups and individuals and their reaction to change. Not everyone is resistant to change and some people actually welcome change, almost any change. A readiness and capability chart for key individuals and groups who will be concerned with the change will be needed (Everard and Morris, 1990; Fidler *et al.*, 1991).

The three basic approaches to change outlined by Chin and Benne (1976) are useful heuristic devices to consider how others are to be influenced. Although there is a natural reaction against the power/coercive, its importance should not be underestimated in combination with other approaches at particular times. Too much reliance would clearly be counter-productive. Neither should the empirical/rational approach be underestimated. Although everyone is aware of the limitations of 'pure brute sanity', to quote George Bernard Shaw, the rationale for a change and the clinching arguments do need to be rehearsed. However, as so many observers have shown, a cognitive acceptance of change does not alone bring it about. Working on attitudinal change or the normative/re-educative approach is likely to be particularly effective. This is associated with changing the culture of the organisation.

The starting point for change is 'unfreezing' or initiation. This is the process of making people uncomfortable with the present state of affairs. For very large changes this may be a substantial and time-consuming task. It should not be rushed. Change is more likely to be successful if people are ready for it rather than still committed to existing ways of doing things.

A commitment chart is worth drawing up for key players in the change in terms of identifying their current position and their desired position. This provides an indication of those for whom 'unfreezing' will be particularly productive. A further device to concentrate efforts where they are most needed is a force-field analysis. From this, weakening resisting forces and strengthening driving forces (in that order) is required.

Planning models

A rough plan needs to be drawn up of the process by which strategy will be created. This needs some sort of time-scale and a pattern of involvement. The person and reference group for the process need to be determined.

The analysis may be begun by a school-based review involving large numbers of people all bringing evidence together and assessing current activities. A group will need to co-ordinate this activity. Whilst this has the advantage of involvement, the quality of the information may be quite varied and managing the process will be demanding.

(a) Time-scale

We think that the basic repeat cycle for the process is a minimum of two years in the first instance. We see a minimum period of about three months as being the appropriate length of time to devise the strategic plan (although as the case study in Chapter 8 shows, this may be a substantial underestimate). This allows time for collecting evidence (environmental scanning, marketing review, staffing review, curriculum review); for full discussion of possibilities; and for the creation and communication of detailed plans. These plans can then be implemented and have a complete year to operate before progress is reviewed and the strategic plan updated (see Figure 4.3).

After this first cycle the plan can be reviewed and updated each year with a major review after about five years (see Figure 4.4).

Strategic Planning for School Improvement

First cycle

	three months	20 months	one month
Evaluate			
Audit	formulate first plan	implement and run	review operation and amend plan
Scan			
Market Research			

Figure 4.3   The time-scale for the first cycle
Source: Fidler *et al.*, 1991, p. 25

Subsequent cycles

		YEARS		
one	two	three	four	five
first cycle		review	review	major review

Figure 4.4   Time-scale of subsequent cycles
Source: Fidler *et al.*, 1991, p. 25

(b) Two models of involvement

At some stage in the process all staff must be acquainted with the strategic plan and give their assent. This is the minimum. Since staff may have much to contribute to the formation of the plan, much greater involvement will in most cases be wise.

Two distinct models of involvement are presented here. One keeps a small group (the strategic planning group or the senior management team) in control of the whole process, but involves substantial consultation. The other model has a larger decision-making group overseeing the process and it is this larger group which sets up smaller groups to work on specific aspects of the process.

Consultation

A small group (strategic planning group) steers the whole process. Larger groups, including the full staff, are consulted and at the final stages participate in setting plans to implement the strategy.

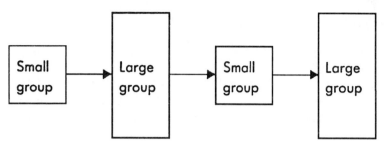

Figure 4.5   Involvement by consultation
Source: Fidler *et al.*, 1991, p. 26

Participation

A large group (probably the whole staff) steers the process and sets up sub-groups to investigate, discuss and report back on specific issues at various stages.

These models represent two different approaches to involvement but clearly there are many other alternatives. In all cases the strategy would require the approval of the governing body, in addition to the work of the groups shown here.

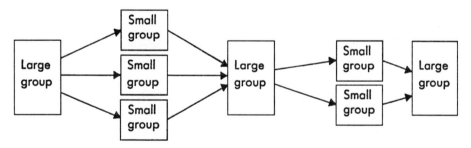

Figure 4.6   Participation in strategy
Source: Fidler *et al.*, 1991, p. 26

(c) Two approaches to strategic planning

There are many possible ways of managing the strategic planning process. Figures 4.7 and 4.8 present two distinctly different approaches. One is a 'grand design', whereby the future direction of the school is planned in general terms before the details are subsequently worked out. The other, in contrast, seeks to 'sum the parts' by producing detailed plans from sub-sections of the school, e.g. departments and pastoral teams, before trying to synthesise the resulting overall direction of the school indicated in these plans. In this method there may be internal inconsistencies which will need resolving. Although one of these may imply a top-down style of autocratic decision-making and the other bottom-up, this need not be the case. A participatory approach could be used to create the 'grand design'. The difference is essentially one of different ways of conceptualising the planning process.

(i) Grand design

This involves planning a strategy for the whole institution, keeping a holistic view in mind throughout the process (see Figure 4.7). Having decided on a strategy for the whole school, the implications for each part of the school are then considered and appropriate sub-plans for departments and other sections of the school are drawn up. In reality such implications, in general terms, should have been considered before the strategy was adopted. This

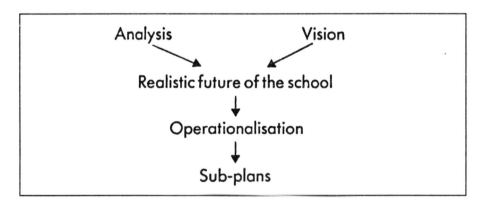

Figure 4.7   Planning by grand design
Source: Fidler et al., 1991, p. 31

approach may be more effective when external forces are strongest and these are the largest factors influencing the strategic plan. It may also be appropriate for small schools where an overview of the whole school is possible for those involved.

However, this overall grand design may not be possible to accomplish if strategic planning skills are being developed for the first time. The alternative method shown in Figure 4.8 is then a way of getting started.

(ii) Reconciling the parts

This method may be better when the strategic plan is being developed in response to internal dissatisfactions with the present state. It is likely to be particularly appropriate when there are well-developed internal sub-units in the school which are accustomed to long-term planning. The risk with this approach is of fragmentation and a failure to recognise or tackle internal inconsistencies and conflicting priorities. The education of the whole child might be the unifying principle. In addition to the contributions of the

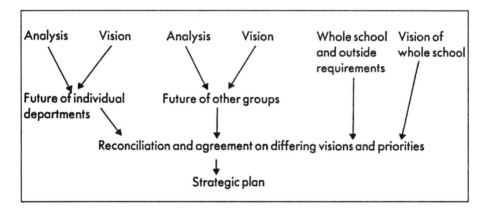

Figure 4.8   Planning by reconciling the parts
Source: Fidler et al., 1991, p. 31

sections of the school, a group also needs to contribute whole-school requirements, since it does not follow that the sum of the individual priorities is the same as institutional priorities. As Eigerman (1988, p. 41) observes in the business world, purely bottom-up processes lead to 'co-ordination by stapler', rather than a more organic reconciling and co-ordinating of priorities.

Collecting data

Evidence can be collected in a variety of forms:

- documents

- questionnaires

- interviews

- observation

- diaries

Inevitably, data collection has to be tailored to the purpose, sources of data and availability of data. A good general book which covers each of these methods, albeit briefly, is Bell (1993) *Doing Your Research Project*. Further details and discussion of each of the data collection methods are to be found in Bennett *et al.* (1994).

It should be remembered that any decisions will only be as good as the information on which they are based. Thus data need to be collected in an informed way and their possible sources of bias assessed. Whilst the aim should be reliable and valid data, the appropriate criterion for assessment is not whether the data would be defensible in a research sense but rather their 'fitness for purpose'. Does it help sufficiently to make improved management decisions? As is well-known, collecting information operates on the principle of marginalism (Simkins, 1981). It is relatively efficient to collect data to begin with, but the search for ever more data becomes progressively more expensive and eventually the cost of collection exceeds the value of the information. Thus in management terms some information is invaluable as an aid to improved decision-making, but a search for all the necessary information is illusory. There are, in any case, limits to the human ability to process data and most decisions involve qualitative evidence and 'soft' data to be weighed alongside more quantitative evidence. Thus ultimately judgements have to be made under conditions of uncertainty. It is only the extent of the uncertainty which can be altered.

5

Strategic analysis and choice

Introduction

This chapter examines in some detail the processes of strategic analysis and strategic choice. Strategic analysis involves an examination of the organisation's current strategic position with respect to its environment and its competitors. But it also involves looking forward to try to detect future important environmental influences.

Analysis also involves an examination of the organisation's culture. Its taken-for-granted ways of doing things need to be made explicit so as to recognise what are the values-in-use in the organisation. The culture provides both a strength when it is successful and a limitation when change is needed.

The result of strategic analysis when combined with a vision of the future together provide the basis for examining possible strategies or courses of action for the organisation over the next few years. Such options have to be generated in a creative way before they can be evaluated for their feasibility, suitability and acceptability.

The *ELMS Workbook: Planning Your School's Strategy* (Fidler *et al.*, 1991) contains exercises to help individuals or groups work on strategic analysis and strategic choice. These provide data collection instruments and simple questionnaires to spur thinking and provide a vehicle to generate staff discussion. These have been extensively used in the school featured in Chapter 10.

Strategic analysis

The three components of strategic analysis involve looking at:

- the environment

- internal resources

- the culture and values of the organisation

This analysis should be going on continuously and not just carried out at one point in time. However, periodically, say every five years or so, a thorough strategic analysis should be implemented, whilst between these five-yearly periods, perhaps each year, some intermediate level of analysis should be carried out to update the strategic plan and take account of factors which have changed in the meantime (to include achievements that have been made and also changes in the environment). But clearly the whole process, if done thoroughly, would take a substantial amount of management time and this could not be justified on an annual basis.

Environmental scanning

The first step in strategic analysis is to examine the environment. This does not primarily mean the local physical environment, but rather the political, social, legal, financial and technological environment, both locally and nationally. This process is called environment scanning. It is difficult to offer systematic advice about how this could be carried out in a truly comprehensive way. It will clearly be a matter of judgement as to what in any particular case is important in the environment for a particular school. However, a systematic set of cues helps to prevent any important issues being overlooked.

The important point to note is that the organisation should be *outward-looking* and *responsive* to the environment. Environmental scanning is also *forward-looking*, trying to predict the ways in which the environment will change in the future such that the match between the strategic direction of the organisation and its environment can be kept as close as possible. In commercial organisations, in particular, a very important factor in the environment is any competitor organisations.

For most schools the following three categories of influences should be considered:

(a) National influences

(b) Local community

(c) Pupil/parental choice and numbers

(a) National influences

A general set of influences for most organisations are PEST—political and legal, economic and financial, social and technological. Technological may seem rather a small influence compared to the others, particularly for schools, but this is an area where new developments can be predicted so that it is important to know what is currently available and how this is changing organisations as well as having ideas on how it might change. For example, take the case of computing and IT: for schools new computer systems are a relatively large investment, particularly installing a network into a school. This needs to be done with a clear future orientation, both in terms of what the developments in technology might bring and also what the school would eventually like to see in its particular situation.

For schools, an additional specialist influence must be educational developments. These involve: national discussion documents from DFEE, SCAA, OFSTED, TTA, STRB etc.; the speeches of ministers and senior officials and opposition parties; professional associations and their campaigns; pilot projects and research reports. A process of political intelligence-gathering is required. This involves assessing the strength of feeling on issues and, in a very general way, predicting the likely pace of developments.

As possible influences on the school are logged this provides a more limited number of influences whose progress needs to be charted. However, this needs to be periodically replenished by new issues which have just appeared and may grow in importance. This is the process of spotting the icebergs and the relief ships before they arrive, rather than after the point of collision. The possibilities are so much more limited the later these trends are spotted. Positioning the school on these issues is more difficult later rather than earlier. The *ELMS Workbook* has some prompts to help spur thinking about such influences.

(b) Local community

A most important factor in the environment of a school is the local community and the expectations of various client groups about what the school can provide for them. The community is both a source of demands on the school and also a source of support and resources.

There are two aspects to environmental scanning:

- checking on the current state
- detecting possible new demands or sources of support

If the school already keeps in close contact through its regular networks, this phase involves only a check to ensure that current intelligence is realistic. The main phase will involve trying to predict future trends.

(c) Pupil/parental choice and numbers

Other educational organisations are likely to be important features of the environment for school. These include both those from which pupils come and those to which children go as they leave. Particularly in urban areas, it is likely that nearby schools that teach children of the same age group will be important factors in the environment. It is vital to keep track of developments in those competitor schools on an informal basis.

Probably the most important strategic consideration for schools will be any intelligence about future pupil numbers. Most LEAs produce estimates, of varying accuracy and of varying future time-scales, of pupil numbers for each school. It becomes more difficult to make meaningful predictions as catchment area policies break down. This will be especially difficult where the more popular schools are not physically full or apply to change their capacity (either up or down). Modern computer-based systems can, to an extent, take parental preferences into account, but these are based on extrapolating past trends into the future and are always likely to have substantial possible errors in areas where there is competition for children. Schools in sensitive positions will find it worthwhile to devote sufficient resources to developing their own intelligence on probable future numbers.

This should start from some assessment of a 'natural' catchment area. What is a reasonable travelling distance? This may lead to an odd-shaped area when local conditions are considered. Any special features within, or at the edges of this area, may be critical, for example any kind of military base where children may come and go at short notice. The greatest difficulty in forecasting numbers is in infants' schools and, to a lesser extent, primary schools. Here particularly information on housing developments and building plans will be important. Indications of numbers from local health authority centre lists may give indications. Building up information over time allows the correspondence between these indicators of future school numbers and reality to be assessed.

An example of recruiting of children out of a 'natural' catchment area is provided by a school in a mature urban estate where the initial children had grown up and the school had increasingly come to depend on children from outside this estate. A key to facilitating this process was found to be adequate road signs because the entry to the school was through a maze of estate roads.

The school drew 55 per cent of children from outside the estate. For first visits a clear map was essential.

Feeder school numbers and estimates from those staff about prevailing trends are highly valuable. Some denominational schools, where there are requirements for eligibility of church attendance or baptism into the faith, will find it instructive to investigate trends in these limiting criteria. If the pool of potential entrants is coming down in a school such as this, a major strategic decision is posed—should the school seek permission to admit other children, and up to what limiting proportion, or should the school try to recruit all eligible children with the consequence that the school will fall in size? This latter is a strategy which has to be carefully managed if the consequences for children and staff already in such a school are to be safeguarded.

Lest all this sound like a statistical exercise, let us redress the balance by making clear that soft information on the popularity of other schools and the basis on which parents and children locally make their choice of school are vital. This provides the base from which to assess reaction from parents to any possible changes by the school (Devlin and Knight, 1990).

Although the first consideration is the number of children attending and likely to attend a school, more sophisticated analysis can then be carried out. The composition of the present intake can be examined in terms of ability range, social class and ethnic composition. This can be correlated with the source of such children and likely future trends in their numbers assessed. As we have seen (p. 25), there is research evidence that the social class (and ability) composition of a school is a small factor which affects its academic results. In general, the performance of all children in a school is higher if it has a higher proportion of middle-class children than a similar school. Although the research was analysed in term of social class it will also be true of higher-ability children.

A secondary school in a predominantly working-class area discovered that as it became more popular and expanded its intake, the marginal children were more able than its typical entry. In view of this (positive) effect for all children, the school had to weigh up the possibility of seeking to restrict the expansion in the light of approaching full capacity, or try to maintain the expansion and seek further accommodation. Whilst expansion has the benefits of economies of scale (Simkins, 1981), and being able to take on new staff (and affect its culture), it is generally a temporary effect. Thus predictions need to be made about the natural limits to expansion and the effects which come from reaching this limit need to be anticipated.

Opportunities and threats

Any organisation will have an existing, possibly implicit, strategy and therefore is broadly heading in a given direction. The environment will pose both opportunities and threats. Opportunities are those facets in the environment that are going to enhance the strategy of the organisation and ensure both its long-term survival and its success. On the other hand, threats are those aspects of the environment which will make the progress of the organisation more difficult and, in the worst possible case, could pose threats to its survival.

Some examples may illustrate the point. The opportunity of applying for resources to become a technology college (DFEE, 1995c) could immeasurably assist a school which had poor facilities but wished to develop its curriculum to make technology a feature of the school. The prospects of a common funding formula to apply to all GM schools in England should be considered an opportunity for those schools in a low-funding LEA. On the other hand, proposals to change an LEA funding formula to reduce the proportion of base funding and increase the income per pupil would pose an enormous threat to very small schools with few pupils, particular small primary schools. The prospects of increasing unpopularity of a middle school to which pupils go on leaving a first school should be regarded as a threat by the first school, since parents, particularly those who are concerned about the whole-school career of their child, are likely to consider other first schools for their child in order to avoid the unpopular middle school.

Resource audit

A resource audit assesses strategic capability. Any strategy will need to rely on these resources for sustainable advantage.

Analysing an organisation's resources goes beyond its buildings or physical equipment and includes the total resources of the organisation, including its staffing and know-how. Thus, the analysis of the resources of a school would start with the school buildings and examine both their location and particular accommodation in terms of specialist rooms and other facilities. The possibilities of finding extra teaching accommodation in very popular schools should be investigated. If there is space, modern mobile classrooms are affordable and can provide a far higher standard of accommodation than in the past. For expansion at sixth-form level, and to provide attractive accommodation, such buildings may be particularly economic.

Staffing resources clearly need a lot of detail. Qualifications, expertise and skills of staff all need to be taken into consideration, and this applies to both teaching staff and non-teaching staff. These should include both formal qualifications and expertise, and also interests and skills which are more amateur in nature.

Also included under the heading of resources are those intangible attributes of the school, such as its reputation and ethos.

There are three aspects to investigating resources:

(a) internal audits and evaluations

(b) external comparisons

(c) external inspections

(a) Internal audits and evaluations

Audits such as a staff audit of teaching and teaching support staff and an accommodation audit of the physical premises can be compiled and assessed. In addition, parental, pupil and staff satisfaction surveys provide a basis for recognising areas of work that the school does well and also areas for potential improvement. The elements of school-based review using GRIDS (McMahon *et al.*, 1984) or some similar practices and instruments for school review can contribute to the evidence here. The *ELMS Workbook* also has exercises.

(b) External comparisons

A useful practice in other organisations is 'benchmarking', or identifying where the practices and performance of a particular organisation stand with respect to industry standards or to other organisations. The STRB have for some time pointed out that school managers are weak on this practice. Partly, of course, this relies on the availability of information about the practices and performance in other schools. However, increasingly now through OFSTED reports and publications, league tables and school performance research and tables, the information base is getting better. The important point is that a school needs to appreciate that such comparisons are necessary and instructive.

A school can use performance indicators (PIs) (Glogg and Fidler, 1990). Indicators of the school's performance should be studied and compared with those of other schools both locally and of a similar type nationally. But it is not simply a matter of trying to maximise all performance indicators. Even PIs which look at output can't simply all be maximised without some valid model of how schools work. Without such a model it is not possible to foresee the consequences of trying to raise some indicators on all the remaining indicators. There will be inevitable trade-offs. Some indicators will go up at the expense of others. Thus, at most, PIs can be an aid to judgment.

Value-added

Outcome indicators such as examination results do not provide much guidance about the effectiveness of the school in allowing pupils to make progress unless there are corresponding input data. Good results might merely indicate good inputs, as was shown in Chapter 2. Only for sixth forms at the moment are there input and outcome scores for a school to calculate its own value-added and compare this with the historic trends of past years and with the performance of other schools (DFE, 1995b; 1995c).

Clearly value-added analysis on outcomes is essentially backward-looking. How far the pupils have progressed is only known in arrears. This is of little value for those pupils, but might help their successors. Some schools are beginning to use the results of baseline testing in a more formative way. If used sensitively this could help raise standards. From previous value-added analysis it is possible to calculate the rate of progress of previous pupils. From this knowledge, predictions can be made about the likely outcome scores for a given level of input score of each pupil. The on-going progress of each pupil can then be compared with this prediction and action taken when pupils fall below the trend line expected of pupils with their input score. Provided that there is recognition of the degree of uncertainty of any test score, and any input score is compared with any contrary evidence, this should be a positive force for raising exam results. It is particularly important for those whose input scores are not high to look out for any evidence that this input score was an underestimate of the true potential of the pupil rather than to have unduly low expectations for some pupils. It also follows that if value-added is to have a positive formative effect, then children probably should be tested every year so that those who are falling behind expectations can be investigated and any remedial action taken.

SCAA (1994) recognises the value of supplementing current examination information in league tables with some value-added data as soon as this is possible. From Scottish evidence (Willms, 1992), schools that initially appear to be obtaining satisfactory exam results when raw scores are compared, may be made to look less satisfactory when value-added scores are compared. Examples are shown of schools near the top of league tables on raw results appearing much lower down, in value-added league tables, when the progress made by their children is compared to that of other schools.

(c) External inspections

Although there may be external inspections from LEAs and others, the main source of external inspections is the four-yearly cycle of national school inspections organised by the Office for Standards in Education (Ouston *et al.*, 1996). OFSTED inspections provide an aid to evaluation but, in their present form, they are not very helpful to poorly run schools. This is because they don't provide much help in making any improvement and, even worse, they fail to provide a worthwhile assessment of management actions and processes that might signal where there are inadequacies.

However, for a well-run school an OFSTED inspection has much to offer, particularly for a new headteacher. Although the OFSTED evidence may not be up to research standards, it is gathered on a systematic basis and subjected to criteria which are made explicit as far as possible. Thus it provides an 'unbiased' account from an external perspective of how the school is operating. Those making the judgements are generally experienced practitioners.

Reports on schools are published and schools are obliged to send a summary to their parents. Many schools have taken the opportunity to comment on the report's findings from the school's point of view. Reports provide a source of information on the performance of nearby schools, including both competitor schools and those from which pupils come or go.

Schools have the opportunity particularly in completing the headteacher's form to signal any areas on which an OFSTED input would be of value to the school. The revisions of the framework for inspections (OFSTED, 1995a; 1995b) propose that more account should be taken in inspections of a school's own procedures for self-evaluation and its own development planning procedures. This should increase the possibility of the inspection having a greater developmental value. Evidence from the first and second year inspections of secondary schools generally indicates that schools on the whole found the experience of value for development (Fidler *et al.*, 1994; 1995).

Strengths and weaknesses

In carrying out this analysis of resources, strengths will emerge by which, compared with similar schools (particularly local ones) this specific school has great strengths. There will also be weaknesses where, in comparison with similar schools, this school is less strong. Such judgements need to be based, as far as possible, on evidence rather than impression.

Both strengths and weaknesses need to be considered from a professional as well as a 'public perception' point of view. In the short term, public perception may be the most influential. The longer-term aim should be to ensure consistency between the two sets of judgements. Any inconsistency indicates either a missed promotional opportunity, if the public perception is not as strong as internal evidence, and a worrying facade where public perception is stronger than the internal picture. Often the two will go together—parental complaints and internal analysis of external examination results may both point to a department with weak leadership, poor teaching and undemanding expectations.

Whilst generally strengths should be exploited, it doesn't follow that all weaknesses should be improved. If both the public and professional perceptions are that some weaknesses are of only minor importance, there may be higher priorities than merely trying to bring all facets of the school's work up to the same high standard.

The publication of examination and other league tables and the work of most school effectiveness researchers has sought to place great emphasis on cognitive learning in pursuit of examination success. Whilst these features may be *necessary* for a successful school they are not *sufficient*. All schools need a wider array of success criteria and for some schools and some pupils these may not be the most important success criteria. This is not to suggest that for all schools and pupils there should not be benchmark standards in appropriate basic skills which all pupils should achieve, but rather to suggest that beyond this basic level there are many ways for schools and pupils to be successful.

A possible list of areas in which pupil and school success can be demonstrated includes:

- academic

- design and technology

- music

- art

- drama

- sport

- charitable work

- preparation for adult working life

Many of these provide pupils and the school with opportunities to put on public performances, displays and exhibitions and to enter competitions.

Often, such activities involve the public and can lead to individual pupils and the school receiving recognition for their achievements.

SWOT and strategic fit

This analysis completes the SWOT analysis of the Strengths, Weaknesses, Opportunities and Threats for the school. Other things being equal, clearly the most favoured strategic direction for a school will be one that takes advantage of opportunities in the environment and minimises threats, and takes advantage of internal strengths of the institution and minimises the weaknesses. This is called strategic fit.

In addition to strengths and weaknesses, Montanari *et al.* (1990) suggest assessing advocates and adversaries (SWAA) to give a service differential assessment. Typically, SWOT emphasises competition and competitors rather than support and supporters and collaboration and collaborators. Such advocates and alliances may be crucial for a school's success.

Culture and values

The third and final component of strategic analysis is to take account of the culture of the organisation. These are the shared, taken-for-granted assumptions made by group members (Schein, 1992). A useful descriptive phrase coined by Deal and Kennedy (1988) based on Bower (1966) is 'the way we do things around here'. This, however, doesn't capture the value dimension which is present in the concept (Willmott, 1993). In other words, 'this is the accepted way to operate successfully in this organisation'. In some senses, organisational culture is the organisational equivalent of personality or character for an individual. It is the characteristic way in which organisation members go about their business that distinguishes one organisation from another or one school from another.

All organisations will have a culture. Usually what is meant is that an organisation has a strong culture, i.e. that the same assumptions are widely shared and articulated within the organisation. Some organisations, however, will have weak cultures. In this case there are no strong beliefs, or else there is a lack of agreement on priorities and a number of competing beliefs. All large organisations have sub-cultures whereby parts of the organisation have some differences of emphasis. These become dysfunctional when they aren't small differences within a largely shared culture.

Strong cultures give a sense of certainty and belief both to organisations and to organisation members. They give a sense of purpose and significance and shared meanings to organisation members (Willmott, 1993). This clear set of expectations of organisation members means that individuals do not have to spend lots of time puzzling out how to behave; the culture makes it relatively explicit. A sense of purpose and stability is highly motivating for individuals.

Willmott (1993) points out that a strong culture provides an alternative and more subtle form of control for organisation members than direct supervision. It means that authority can be delegated in the knowledge that decisions made will have a degree of consistency, because they are made within a shared culture. Some authors, e.g. Peters and Waterman (1982) have gone on to identify what they consider to be successful cultures. Cultural change programmes have become very fashionable, despite frequent reports of a lack of success.

There are two major reasons why a study of culture in a school is important:

1 SWOT and strategy are dependent on culture.

2 Major changes will involve attempting to change the culture.

There is evidence from studies of other organisations that how the elements of SWOT are perceived depends upon preconceptions which are a function of organisational culture (Stevenson, 1976; Ireland *et al.*, 1987) and that the subsequent formulation of strategy also depends on culture (Sapienza, 1985). The crucial point is that by trying to make the culture more explicit, such preconceptions can be challenged or at the very least acknowledged. This may help prevent disasters.

There are two kinds of danger. One is that a school may be going downhill and need a radical change (including a change in its culture) without being aware of it. This is less likely to be appreciated unless the previous 'recipe' is recognised and challenged. Second, there is a tendency for successful organisations to continue to do what they were good at long past the time when this was an advantage (Miller, 1990; 1994). Recognising the culture and what it represents, in conjunction with external evidence from other aspects of the analysis, may begin to sow the first seeds of doubt. As Stacey (1993) points out, the art of successful strategic change is to detect and act on these signs rather than rationalising and dismissing them as temporary problems.

The second reason that a study of culture is important is in preparation for a possible change in culture. It is important to analyse the present culture because it may be that, in order to make strategic changes, this culture will need to change. To recognise the culture within which one is operating, it is helpful to think about the sorts of descriptions people would give about how the organisation operates. These descriptions will cover traditions, rituals and possibly myths about times past. Such widely shared understandings of how the organisation operates are important in making this assessment. Thinking about the induction of new staff may also be helpful in thinking about the culture and values of the organisation. What would they need to be told so that they would operate like other people in the organisation? The perceptions of newly appointed staff are particularly useful in surfacing critical differences in the operation of different schools and their underlying assumptions.

Organisational culture and climate are related concepts. Owens (1991) sees climate as being more concerned with the *perceptions* of organisation members and the extent to which they find the way that the organisation operates is *satisfying* to them. Climate concerns attitudes to culture. This distinction is shared by other writers (e.g. Sergiovanni, 1991). Unfortunately, early work on climate and culture in schools did not perceive this distinction and so the two concepts were used interchangeably.

The combined effects of past experience and the culture of the organisation give rise to the 'recipe' or paradigm (Johnson and Scholes, 1993, p. 165)—see Figure 5.1. In the figure, the headings are generic and the particular illustrations are for a regional newspaper.

The recipe evolves over a period of time as the way of seeking solutions to problems and decisions are made in accordance with the recipe. Difficulties arise when the environment has changed and the recipe no longer works satisfactorily. The effects of the ERA will almost certainly have led to this situation in schools. For strategic planning it is particularly important to be aware of the implicit limiting influence on thinking which the recipe gives.

How useful is culture as a concept?

Increasingly culture has been regarded as a critical factor associated with organisational success. As more and more emphasis is placed on its importance it becomes so all-encompassing that it is more and more elusive in terms of being a useful operational concept. It is the organisational equivalent of personality or character and suffers from the same problems of being so subtle that attempts to reduce it to examples lose as much as they gain.

Can culture be managed, or only influenced?

Schein (1992) has stated that the most important thing that a leader can do is manage the culture of the organisation. However, there is some disagreement about whether culture can be managed or only influenced (Wilkins and Patterson, 1985). Even if it can only be influenced it is important that all

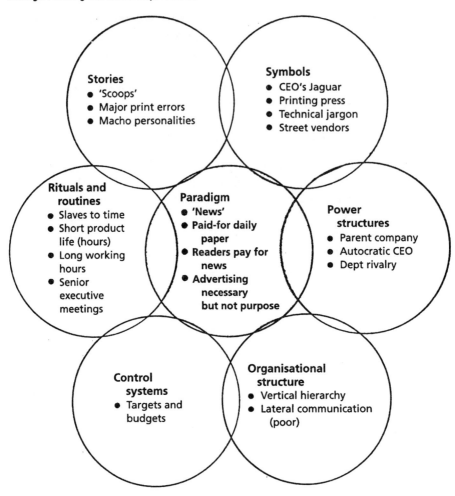

Figure 5.1 Components of organisational culture of a regional newspaper

Source: reproduced from Johnson and Scholes, 1993, p. 165, by permission of the publisher, Prentice Hall International, Hemel Hempstead

opportunities are taken to influence it consistently, rather than mixed messages being transmitted.

All are agreed that major changes to culture are extremely difficult. Some appear to pay lip service to this but then offer quick and easy means of changing. We offer some tentative means of changing the culture of a school in the next chapter.

Stakeholder expectations

An environmental scan will have implications for each school and resource capabilities will depend on each individual school, but no two schools would respond in the same way to identical findings. This is because the people associated with each school have their own expectations about how their school should respond. This political dimension needs to be investigated by a stakeholder expectations analysis. A stakeholder is anyone who has an interest in the performance of the organisation. Thus parents, children, staff and many other groups are all stakeholders. As Johnson and Scholes (1988) point out, 'Strategy is also a product of what people want an organisation to do and what they feel the organisation should be like' (p. 113). Thus their views, particularly in a non-profit-making organisation, are going to be important in identifying a successful future strategy.

Johnson and Scholes (1993), based on work by Mendelow (1991), offer help on how to prioritise stakeholders for this purpose. By examining interest and power as two independent dimensions on a matrix, they identify four groups that need different kinds of involvement. Since there is such a large number of groups and individuals who are stakeholders in a school, this is a useful device to help prioritise efforts.

Formal surveys of parental and other opinion are likely to be required, but the importance of 'soft data' should not be underestimated. For example, the questions which prospective parents ask as they are shown round the school

Level of interest

	Low	High
Low	Minimal effort	Keep informed
High	Keep satisfied	Key players

Power

Figure 5.2   Stakeholder mapping
Source: based on Mendelow, 1981

103

are valuable pointers. There may be groups able to contribute opinions in addition to individuals. The quality and clarity of responses are likely to be more important than sheer numbers of fairly bland and anodyne responses.

The staff of the school are likely to be the major contributors to the formation of strategy. However, they are unlikely to contribute with equal voice because of the differences in status, power and influence. Nevertheless, all the processes of micro-political power can be used to influence strategy.

Finally, but not least, pupils and young people in the school should be consulted in some way. Surveys of pupils' satisfaction with their schools show substantial differences. Other things being equal, schools with a higher degree of pupil satisfaction are likely to achieve their purpose more readily than those that seek to operate despite their students' opinions. The extent to which young people might contribute their views and the weight which should be attached to such views will probably depend on their age.

Strategic choice

Strategic choice is concerned with:

- generating options
- evaluating options
- making a choice

Generating options

Following strategic analysis, it is necessary to look at various broad courses of action that the organisation might choose to follow as a result of that analysis. For business organisations, Johnson and Scholes consider that there are three possible considerations for generating strategic options. The first of these is to identify a generic strategy; the second is to look at alternative directions in which the organisation might develop; and the third is to look at the methods by which the development could be achieved. For schools, the generic strategy would have to be based upon differentiation and focus, i.e. in what ways a particular school could be better than other similar schools of its type. Moreover, it needs to establish whether it is to achieve these advantages on a broad front or whether it is just to identify certain areas where it thinks it has something rather special to offer and concentrate its success around these.

Murgatroyd and Morgan (1992) outline four generic strategies for schools. Their choices depend on decisions about access and curriculum. The degree of access (open to all applicants or restricted by selective entry) and curriculum (balanced or specialised) leads to a four-fold typology covering general differentiation and niche differentiation. They give four examples from secondary schools in the UK and North America, which illustrate each of the four types. Figure 5.3 gives examples for school types in the UK.

open	comprehensive school	technology or language college
restricted	grammar school	music specialism
	balanced	**specialist**

access (label on left side)

curriculum (label at bottom)

Figure 5.3   Examples of differentiation and niche differentiation of schools in the UK

A starting point for a consideration of alternatives is to propose no changes and to continue on the present strategy. That might prove a useful baseline against which to judge alternative directions. There are certain broad strategies which can apply to any organisation. These are:

- *Specialise*
  by subject specialism, learning style, special activities
  by type or age of pupil

- *Merge*
  with another school or educational establishment

- *Diversify*
  teach additional age groups or subjects

- *Federate*
  join with schools of a similar kind

- *Integrate (vertically)*
  join with schools with complementary age groups

- *Liquidate*
  close the school

The present range of major changes which schools are currently making were reviewed in Chapter 1, and include changing status and taking an additional age range of children. These alternative directions could range from seeing future closure as the most likely development, to seeing an expansion in size. Within such a spectrum it may be possible to see an expanded and related role for the school, perhaps taking account of a greater community element—what would be referred to in industrial terms as diversification. In terms of the alternative methods by which this might be achieved, the first would be by working with the existing organisation and developing it. The second would be by seeing a merger or takeover of another school or college and working towards an acquisition. The third alternative method would be to see joint working with another institution whilst remaining separate entities, but nevertheless collaborating for the joint good of both institutions.

Given the dependence of finance on pupil numbers, this aspect has to be the primary determinant of any strategy. Where the school roll is falling, finance has to be the first priority. Can and should the decline be arrested? When numbers are satisfactory or growing, other possibilities can be pursued. A second priority is probably pupil behaviour in and around school. Where a school has a bad reputation locally for behaviour, or children are insufficiently well-behaved to benefit from education, this has to be a priority. Next in order may be academic progress and results, and only when these are good can other possibilities be pursued:

- numbers

- behaviour

- academic results

- community involvement

For most schools the choices will be very wide. A curricular specialism or emphasis offers the widest possibility. Some choices will emerge from the analysis, but these may need to be refined or supplemented by some more creative process as indicated below.

The whole aim is to develop a range of options which might be related and go together as a generic strategy, but essentially a series of options from which choice can be made.

Mixture of vision and evaluation

Some ideas for improvement may come from:

- dissatisfaction with the present in the form of clear problems
- evaluating present operations
- comparisons with other schools
- a vision of how things might be

It is some combination of all of these sources that leads to the creative process of forming a realistic vision of how things might be in the not-too-distant future and within current or obtainable resources. As Mintzberg (1994) has remarked, the process of moving from analysis to creation and vision is the least described and researched part of the whole strategy process.

The range of techniques to aid the process are:

- strategic issues (decision-making helping to prioritise issues)
- goals (where there are clear single goals to give guidance)
- SWOT (resulting from analysis)
- vision (creative element)

Strategic issues

Strategic issues are crucial questions which, when answered, help define strategy. The questions need identifying and then placing into some kind of logical order such that resolving one question leads on to the next and so on. Bryson (1988) considers that the identification of strategic issues is a vital step between strategic analysis and the development of strategy in not-for-profit organisations. Strategic issues are the fundamental policy questions affecting the organisation's mission and values. These by definition involve differences of opinion and interpretation. They may involve ends (what) and means (how). Each issue should be framed as a question. These should be prioritised according to the consequences of failing to address the issue. 'The strategic issue identification step therefore is aimed at focusing organisational attention on what is truly important for the survival, prosperity, and effectiveness of the organisation' (Bryson, 1988, p. 57).

Some examples of large strategic issues are as follows:

- should the school seek GM status?

- should the school seek to expand?

- should the school try to attract more able pupils?

- should a Roman Catholic school take non-Catholics?

- should a junior school merge with a nearby infant school?

- should the school seek greater parental involvement?

Goals

Commercial organisations tend to set single goals such as profitability or turnover or share of market as the summary measure of strategy. Perhaps for schools, pupil numbers for schools with falling rolls might provide such a goal, or the percentage of children getting a certain percentage grade A–Cs. Where such a clear goal is appropriate, strategy involves identifying the means for achieving the goal. In what ways could the examination results be improved? This broad question would involve looking at teaching methods and the curriculum in addition to smaller-scale and more direct actions. For the case study in Chapter 8, the main goal was an increase in pupil numbers.

SWOT

Although SWOT is an analytic tool, positive courses of action may emerge. However, the process may reinforce failure. There is a need to understand thoroughly strategic ideas and the culture of the organisation, or else the SWOT analysis may be carried out looking through blinkers. SWOT is a way of summarising pointers which have arisen as a result of the detailed process of strategic analysis of the environment and resources.

Vision

Vision is important, otherwise strategy may be merely reacting to conditions or clients. Vision is the creative, proactive part of devising strategy. Thoughts may be stimulated by trying to describe what the school might be like in five or ten years' time. It can be made more elaborate by scenario planning. This can incorporate contingency planning, depending on the turn of events in critical incidents.

Scenario planning or developing a 'vision of success' (Bryson, 1988), in other words, trying to paint a picture of what might happen if the chosen course of action was pursued, involves some of the following questions. What would the end result look like? Would the scene then carry credibility? That might also lead to some contingency planning. If various steps on the way to the scenario went in different directions from the assumed ones, what contingency plans could the school develop in order to cope with this?

Evaluating options

From the series of options that have been developed it is then necessary to look at which of them is likely to prove the most viable. Johnson and Scholes suggest three broad criteria for making this choice:

- suitability
- feasibility
- acceptability

The test of suitability asks how far the chosen course of action maximises the SWOT analysis (strategic fit). The second criterion is of feasibility, in other words, do the resources and other changes that would be required to make the strategy work appear feasible. If for example more resources are required, then a credible source has to be identified. The third criterion they suggest is of acceptability. This has to include both internal acceptability in terms of the culture of the organisation, and external acceptability to governors and the wider community, including parents.

One technique which can help to decide between some options is cost-benefit analysis.

Cost-benefit analysis

Where there are a number of ways of achieving the same ends, these can be costed to see which can achieve the chosen results at lowest cost. In an example given by the National Audit Office (1994), a primary school which had decided to raise reading standards examined different ways of achieving this and carried out costings to use cost-benefit analysis in order to choose between the various alternatives. The school in Chapter 9 used cost-benefit analysis to assess the various curriculum options.

Choosing options

Finally, the selection of strategy has to be partly a rational process and partly a political process. Clearly the values espoused by the leaders of the organisation are going to be particularly influential in any strategy. In the case of schools, this should be the role that the governing body plays. Various strategic options could be worked out in some detail and left to the governing body to make the final decision on the strategy. It is important that a clear decision is made and communicated in order to conclude these first two stages of strategic management before moving on to implement the chosen strategy.

6

Strategic plan and implementation

Introduction

This chapter looks at the issues involved in implementing a strategic plan. It begins by examining organisational culture and proposes a range of ways of changing the culture of a school. This is the most major of changes. The individual components of strategic implementation—organisational structure, people and systems, and resources—are considered, with the major emphasis being on deploying resources for development.

Finally, school development planning is seen to have a role as an action-planning sequence to implement the components of a strategy.

Strategic plan

The strategic plan contains the aims and values of the organisation and the 'glue' which binds together and co-ordinates the other sub-plans. The distinguishing features of a strategic plan is that it involves:

1 the long term

2 the future of the whole school in an integrated way

3 taking account of future trends in the world outside the school

4 taking account of the school's present, and likely future, resources

The school will have a **mission statement** which gives its long-term purpose and the groups which it intends to serve. This will have been questioned as part of the strategic analysis. In addition, the strategic plan will involve the creation of a short, compact, memorable, meaningful **focus statement**, outlining the specific development of the school in this strategic plan. The wording of this statement should have been refined to be as concise as possible, whilst retaining as many as possible of the nuances which are the keys to the direction of many other aspects of the school's work. It should be capable of being 'unpacked' to yield the core values of the school and its vision of the future. The most basic feature of the statement is that it should be a **guide to action**.

The importance of this process is described in Chapter 10. It corresponds to the situation described by HMI at Newall Green High School (OFSTED, 1994b), where everyone in the school knew where the school was going. This is the situation which Harvey-Jones (1988, p. 55) describes at ICI when major change is contemplated:

> *We need at the end to have simplified to a stage where one sentence, almost a slogan, will describe what we believe, and what we can accept and work to. This process of simplifying down involves attacking the 'weasel words'. We aim to make the simplifying process one of distillation and concentration, rather than trying to make 'umbrella' statements which are unobjectionable. We haggle and argue over single words. But we know when we have 'got it', and when we have 'got it' we believe it and can work to it.*

The strategic plan should have implications for each of a series of more detailed sub-plans. It should include implications for both what to do and also what not to do. In short, it should indicate (implicit) priorities.

The focus statement may be amplified by lists of long-term objectives which indicate intended progress on a range of fronts. These should be consistent with each other and, where there are potential internal inconsistencies, the means by which these are to be resolved should be indicated.

The first level of detail of the strategic plan is the plan of the organisational structure and decision-making machinery of the school, including the involvement of governors. The strategic plan will have implications for the structure of responsibilities in the school and that, combined with the culture of the school, will have implications for how decisions are made and the involvement of governors. Where this implies a change in the culture of the school, this should have been recognised at the choice stage and the extent of the implications of the change recognised.

Changing organisational culture

There is widespread acceptance in the literature that it is difficult to change the organisational culture of an institution. Some argue that it is possible only to influence culture and not to change or manage it. However, as a number of authors note, after a ritual acceptance of the difficulties, many authors then proceed with great certainty to offer changes and many consultants offer change programmes. After looking at what writers have said about changing an organisational culture we shall offer some tentative ideas which might be used in schools to change culture.

Influences on culture

In order to begin to understand the deep-seated nature of culture, Schein (1992) suggests conceiving culture at three levels (p. 17):

Artifacts	Visible organisational structures and processes (hard to decipher)
Espoused values	Strategies, goals, philosophies (espoused justifications)
Basic underlying assumptions	Unconscious, taken-for-granted beliefs, perceptions, thoughts and feelings (ultimate source of values and actions)

This makes clear that the organisational structure is at the most superficial level of culture and that, although this may need to change to influence the culture, this alone cannot change the culture. Thus changing roles and responsibilities or even decision-making machinery will only influence and not change culture. There is universal agreement that changing the culture of an organisation is a lengthy process and one that takes a great deal of organisation members' time. Three factors which Deal and Kennedy (1988) identify as affecting the difficulty of changing the organisational culture are:

(a) *Evident crisis*: where an organisation is evidently in trouble or heading for trouble, there is a greater willingness to consider deep-seated change.

(b) *Attractiveness of change*: the proposed change needs to have all its highly desirable features emphasised.

(c) *Strength of present culture*: the stronger the present culture, the more difficult it is to change.

There are two instances which may affect schools and which need rather different treatment:

1 *Evolving the present culture*: this would be the case where some features of the present culture are being emphasised and others de-emphasised, e.g. teachers working in each other's classrooms goes on to a limited degree, but is to be encouraged to encompass more people on more occasions.

2 *Radical change to the present culture*: this would be the case where major features of the present culture need to be overturned, e.g. an academic sixth form broadened to give equal status to a vocational sixth form (the radical change is in giving parity to both types, not in introducing a clearly lower-status sixth form).

Schein (1992) poses ethical issues for consideration before embarking on a study of an organisation's culture. The consequences of what might emerge from the study need to be foreseen and an appropriate ethical stance adopted. Willmott (1993) goes on to pose ethical issues involved in attempting to change a corporate culture. These issues will be most serious where a powerful senior group decides to change the culture for existing staff. Where this is done in an open way and where everyone is involved in the decision to change, such issues will be resolved with less difficulty. It should be borne in mind by those worried about the morality of attempting to create a culture, that the actions of a leader will be subjected to scrutiny and inferences drawn no matter what they do, whether planned or unplanned. It is not possible to have no effect. Thus the consequences of some random set of chance acts being analysed by others and their resulting actions should also be evaluated.

A further point on ethics and efficacy should be raised. The actions of the leader and statements made about what the organisation stands for and which attempt to influence culture should be genuinely meant. Deal and Kennedy (1988) point out how any inconsistencies between what is espoused and subsequent actions will be greeted with cynicism, and a search will continue to find the culture-in-use rather than the espoused culture. Saying that some things are high priority and then failing to reward them in some way will cast doubt on the espoused priorities. Consistency between words and actions is reinforcing. As Watson (1994) points out, where attempted changes carry no credibility, an unofficial culture will develop.

How culture is transmitted

Schein (1992) identifies stages in cultural growth depending on the age of the organisation:

1 founding and early growth

2 midlife

3 maturity and decline

Since the founding of a new school is relatively rare, it is easy to forget the very formative period that the early stages of a school represent. In a lesser way, a very large expansion in an existing school is a similar experience and needs similar thought and planning. The three stages above present different challenges.

1 Founding and early growth

Schein (1992, p. 231) identifies the following primary embedding mechanisms:

- what leaders pay attention to, measure and control on a regular basis

- how leaders react to critical incidents and organisational crises

- observed criteria by which leaders allocate scarce resources

- deliberate role modelling, teaching and coaching; observed criteria by which leaders allocate rewards and status

- observed criteria by which leaders recruit, select, promote, retire and excommunicate organisational members

At this early stage leaders are very influential in creating the culture. As Deal and Kennedy (1988) point out, the external environment should be the largest single influence on the conscious choice of culture, since it is intended to provide the organisation with an advantage in competing with other similar organisations. Thus the culture should represent the set of assumptions that, if acted upon, would make the organisation successful.

Torrington and Weightman (1989), following their study of secondary schools in the mid-1980s, caution against placing all the expectation of cultural leadership on the headteacher. They point out that other respected teachers will also exercise cultural leadership. They also note that in schools there are at least two distinct cultures—the children's and the staff's. Traditionally, the culture for the pupils and students of schools has been called ethos. There may be a number of sub-cultures within the staff group. Torrington and Weightman particularly noted differences between the cultures of teaching staff and teaching support staff.

Differences in sub-cultures within teaching staff need some discussion. As we have noted, a strong culture is a strength in an organisation in times of success and a great difficulty when a major change is needed. Culture is an agent of stability. One of the means of change where there are different sub-cultures within an organisation is to seek to spread more widely a sub-culture that is favourable to a new organisational direction. This is not possible where there is only one monolithic culture. In that sense, sub-cultures are an advantage, but they need to be sub-cultures rather than totally different cultures. There need to be shared assumptions across the organisation with some differences of emphasis. An appropriate metaphor would be to speak with the same language but different dialects, rather than speaking different languages.

Schein (1992) also lists what he terms 'secondary mechanisms'. These do not create the culture, but are means to reinforce it. They work only if they are consistent with the primary mechanisms. The secondary articulation and reinforcement mechanisms are:

- organisational design and structure
- organisational systems and procedures
- organisation rites and rituals
- design of physical space, facades and buildings
- stories, legends and myths about people and events
- formal statements of organisational philosophy, values and creed

As Torrington and Weightman (1989) point out, formal policies are the last on the two lists and yet in their experience these were the first action of schools trying to change. There is nothing inconsistent about this, providing that such school aims are the starting point of a whole series of actions which are to establish a different culture, rather than seen as a change in the culture itself.

2 Change in midlife

When the period of early growth is over, the culture of an organisation will be established and changing it will be more difficult. The suggestions from Schein (1992) are the following:

(a) *Systematic promotion of a suitable sub-culture*
   Where a sub-culture is better adapted to prevailing conditions, either this can be spread or the chief proponents moved to a more central position in the organisation.

(b) *Creation of a parallel learning system in part of the organisation*
A trial can be mounted in part of the organisation to test a new way of operating.

(c) *Technological seduction*
Change involving either a new physical technology such as IT, or a new human technology such as total quality programmes can be used to give training and emphasise new ways of doing things.

3 Change in maturity

This is the stage when change is most difficult of all. Schein's suggestions are:

(a) *Infusion of outsiders*
New people in senior positions can be brought into the organisation. They are likely to be chosen for their culture change possibilities.

(b) *Scandal and explosion of myths*
Where the difference between the espoused culture and the culture-in-use is exposed as a sharp contrast, this frees up the existing espoused culture.

(c) *Coercive persuasion*
This is exceptional, but represents the situation where people are compelled to follow new ways of working.

(d) *Turnarounds*
There are two forms: (i) a new visionary leader with a new and appealing message appears in adverse circumstances; (ii) fuzzy vision model—the solution has to be devised, but there is a clear determination that 'something must be done', usually with a new leader from outside.

Changing school culture in North America

Fullan (1992) cites work by Leithwood and Jantzi on principals who transformed culture towards school improvement in North American schools. The mechanisms involved:

1 strengthening the school's improvement culture

2 using a variety of bureaucratic mechanisms to try to change culture

3 fostering staff development

4 engaging in direct and frequent communication about cultural norms, values and beliefs

5 sharing power and responsibility with others

6 using symbols to express cultural values

Firestone and Wilson (1985) offer some suggestions about how US principals could change the culture of their schools, particularly with respect to teaching in their schools, although they recognise that the principal will need a high energy level and self-confidence to do it. They think that it may need a group to achieve the change rather than one person. The mechanisms are:

- manage flow of stories and other information in schools—initiate and emphasise some and suppress others

- create and manipulate rituals and symbols

- actively communicate culture—principals move around and have the opportunity for informal conversations

Changing a school's culture

Changing a school's culture should not be an arbitrary, isolated act. It should be associated with a strategy for the school which will enable it to be successful in the prevailing conditions and in the future. Any change in culture should be contingent on the choice of strategy and be necessary to implement the strategy. Changing the culture and the strategy are both means to ends, not ends in themselves.

Preparation

Clearly changing a school's culture has to be contingent on whether the change is to be evolutionary or radical, and that in turn depends on the current success of the school and future prediction of its success in a changing environment. The advice from Deal and Kennedy (1988) is not to attempt to change the culture unless it is essential. Where there is a crisis such as falling rolls, poor reputation, poor exam results, large-scale absenteeism, a poor inspection report, any decision to change is easy—there is a clear and self-evident need. However, the position is much more difficult where the picture is less clear-cut. This book is about strategy, and this is precisely the occasion to look forward and foresee problems before they happen. The strategic management process outlined in this book provides a systematic way of accumulating and sifting evidence, examining alternatives and testing out future courses of action. Thus, the need to change should be pointed up more clearly than relying only on personal subjective reaction, but ultimately the need to change is a matter of judgement.

Having made any decision to change the culture, further decisions are contingent on the current state of the school and its recent history and future opportunities. However, as we have seen many times before, once an intention exists opportunities can be recognised as they occur, e.g. any staff leaving can be seen as presenting an opportunity.

The starting point for any such change is how far the organisation is ready for change. The strategic management process should have heightened awareness, and the difficulties involved in changing culture as part of a strategy should have been considered before the strategy was chosen. Nevertheless, the first consideration must be how far further 'unfreezing' is needed before the change has a chance of success.

Possible actions

Based upon the foregoing, there are a number of possible actions that could be taken. Individual actions may be evolutionary; only a concerted number of actions could be radical.

1 Staffing

(a) Existing staff

Any incompetent staff in senior positions have to be tackled. Such people are a double handicap. They are not able to play the positive part in the change that they should and they are a symptom for all to see. Tackling such staff also has the advantage of symbolic value, in that it marks a decision to confront difficult issues and is generally welcomed by staff who are equally disadvantaged by incompetence. Incompetence here is intended to mean precisely that—an inability to do the job (Fidler, 1992a).

Senior staff who do not share the view that the school needs to change or to change in a particular direction are not to be included in the above category. Where such staff have been involved in all the deliberations leading to the choice of strategy, they have had their chance to mobilise support for their views and if these have not carried the day, they need to abide by the legitimate decision. If necessary, they need to be reminded of their obligations of loyalty to legitimate decisions.

Staff development of existing staff can be a major force for change. This can mean encouraging those who are receptive to new ideas to study and provide outlets in school for them to use new skills or persuade others to change. The effect of more than one member of staff taking the same course more than doubles its value. They have a shared language and shared ideas which can help reinforce each other's commitment and confidence.

If groups of staff are to work as teams, team-building activities can be undertaken. Although these can be planned and undertaken by members of the group, an external facilitator is most often used to plan and organise the activities so that all team members can take part (Everard and Morris, 1990). Although the idea of a team may have a reassuring sound, this form of close working may not be suitable for all circumstances. For many purposes a co-operative group may be the most appropriate form of working (Fidler *et al.*, 1991).

Those who are resistant to change can be sent on courses in the hope that they will be influenced by mixing with others of more progressive view, hearing of practices in other schools and learning new knowledge. Whilst this may not be totally effective, it may be better than any feasible alternatives, and, coupled with other actions in the school, may have a higher success rate. Finally, there are whole-school staff development activities. The statutory inservice days provide an opportunity to programme all staff, but to have any lasting effect there has to be follow-up from any particular event. The choice of activity for the day, the interaction pattern of staff, how the day concludes, and how this leads on to the next steps are all crucial in planning to gain the maximum advantage from such an occasion.

(b) New staff and induction

New staff are a potent force for change, the most far-reaching being the appointment of a new headteacher.

(i) *New headteacher*: staff expect change with a new headteacher. Weindling and Earley (1987) noted that newly appointed secondary heads that they studied had intentions to take stock of their new schools before taking action, but tended to be precipitated into action earlier than they had intended. As we have seen, some decisions are strategic and, once made, will have a long-term impact. Many such decisions, especially if they come from outside the school, cannot be postponed, nor can a neutral decision be made. Thus heads cannot just take stock as they take up their post. Beginning with either an informal or a formal strategic analysis of the current position is an excellent way of:

■ gathering evidence in a systematic way

- most quickly becoming acquainted with the strategic position of the school

- recognising strategic decisions for that school

Heads who are new-to-post are more positive in their views about the value of school inspections by OFSTED than those who have been in post longer (Fidler *et al.*, 1994). As we have seen, such inspections can play a part in gathering evidence for a strategic analysis.

(ii) *Other staff*: all new staff present an opportunity, but senior staff can be particularly influential. In appointing such staff, their fit for the school should be a major consideration (Fidler, 1992c) in addition to assessments of their competence and ability to do the job. In many cases this will involve an assessment of their fit with the present culture of the school with a view to continuing the culture, but the dangers of having groupthink and an absence of sub-cultures on which to build should caution against having too many like-minded people working together in what might be a stable staff. Where an appointment is made in the context of a need to change the culture, choices are much restricted. The person must represent a move in the desired direction, have personal skills to make this more widely acceptable, and possess the determination to carry through new ideas (with support from the top).

In all cases of new staff being appointed, a much neglected process from the point of view of culture is the induction process. This is the opportunity to induct staff into the culture of the school. This can either be left to chance or it can be managed. It represents an opportunity to transmit an espoused culture and to indicate a small change of emphasis. This is likely to be effective since new staff are not immersed in the present culture. They are susceptible because they are in new surroundings with the added effect of interpersonal influence. Thus who inducts, what goes into an induction programme and whether new staff have a mentor will all be important decisions.

Appointing new staff will represent a much larger opportunity in a school with a small number of staff and in a school with a very stable staff than in larger schools or in a school with a higher turnover.

2 Internal 'marketing'

Although promotion and marketing are generally thought of as activities intended to influence those outside the school, influencing those inside the school, or internal marketing, can also be important (Bowles, 1989). Briefing meetings, staff meetings, newsletters and public events can all be used for internal marketing. They can be used to emphasise certain aspects of culture.

This may be in the form of information which was not widely known, an attitudinal gloss on events or reporting the views of others about the school. It can contribute to insiders seeing the school and themselves differently.

3 Organisational structure

This is the formal means by which a school expresses how it works together (Fidler, 1992b). It expresses the relationship between the posts of responsibility within a school. It sets down formal accountabilities and indirectly it determines who will work closely together. Decisions are required both about the design of the organisational structure and also about how the positions of responsibilities should be filled. Design involves considerations of how sections of groups should be related and to whom they should be accountable. The grouping of people together into departments or sections and the formation of committees and working groups has a great bearing on who will work together and who will influence whom. The organisational structure also indicates the formal decision-making structure of individuals and groups.

Thus changes to the organisational structure should, in principle, be a very powerful influence on culture. They can also be a way of placing people in influential positions to evolve or change the culture. Changes can be made by grouping some staff under a new leader. Opportunities for this are provided for by positions of responsibility in the formal organisational structure and also by chairing committees and working parties.

4 Decision-making

The organisational structure gives the formal decision-making machinery in a school. Involvement of staff in decision-making can take two basic forms—consultation and participation. Although sharing the responsibility of decision-making with others through participation gives a greater sense of ownership for other staff, its consequences should be foreseen. If the agents of change are not sufficiently strong, any sharing of decision-making runs the risk, at this stage, of being thwarted by conservative forces. Thus the stage at which any participation is contemplated needs consideration.

5 Systems, policies and documentation

These are part of the organisational structure, but it is convenient to separate them. Systems set out the school's procedures for carrying out tasks. These can be changed.

Where documentation does not exist and knowledge passes on in an informal manner, the creation or revision of documentation provides an opportunity to reflect and codify either how the school does do things, or how the school should do things and intends to do them in that way in the future.

Revising documentation and producing policies alone will not make change happen; however, as Firestone and Wilson (1985) point out, these can reinforce other levers on change. All the forces of change need to be consistent with each other and support each other. In this way the combined effect is stronger than the sum of the parts.

6 Rewards

Rewards encourage behaviour. They are important because they indicate the school's priorities. Rewards can take many forms and be monetary or non-monetary. Rewards both motivate the individual who has been rewarded and provide a clear message to others about institutional priorities.

The symbolic aspects of who gets rewarded and why should not be overlooked. People will make all sorts of inferences as to why decisions have been made unless there is (and even in spite of) a clear explanation.

7 Symbolic acts

In the midst of rational planning there is a great tendency to neglect the symbolism of actions. Some trivial changes may be deliberately made so as to cause comment and make staff stop and think and recognise that change may be irresistible. Where the reasons for actions are not clear, many staff will ponder and come to their own conclusions. This needs to be considered for its possible symbolism, or an explanation given if this is not to be seen as symbolic.

Visionary leaders will be very conscious of the effects of their actions and how they may be viewed. Staff can accomplish great feats if they have confidence in a leader and it would be foolish to think that such confidence was all built up on a purely rational level. Some events may need to be 'stage-managed' so that they have the appropriate effect.

An articulated vision of how things might be is a powerful influence on culture. Dwelling on events and people in the past or present draws attention to them and has an influence on the culture.

8 Interpersonal influence

Finally, the direct interpersonal influence of the headteacher talking with individual members of staff and using the power of persuasion, discussion and argument should not be underestimated. Such frequent informal work with substantial numbers of people can have a powerful effect.

Strategic implementation

For a major strategic change the task of changing the organisational culture, dealt with in the previous section, is likely to be a substantial element. It would also need to be associated with resource deployment (see below) to encompass the major elements of strategic implementation. For lesser changes, the following three elements may be more readily associated with strategic implementation. The first is concerned with the organisational structure, the second with people and systems and the third with resource planning.

Organisational structure

Clearly, the structure of an organisation—the relationship of people and tasks—is intended to facilitate the work of the organisation. If the generic strategy that has been developed involves a change in direction for the organisation, then the organisation structure will have, at the least, to be reviewed and may need substantial change. Thus, the basic structure of an organisation needs to be considered first, and then individual jobs within the organisation. The whole structure may need changing rather than an extra post being added on to the existing structure. If a change in the basic structure of the organisation is required, this may be a long-term process by which over a number of years a structure is gradually put in place as opportunity allows. Existing personnel may mean that any change cannot be achieved by a simple restructuring at one point in time, but to the prepared mind opportunities can be seized as they present themselves.

The basic organisational structures are: a functional structure, a divisional structure and a matrix structure (Fidler, 1992b). A functional structure divides the work of an organisation into its basic tasks. Thus for example, for a school, they might be:

■ teaching

- marketing and external relations

- finance and premises

- personnel

These comprise four large components of the work of the organisation, of which teaching would clearly be much the largest.

A divisional structure has sections which carry out work in parallel. The basic departmental organisation of secondary schools, by which teaching is divided up into its various subject areas each with its department head, is a divisional structure.

Where individual members of staff carry out more than one job, complications arise. They have at least two people to whom they are then accountable for different aspects of their work. This is called a matrix structure, since it is most easily represented as a grid in two dimensions. The typical work of a secondary school operates as a matrix where there are subject department heads responsible for the subject teaching work and pastoral heads responsible for the pastoral work carried out by staff. Each member of staff is responsible to a head of department and a pastoral head.

All organisational structures are compromises. The basic tension is between co-ordination and control. It is possible to increase one at the expense of the other. Choices of organisational structure and the nature of the compromises and difficulties are more fully discussed in Fidler (1992b).

Allied to the basic structure are the job positions within the school. This introduces the element of delegation, and how far the organisation is decentralised with each individual operating in a given area with a large measure of autonomy, and how far things are tightly controlled from the centre. From all that has been said previously about shared values in an organisation and a clear strategic direction, it should be clear that within such a framework, delegation substantially increases the capabilities of the whole organisation since there are then many managers at work and not just one. But it also follows that delegation without a clear strategic direction for the organisation may be counter-productive.

People and systems

Clearly the most potent elements in implementing any strategic change are people and systems. Systems ensure that the tasks people are doing are co-ordinated and reinforce each other, that they are consistent with the strategic direction of the organisation, and that other actions are discouraged. This means reward systems, monitoring and control must all be facing in the same direction.

The skills of existing staff will have been noted at the analysis stage and thus future demands for additional skills can be predicted. New people may need to be employed and those already in position may need to be trained and develop any new skills that are required. All of this needs to be planned, in general terms, at the stage of choosing a particular strategy, and subsequently implemented.

As predicted at the time of financial delegation to schools, the use of non-teaching staff has expanded substantially. In classrooms, classroom and special needs assistants have increased, particularly in primary schools, whilst in secondaries the range of office staff, technicians and finance staff has increased. In many schools these trends have further to go and may form aspects of a number of strategies.

If the new strategy requires a change in the organisational culture, then that has to be thought through as a major change process as we have indicated above. All that is known about change suggests that people do not generally welcome it and the way has to be prepared very carefully and thoroughly for change to be successful. To indicate that change is happening and to help the process along, some symbolic acts may be required by the leadership to indicate that things cannot remain the same and to reinforce the sorts of actions that are going to be highly regarded in the future.

Resources

Clearly, to achieve the strategy, resources will be required and will need to be allocated (Knight, 1993). This of course takes us right back to financial delegation, because this provides the possibility of directing resources to where the school decides they are most needed. Although it is well known that the extent of redirecting resources is limited in any one year, this is where the long term becomes important because, if resources can be re-allocated at only 2 per cent a year, then over five years 10 per cent could be re-allocated.

> In the short-term nearly all costs ... are fixed; in the long-term, all costs become variable. Thus, a particular split between fixed and variable costs is valid only for one particular time horizon of decision. (Emmanuel and Otley, 1985, p. 88–89)

The degree of difficulty in re-allocating resources is likely to be affected by whether or not the school is static in size, or whether the school is growing. If the amount of money, in real terms, is likely to remain constant, then spending on a different course of action can only be achieved at the expense of cutting some present expenditure, whereas if there is additional money appearing, then it is possible to look at a standstill budget to keep existing activities functioning and to apportion further money for new developments.

It would be prudent to plan for little real expansion in spending over and above that generated by additional pupil numbers, in which case resourcing a strategy is likely to involve the transfer of some expenditure from one current heading to a future one. The inter-relationship between resource planning and allocation and the initial analysis of resources and their use should be quite clear. Some kind of very simple network analysis (Fidler *et al.*, 1991) might be quite useful to indicate stages in the achievement of strategy. It is then possible to look at the spending implications of each of these stages to make sure there isn't some hiatus towards the end because of some intermediate step which should have been funded.

Short-term development projects

Where the strategic plan requires new activities or extra funding of existing ones, extra finance may be needed. In an expanding school there may be additional funds which can be used for this purpose. For a school with a fixed budget, such funding has to come from existing activities. This can be done by creating a 'development budget'. This is a heading within the draft budget which can be allocated to whatever are the development priorities in a particular year. However, as school budgets are generally tight, where is the development budget to come from? There are a number of systematic answers to this question:

- arbitrary cut in recurrent spending
- base and development budgets
- programme budgets

Arbitrary cut in recurrent spending

In order to free up 3 per cent of the budget for development, the spending allocation for the coming year can be planned to consume only 97 per cent of previous spending. If this is done too quickly, it will lead to the oft-noted effect that those budgets that are 'easy' to cut are cut rather than those budgets that ought to be cut. Thus some activities may be only partially funded. This is the least efficient way of operating, since resources are being consumed but the activities cannot take place as intended because one element of resourcing is missing. The computers have been purchased but not the software, for example. A programme budget (referred to later) is a way of preventing this happening.

Base and development budgets

The Audit Commission (1991a) has suggested that schools should construct a budget called a 'base' budget that represents their minimum spending level. Contrary to what many in schools might think, this is not their current spending level, but is the level below which they could not offer a satisfactory education, or below which teacher unions would not co-operate (for example if class sizes were too great). The Audit Commission recognises that a school might not be able to operate in this mode immediately even if it wished, because it would involve breaking contracts etc. However, the value of such an exercise is to show up the ways the school is currently spending resources in excess of the minimum needed, so that these can be subjected to scrutiny and changed.

The difference between the actual income to the school and the projected base spending level represents, in principle, the sum available for development. A plan could be drawn up to release this sum and to deploy it over a number of years.

The Audit Commission illustration covers a primary school where most resources are committed by the fixing of class sizes. In secondary schools the situation is more complicated. There are two techniques which provide assistance:

- staff deployment analysis
- activity-led staffing

Staff deployment analysis: this is more commonly known as COSMOS analysis after the committee which first introduced the techniques devised by T.I. Davies (1969). They have been reproduced in the OFSTED handbooks for school inspections (1992; 1994a; 1995a). This technique recognises that the main curriculum cost is not in differences between subjects offered, but in the sizes of teaching groups. Decisions about how many teaching groups to divide a year group into, and how large to have as a maximum for a particular subject, are often defended as rational decisions. However, schools rarely understand the 'cost' of these decisions and are often unable to recall when and on what basis such decisions were made in the past. Hutchinson (1993) investigated two similarly sized secondary schools and discovered that in one the smallest teaching groups were in maths and in the other they were in CDT. Whilst these may have been rational decisions at some point in time, they tend to get perpetuated year after year and cease to have a clear rationale years later. Staff deployment analysis provides a conceptual framework to investigate the deployment of staffing resources between year groups and can be developed to compare the use of resources between different curriculum subjects in the same year (Griffiths, 1995). Staff deployment analysis provides information to improve judgement. It does not replace judgement.

Activity-led staffing (ALS): activity-led staffing (Audit Commission, 1986) goes one stage further than staff deployment analysis to include non-teaching activities. It is mainly intended as a planning tool, but can be used to analyse an existing situation. In planning mode, decisions are made about the number of teaching periods offered to each year group in each subject of the curriculum, and also the maximum size of teaching group for each subject each year. The maximum number of teacher periods to staff this curriculum can then be calculated.

The secondary stage of the calculation is to estimate the amount of time which should be allocated to cover school tasks, teacher-related tasks and pupil-related tasks. Since the original proposal, 'directed time' has appeared (DES, 1987) and the time allocations could now be made to time during the school day or other directed time. However, in principle the total time taken for teaching and non-teaching tasks can be aggregated to ensure that school resources are sufficient to cover the total. The value of ALS is that it focuses on the whole-school task. There is a tendency in allocating resources to provide staff for teaching to allocate up to a historical proportion of time. Recently this appears to have taken account of the extra time taken to cover classes for absent colleagues (Newton, 1986; DFE, 1993). Allocating time for teaching and assuming that other tasks can be fitted into the remaining time is unsound. This should be regarded as an empirical question rather than the answer being assumed. The relative proportions of teaching and non-teaching time need investigation and judgment rather than relying on historical precedent from ten or more years ago. Managing school time is a fundamental decision (Knight, 1989).

Programme budgeting

Programme budgeting is a way of costing areas of activity. Thus the cost of educating a year group could be calculated. The cost of providing the activity is built up from the cost of each type of resource required, e.g. teaching staff, teaching support staff, training costs, equipment, supplies and services, and overheads to provide premises etc. (Fidler *et al.*, 1991). This is a way of ensuring that the appropriate resource mix is available, rather than discovering that there are plenty of teachers and classroom assistants in well-equipped and furnished classrooms, but no paper or pencils. Programme budgeting is a form of zero-based budgeting (Simkins and Lancaster, 1987). This involves devising the cost of carrying out an activity without any prior (historical) assumptions. Although this is unrealistic in that teachers are already employed and other expenditure is committed, a programme budget does then provide a target budget towards which to aim as circumstances allow.

Resourcing of primary schools

LMS has exposed the inequities of funding the education of primary-aged children compared to those of secondary-school age. A recent Parliamentary Select Committee Report (House of Commons, 1994) has drawn attention to this disparity. Attempts to investigate this situation in LEAs have generally foundered on the unwillingness of secondary schools to contemplate any diversion of their funding to primary schools. Unless additional resources are forthcoming from central and local government, the only way in which primary funding can be increased is at the expense of secondary funding. Probably a combination of some new money and a redistribution is most likely. Thus in their strategic planning primary schools should develop ideas on how they would use additional resources if they were to become available, and secondary schools should assume a more level funding than they might wish.

Raising extra finance

Some schools are in positions where raising extra finance by a variety of means can be contemplated (Braund, 1989). Clearly, where special grants are made available by central government it should be regarded as a strategic decision whether to apply for such funding. For example where there is a specific grant to facilitate specialisation, the school should have identified this as a viable route for the school to follow before applying for the finance.

In some situations parents may be a source of substantial extra revenue for the school. One of the niche scenarios painted by Murgatroyd and Morgan (1992) is of a school which offers certain facilities and activities to pupils, in return for a modest financial contribution from parents. Such a possibility will depend on the school's situation. Many schools can count on substantial sums from their PTAs but, as we concluded when discussing this in the *ELMS Workbook*, generally the sums are not so large that they should be allowed to disrupt the school's basic operation. A sense of perspective demonstrates the relatively small proportion of a school's expenditure which these activities generate. Its principal attraction is that it is new, uncommitted money. However, our basic advice is that such activities should serve additional purposes to those of raising money, for they have the potential to distort the school's activities and become ends in themselves rather than means to an end.

Business and industry can be used as sources of funding, but again their help and support should be sought on additional grounds than finance if the relationship is to be mutually beneficial.

Development planning

School development planning was devised in the mid-1980s and publicised in two pamphlets from DES in 1989 and 1991 (Fidler, 1996a). School development planning built upon a base of previous experience of school self-review. In a sense this is analogous to strategic planning which builds on a base of school development planning. However, as Constable *et al.* (1991) have pointed out, not all experience is good or developmental and may not necessarily lead to better development planning. However, successful experience of development planning should have two advantages:

- strategic planning can be regarded as a deeper, more comprehensive form of development planning
- action planning within development planning can be used to implement aspects of strategy

Unsuccessful experience of development planning, on the other hand, would be a handicap. In this case the differences between school development planning and strategic planning should be stressed.

There are large conceptual differences between the form of school development planning outlined by Hargreaves and Hopkins (1991) and strategic planning. Compared to school development planning, strategic planning is:

- *Forward-looking*: environmental scanning tries to spot future influences.
- *Outward-looking*: data are collected from parents and others; the consequences of the schools' actions on others are considered.
- *Proactive*: the school is regarded as an initiator—recognising opportunities and taking advantage of them; reviewing possible impositions from outside and taking a stance on them rather than acquiescing.

- *Creative*: vision is a creative element to balance improvement which would otherwise be based on analysing and improving present practices rather than doing something radically different.

- *Holistic*: it deals with all the school's operations rather than mainly being concerned with curriculum and staffing; it also tries to view the school's operations holistically.

The similarities are that both involve:

- an evaluation of current activities

- prioritising areas for development

- creating action plans

- identifying staff development needs to implement action plans

- implementing action plans

Most schools are familiar with some form of development planning (MacGilchrist *et al.*, 1995). These techniques can be used to implement the various parts of the strategic plan.

Monitoring and evaluation

Responsibilities should be allocated for monitoring the implementation of the strategic plan and the modification of the plan in the light of progress in implementation. The plan should have within it progress checks so that the extent to which it is on course can be assessed.

The plan should have within it a clear rationale which can be used as the basis for evaluating the working of the plan in the future.

7 Primary school case study 1

Client orientation in a first school

Maureen Edwards

The context of the school

The subject of this case study is a small first school taking 5–8 year olds with 150 children on roll in five classes. It is situated in the north end of a small town and has a mixed catchment area. It serves a council estate with a high proportion of problem families and social hardship. The school, over a period of eight years, has experienced a falling roll brought about by middle-class drift to schools in more affluent areas of the town, now that open enrolment provided parents with a greater choice than the local catchment-area school. The roll has now stabilised and numbers have remained at 150 for the last two years. In 1988 the number on roll was 200 and the school had seven classes. The school shares a joint governing body with its associated middle school, which is situated on the opposite side of the road. The middle school has very similar problems and is still experiencing a falling roll. It is generally acknowledged that the town has surplus capacity within its schools. There are two other first schools in close proximity, one of which suffers a similar problem of a falling roll.

Adopting a strategic management approach

The 1988 Education Act has had a dramatic impact upon the way in which schools need to operate. National Curriculum, open enrolment, formula funding and local management of schools have all played a part in pushing schools towards adopting a more market-based approach to education.

Formula funding, which is closely linked to pupil numbers, has posed a great threat to schools in a falling roll situation and for the past eight years the school has had to accommodate significant cuts in its budget. This has highlighted the need for identifying and responding to the factors which influence parental choice of school. Local management of schools (LMS) has, however, also brought about greater opportunities for schools to take decisions. Schools are now in a position where they can have a much greater influence on their future, and are able to have much more control over their own destiny. These new responsibilities require a greater knowledge and understanding on the part of school management teams of the management techniques and approaches used in other organisations.

In 1990 I was appointed headteacher of this school. For the first three years of my headship the school was heavily involved in implementing the National Curriculum and National Curriculum Assessment procedures and in setting up a system for managing a delegated budget. It was a period of 'reactive' development planning driven by a need to meet legal requirements rather than a proactive approach. With curriculum policies in place by 1993 and financial procedures established, the time was right for the school to consider its position in a wider context and in a more structured way.

Before 1993, the school development plan provided an annual forecast of what the school intended to focus on during the next twelve-month period. It was written by the headteacher after consultation with the staff and was largely concerned with curriculum development and staff training needs. It followed a county-approved format and closely reflected the school's GEST allocation. Governors took little interest in the drawing-up of the document and it was approved as a matter of course at the appropriate governors' meeting, usually without question or comment. Table 7.1 provides an example of a development plan for a previous year.

In April 1993, the school needed to produce another development plan for the academic year beginning September 1993. Since the 1988 Act, governors were gradually becoming more involved in the organisation of the school, and by 1993 there were five governing body committees with delegated responsibilities for premises, finance, personnel, curriculum, marketing and promoting the school. The need for a new development plan was first discussed at a staff meeting, which included the governing body curriculum committee. Following this meeting it was agreed that the vice-chair of governors, who was a member of the curriculum committee, would represent the governing body in future discussion and formulation of the plan. A meeting between head, deputy head and vice-chair of governors was

	Next Year	Support training	Longer term
Curriculum	Review of Science, RE and update policy statements Technology and IT: complete review of resources, policy statements and record-keeping	IT INSET for new staff	History and Geography review of practice and resource needs
Management e.g. organisation personnel staff development governing body development	Formalise a scheme of non-contact time for co-ordinators to work with colleagues Adopt a system of focused visits for governors	Use of INSET supply budget Focused visit Governor training (video and discussion)	Provide time for Deputy Head to acquire working knowledge of school finances
Community e.g. parents local community wider community	Complete the 'Getting-Started' package—extending time in school Improve links with the Middle School	Supply cover for Reception Class teacher to liaise with playgroup Supply cover	Introduce a Mother and Toddlers' Group to the school
Budget management e.g. staffing premises supplies/equipment generating income	Maintain staff levels Budget for additional 10 hours' welfare Upgrade Beech Room for Technology Buy computer		Replace classroom furniture in top block (chairs and desks) Generate £2,000 for above from Parent Association events

Table 7.1   School development plan

arranged and this resulted in the decision that a one-year plan with a focus on curriculum and staff training was not adequate. The school needed a more long-term view.

It was decided that a four-year plan would better meet the school's needs and concerns. A four-year cycle was chosen as a suitable time-scale because it fitted in with the OFSTED cycle of school inspections. No very clear views were expressed on how the plan should be formulated and a second meeting was arranged so that each member of the group could have some thinking time. At the second meeting, a further governor who worked in industry, and had considerable management experience, was co-opted. Strategic planning was suggested as the best way forward. This led to a small working party— myself (headteacher) and the governor with management experience putting together a draft format for creating a four-year strategic plan.

A meeting was arranged to explain the new format to the teaching staff and to invite comment on the new approach. It was made clear that responsibility for collecting and disseminating the information would be delegated. Staff input at this meeting was very limited. There was no obvious resistance, but I suspected that everyone was trying to gauge what it all meant in terms of their workload. The autumn term (September 1993) was designated as the best time to undertake the analysis. This allowed a period of time for staff to take on board the new ideas, and for me to try and generate a positive response for the initiative. It also allowed me a time to reflect on strategic planning and to become more familiar with the literature on the subject, and reach a better understanding of what it was likely to entail. The staff meetings for the remainder of the summer term included some reference and discussion of strategic planning. They were intended to inform staff more fully of the issues that surrounded strategic planning, in the hope that greater knowledge and understanding of the process would lead to greater commitment and enthusiasm for the delegated responsibilities each teacher was being asked to undertake. The idea that there were key stakeholders, who were affected by, or who could affect the organisation, was debated at length. The influence that parents and governors should have upon the organisation was particularly contentious.

Strategic analysis

Literature relating to strategic planning suggested a need to focus on:

- action
- the consideration of a broad and diverse set of stakeholders
- attention to external opportunities and threats and internal strengths and weaknesses
- attention to actual or potential competitors

(Bryson and Roering, 1987)

The Johnson and Scholes model for strategic management seemed to provide a workable format and was adopted to carry out the strategic analysis required for the formulation of a long-term development plan.

Following the model:

1 An audit of resources, human and physical, was carried out and a human resource register compiled.
2 The organisational culture and the degree of satisfaction with it was considered.
3 Key stakeholders were consulted to establish the needs which had to be met in order to gain stakeholder satisfaction.

Internal stakeholders were identified as:

1 children attending the school
2 teaching staff
3 ancillary staff
4 governors

External stakeholders were identified as:

1 parents
2 playgroup personnel

Ascertaining their views required several different approaches. The best ways were discussed by staff, and the following identified:

Children:

- oral and written communication
- class-group discussion

- fact-finding sheets/questionnaires
- drawings, writing about school

These were all used to gain knowledge of the child's satisfaction with the *status quo*.

Class teachers were involved in collecting this information and a designated member of staff collated and analysed the results.

Teaching staff completed a questionnaire and a SWOT analysis. They participated in staff meetings and individual consultations. The information gained from teachers was processed by the headteacher.

Ancillary staff were asked to complete a questionnaire and invited to give their views at a focused staff meeting.

Governors' views were sought at governors' meetings and at committee or working party meetings. They also carried out their own SWOT analysis and the comparison with teaching staff analysis provided an opportunity for a meeting of staff and governors to discuss the school's future.

Parents' views were sought by:

1 questionnaire

2 a formal meeting with governors/staff

3 informal meetings

The questionnaire was produced through consultation between a governors' 'Promoting the School' working party and teaching staff. Its purpose was to try and ascertain the level of satisfaction with the education (product) offered, to highlight the school's strengths and weaknesses as perceived by parents, and to provide parents with an opportunity to make suggestions for further development.

The formal meeting was designed to provide an opportunity for parents to meet the staff and governing body who gave a short presentation of their role in the school. It was intended to provide the opportunity for parents to question and comment on the service provided by the school.

The Parents' Association provided a parent to look after the interests of each class. These class representatives were responsible for arranging coffee mornings. In an informal atmosphere school issues were discussed. As part of the strategic analysis, class representatives were asked to hold a coffee morning and were briefed to explore general perceptions of the school—the things it did well and the things it could do better. A key question for the first term's coffee meeting was 'How does the school meet the needs of parents?'. Class representatives fed back information to class teachers, who in turn fed back to the whole staff.

The playgroup

The school had an independent playgroup renting one of the classrooms. As potential customers, these parents and children are key stakeholders. Their perceptions of the school were sought by the headteacher at a meeting 'Getting Started', which focused on the first year of schooling. An additional purpose that term was to establish what parents expected to receive, both in terms of the curriculum and the other services that the school provided.

Ideally the perceptions of the wider local community would have been tapped, but a way to achieve this was not readily forthcoming and therefore not pursued.

Future pupil numbers

Two measures were planned to provide this information:

1 acquiring the local authority estimates
2 using the school's street representatives' records of children in the catchment area

Resources

An audit of both physical and human resources was undertaken in September. Curriculum co-ordinators were responsible for the curriculum areas. An assets register was compiled and a 'Needs' list established.

A human resource register was also compiled. This became my responsibility. The information was gathered by asking all staff to complete a standard format form which asked for:

- Present responsibilities
- Specialisms/skills
- Clubs they could offer
- Responsibilities they would like to have
- Training needs/courses they would like to attend

Time for individual interviews with members of staff to renegotiate job descriptions for the year had already been built into the September schedule. This also provided an opportunity to include discussion of the information sheets and the valuable part each member of staff would play in the successful operation of the new plan. In addition, it allowed each member of staff to put any questions they had directly to me.

A parent letter—asking for parents to register any skills they could offer or help they could give—was also circulated in September.

I collated the information with the help of the deputy in October.

Reputation and ethos

Establishing a common view of intangibles is never easy. In July 1993, I began headteacher appraisal. The time-scale of the appraisal meant that the final statement would have been written by the end of October. The focus of the appraisal was: How the school's ethos is communicated by the head to parents, children and staff. This information was to be gathered and collated by a headteacher colleague and an LEA adviser. All relevant findings were fed into the strategic analysis.

Organisational culture

Information on this aspect of the school was gathered from:

1 staff

2 children

1 Staff

A staff Inset day had been planned when each teacher was asked to talk for a few minutes on:

- what they believed the school's mission to be
- what they saw as the school's central concerns
- how they would sum up 'What we're about?'
- how the school met the needs of parents

The minutes of the meeting provided the record which was used as part of the analysis.

2 Children

The topic for the first half-term of the school year, September to November 1993, was 'Our School'. As part of this topic, children were consulted along similar lines as the staff. This was carried out in school assembly discussion times.

Pooling the information from the children and analysing it took place during staff meetings scheduled for the end of October.

Response to, and results of, the strategic analysis

The results of the analysis of these measures identified four key factors:

1 Parents felt the school curriculum was mostly good, but parent liaison and influence within the school were satisfactory to poor. There was also some concern about standards of behaviour, extra-curricular activity, and discipline.

2 Children wanted a wider range of non-academic services (clubs).

3 Teachers were more critical than parents of the curriculum provision offered, but felt that parent influence and liaison was at a high level.

4 Governors were most concerned with the falling roll and the need to promote a higher profile for the school within the local community.

Both parents and children were indicating needs which were not directly related to the National Curriculum.

Parents

The informal coffee mornings were attended by 41 per cent of parents. Reception and Year 1 parents had a slightly higher attendance figure than Years 2 and 3. The questionnaires had a disappointing response. In total, 102 were sent out and 39 returned. The governors' meeting for parents was particularly disappointing. Approximately twenty parents attended, all of whom had connections with the governing body or the parents' association, and were therefore particularly 'active' parents.

Children

An invitation for the children to participate was enthusiastically received. Little information was gained about their perception of the quality of curriculum provision, but what surprised staff was their knowledge of what other schools provided in the way of 'extras'.

The dissatisfaction felt by the children at not having clubs was not anticipated and came as a great shock. The children's response, more than any, highlighted how out of touch the school was with its local 'competitors'. There was a feeling amongst staff that good schools were synonymous with a good curriculum, and a reluctance to accept that extra-curricular activities played an important part in determining a school's reputation.

Teachers

The initial response to their role in carrying out the analysis was compliance rather than commitment.

Questionnaire responses showed a very marked similarity of teacher responses in terms of curriculum provision training needs and involvement with the parent group. All teachers felt that the core curriculum subjects (along with PE and Art) were well taught, and all were unanimous in saying that Technology, Geography and History needed further development and clarification. Four of the five teachers also felt that parent liaison, and the school's involvement with parents, was at a high level. This was in marked contrast with what the parents were indicating. The staff Inset session relating to the organisational culture of the school showed that there was not a very clear view of what we were about. The staff handbook was mentioned by all staff, together with the good team spirit amongst the staff. These two aspects were a direct result of the cycle of change that the school had undergone in the previous two years. Nebulous statements about children reaching their potential and a broad and balanced curriculum were also offered. It indicated that, as a manager, I was not giving a clear lead, and that I needed to be more articulate in communicating my vision for the school. It was encouraging to note that a previous change (team planning) was now viewed as a strength, and this provided me with positive feedback about accepting change.

Governors

Their views more closely matched those of the parents. This, with hindsight, was probably not surprising, since the school has a high proportion of governors who are parents, as well as the statutory number of parent governors. Governors, like parents, identified a need for more liaison with parents, and for greater opportunities for parents to express their views. The governors' questionnaire had an 80 per cent response. There was a very marked difference between their views of liaison and influence of parents compared to that expressed by teaching staff. Governors quite clearly wanted a more public and diverse role for the school and were very aware of market forces.

The gathering of information and the processing of the information, in order to make a strategic analysis on which to base a strategic plan, proved more difficult and time-consuming than I had supposed. Moreover, the information proved to be problematic, in that it identified several mismatches between the views and priorities of the stakeholders involved in the analysis.

Strategic choice

A further meeting of the strategic development plan working party discussed the issues. There was concern about how valid and representative of stakeholders' views the information might be. I was very aware of the lack of experience we had in collecting data of this kind. Small schools, unlike many profit-making concerns, are not able to call on the resources, skills and services of a top management team. There was concern about the low response rate of the parent questionnaire (38 per cent). The reliance on oral feedback in the form of meetings, interviews etc. also led to discussion on how far the eloquence of the interviewer and interviewees might have influenced the outcome. However, it was agreed by all that this analysis was the most thorough and wide-ranging the school had ever carried out, and however imperfect it might be, it was more likely to provide a more accurate forecast of future needs than those defined solely by the head and teaching staff.

Arriving at a plan that would integrate policies, goals and actions was very time-consuming. Trying to match a long-term direction with the current environment was problematic, in that there were several mismatches between present skills and attitudes, and those required if the school was to identify more closely with the needs identified by external stakeholders, and take on a wider role than achieving sound academic progress. The choices to be made were put to staff in November staff meetings in the form of a draft plan for the next four years. We were very aware that this was a critical point and that everyone needed to consider themselves part of the process, and time was taken to explore each issue in detail.

The main thrust of the plan was to try and increase the pupil numbers by concentrating more on the factors which parents, governors and pupils deemed important to make the school successful, whilst at the same time maintaining and building on the academic progress and curriculum development already achieved and viewed as important by the teaching staff.

Key issues therefore were:

1 Extending the role and skills of class teachers, so that they are able to become more involved with parents, and build a positive partnership between home and school.

2 Providing opportunities for parents to participate more fully in the school, so that more positive attitudes and a sense of commitment might be achieved.

3 Providing a wider range of activities in the form of clubs for the children.

4 Informing the local community and parents more fully of the initiatives taking place within the school, paying particular attention to the successes achieved in areas such as behaviour.

This was thoroughly discussed. It became clear that to implement the plan fully, there would need to be significant changes in school practices and staff attitudes.

As a headteacher, the problem I needed to address was how to manage successfully the process of change required to implement the plan. The teaching staff had already experienced a period of change during my headship. The curriculum had been overhauled and team planning introduced, both of which had achieved a high measure of success. In many ways, a period of stability with no changes might have seemed a more sensible option. There was, however, overwhelming support from the governing body to move forward. Teaching staff also had a feeling of great urgency about increasing pupil numbers.

Literature related to achieving change in an institution stresses that bringing about successful change needs to take account of factors relating to the individuals involved. Change has a profound effect upon the individual. To accomplish successful change, managers will, therefore, need to have some understanding of the individuals involved in the change.

Fullan (1991, p. 117) quite rightly states 'educational change depends on what teachers do and think—it's as simple and as complex as that'. Everard and Morris (1990) remind us that change usually leads to temporary incompetence and that this is uncomfortable. Grundy (1993) states much the same: 'performance is adversely affected by change and sometimes in a profound way' (p. 49).

Everard and Morris (1990, p. 232) identify nine factors that they believe to be common to any change, and point out that participating in change engages both the intellect and the emotions. These factors were borne in mind when promoting the desired changes.

It seemed a daunting task at the outset and I felt a need for clear guidelines on how to move forward. The previous changes made within the school had been more closely aligned to what the staff felt educational institutions were concerned with—improving academic standards, defining and delivering the curriculum. There was no previous tradition of opening up the school and extending the range.

Parental involvement was only beginning to take root. The previous head had not felt a need for parents to be closely associated with what went on in school, and had been reluctant even to accept a parent fund-raising association. Discussions arising from views about stakeholders suggested that at least two members of staff felt that closely involving parents would, in some way, demean their professional status.

Managing the process of change

After reading several authors' views on strategic management and implementing change, Grundy's five-stage model of strategic change seemed to be the most straightforward framework for moving forward (see Figure 7.1).

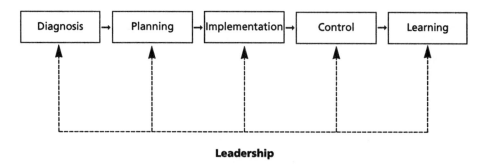

Leadership

Figure 7.1   Key elements in managing change successfully
Source: reproduced from Grundy, 1993, p. 53, by permission of the publisher, Kogan Page Ltd, London

Grundy's five-stage model

1 Diagnosis

2 Planning

3 Implementation

4 Control

5 Learning

These five stages are supported by the key co-ordinating mechanism of leadership.

Grundy offers the following definitions for each of the stages.

Diagnosis is the process of understanding the rationale (that is, why we are doing it) and implications of the change. Effective diagnosis involves exploring the forces which may enable or constrain the process of achieving the change objective (that is, what we want out of it). This may also involve exploring the stakeholders in the change and the impact of the change on the organisational paradigm.

Planning is the programming of one or more change thrusts or projects to mobilise resources, co-ordinate activities and to achieve desired milestones and outputs.

Implementation is the execution of change programmes and the management of barriers to change.

Control is the checking back to ensure that the change process is on track in terms of its benefits and costs (both expected and unexpected) and time-scales.

Learning is the systematic review of lessons gained from the change, both in terms of the change rationale and also of the effectiveness of the change process. (This does not mean there is no learning in earlier stages; simply that a more formal learning review is appropriate.)

The diagnosis stage of the Grundy model fitted well with the Johnson and Scholes model for strategic analysis which had been used for collecting the raw data. The diagnosis phase of the Grundy model was the responsibility of the working party. The three questions addressed were 'Where are we now?'; 'Where do we want to be?; and 'How ready are we for change?'. To make the diagnosis, SWOT analysis, force-field analysis, commitment and capability charts were used.

The measures outlined provided the answer to 'Where are we now?' and 'Where do we want to be?'. The following statements were the view reached from an analysis of the information.

Diagnosis

Where are we now?

The school is a small school which has had a declining roll and shrinking budget for ten years and a poor reputation in terms of catchment area and educational standards. The teaching staff recognising this description have channelled their efforts into curriculum development in the belief that raising the quality of provision offered will enhance the performance of the children and *in time* improve the reputation of the school.

The parents who responded to the consultation measures—questionnaires and coffee mornings—expressed a satisfaction with the curriculum offered (with the exception of RE), but are less positive about the degree of influence they have in the school and the opportunities they have for parent–teacher liaison.

The children in school are more concerned with the provision of extra-curricular activities in the form of clubs than either curriculum or other factors.

I (headteacher) have been in post since September 1990. The school has in my view successfully completed my initial long-term objective—a significant increase in pupil performance—brought about by building a commitment to team work and shared curriculum expertise in planning and delivering the National Curriculum. Financial priorities have been weighted in favour of resourcing the curriculum and meeting staff development needs in terms of curriculum expertise. A SWOT analysis verifies the view that staff now regard themselves as a committed team. It also shows that staff have a poor perception of the parental client group.

Force-field analysis indicates that enabling forces for the proposed change are stronger than the constraining forces, but highlight the need for a shift of emphasis in providing people expertise and resource provision.

A capability chart highlights the need for further staff development (three of the six key players not capable of meeting change requirements). A commitment chart reflects the capability chart with three of the six key players not totally committed to the shift of emphasis.

Where do we want to be?

Mission statement

We aim to educate children to achieve a high standard academically, socially and morally and provide a safe, happy environment in which children, teachers and parents feel valued and work together to achieve this common purpose.

Prior to carrying out a strategic analysis, the school did not have a written 'mission' statement. 'What we were about' was implicit, and so mixed messages were fed back. The mission statement needed to be short enough to memorise, but it also needed to be more than just a nebulous statement that could be conveniently repeated. The wording of the statement was agreed by the strategic development plan committee. I felt that the statement needed further explanation, therefore when it was presented to staff the additional four statements were added, along with a definition of the change that needed to occur and the justification for doing it.

What is the change?

The school is extending the range and scope of the product it offers to children and parents.

In response to current demands, both nationally and locally, the school will not only provide a broad and balanced curriculum in keeping with the National Curriculum requirement, but also offer children a range of extra-curricular activities in the form of clubs. It will also provide parents with a greater say in how the school operates by responding in a positive way to their expectations and needs from education.

This means that teachers will need to extend their role to include the communication skills acquired by and expected of service-sector workers.

Why are we doing it?

Schools now by law have to be more accountable to parents and provide a curriculum and services which are in tune with local demands. Open enrolment means that schools are no longer guaranteed a monopoly of the local children, but have to compete with market forces.

In the next four-year cycle, I would like the school to maintain and build on the improvement in academic standards already achieved so that in four years' time, the gate gossip will be 'the school is a successful school where disadvantaged children are offered and profit from the same benefits as their more middle-class counterparts'.

In four years' time, the school will be an asset to the local community, with parents and the school's neighbours sharing and enjoying a sense of pride in the facilities the school has to offer.

In four years' time there will be a tradition of staff working in close partnership with parents in an atmosphere of mutual respect.

Parents will feel a sense of commitment and responsibility for ensuring that their child is fully benefiting from the educational provision offered, and will feel empowered to offer help and support to class teachers. The success of the school will be reflected by an increase in pupil numbers and a correspondingly more healthy budget.

How ready are we for change?

This was gauged by using the following techniques:

1 force-field analysis

2 SWOT analysis

3 commitment chart

4 capability chart

The Grundy model we were following reinforces the need to define the change objective clearly (where you want to be or need to be). 'It is worthwhile re-emphasising that unless the change objective is clearly specified, the force-field analysis will become unfocused and non-specific' (Grundy, 1993, pp. 83–84).

Grundy suggests that the relative strength of a force may be evaluated successfully either by:

■ scoring each force as high, medium, low; or

■ scoring each force on a 1–5 scale

In analysing the forces, he suggests questions such as:

■ Why is it an enabler or constraint?

■ How important an influence is it on the change process?

■ What underlying factors does it depend upon in turn?

A force-field analysis (see Figure 7.2) was carried out by myself (headteacher), the deputy and vice-chair of governors who is a parent governor and an active member of the 'Promote the School Committee'.

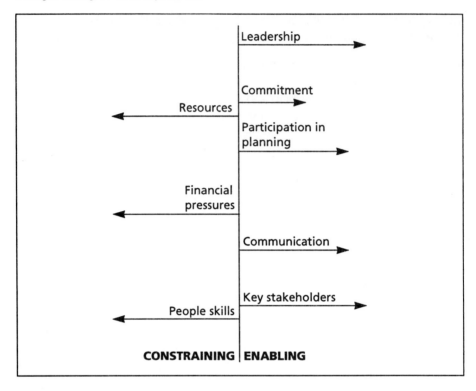

Figure 7.2   Force-field analysis

The key areas identified were:

- resources
- people skills
- financial pressure
- leadership
- communication
- commitment of staff
- participation by staff in planning
- backing of influential stakeholder

In drawing the diagram, scoring each force was in terms of high; medium; low.

As can be seen, there is on balance a movement in the right direction with enabling forces stronger than constraining forces. The finance constraining force is not easily overcome. An increase in pupil numbers or measures to generate more income are the most obvious solutions, but neither is realistic in the present climate. People skills were seen as a constraining force, as there needed to be a significant shift in the way teachers perceived parents and in their approach to them, particularly in less formal contacts. Staff Inset training needed to be initiated so that there would be a greater awareness and sensitivity on the part of staff when dealing with parents.

The SWOT analysis showed:

1 Teachers were united in feeling a sense of well-being about the school's approach to curriculum development, planning and implementation. Even the newest members of staff identified the team as a strength.

It demonstrated that the staff had accepted a previously imposed change as a benefit and success (i.e. team planning). All who took part in the analysis identified the team as a strength.

2 Every teacher made some negative comment in terms of a 'weakness' or 'threat' about the parents in the catchment area. This highlighted a significant gap between the school's present position and where we needed to be, and called for careful consideration at the planning stage and sensitive handling during the implementation phase. Other readiness indicators showed positive features.

An analysis using Leithwood's (1990) career cycle suggested three of the five staff were in an active career phase, either launching or looking for new challenges. Bolam's (1990) job stage showed a similar trend with teachers in the induction phase and one transitional seeking promotion. Plotting a commitment chart showed that no-one would oppose the change and three out of five staff had reached the desired position.

Taken collectively, these indicators pointed in the right direction for change to occur.

The SWOT analysis, however, suggested that the rate of change might not be rapid, since a changing of attitudes (e.g. the negative view of the staff concerning parents) would take time.

The Grundy model of managing strategic change points out that in order to implement a change, a 'paradigm shift' might be required. Grundy (1993) defines a 'paradigm' shift as 'a concerted attempt to move the paradigm from one state to another whilst retaining some, but not all of its core features'. A 'paradigm shift' was needed in order to implement this change successfully, so that 'the way we do things around here' adopted the view that parents are valued and work in partnership with teachers to achieve high academic, social and moral standards for all the children.

The change in working procedures that the 'paradigm shift' required needed to be communicated ('sold') to staff in terms of the tangible benefits, for as Everard and Morris (1990) point out: 'Effective educational change cannot occur without improvements to the teacher's working life.'

Planning

The spring term was set aside for planning the implementation of the new strategic plan. The planning for change was my responsibility. The four-year cycle was agreed as the time required to get from 'Where We Are Now' to 'Where We Want to Be' and the changes were planned in four phases—one for each year.

The strategic plan

PHASE 1	Apr 1994–Mar 1995
PHASE 2	Apr 1995–Dec 1996
PHASE 3	Jan 1997–Mar 1998
PHASE 1	Setting up system. Transition phase.
PHASE 2	Monitoring success and extending range.
PHASE 3	Perfecting the system.
PHASE 4	Audit and review. Planning to move on.

In arriving at the plan, Carnall's checklist was adopted (1990, p. 201):

1 Does the plan identify clear aims and deadlines?

2 Is the timetable realistic?

3 Is responsibility for change clear?

The first year's plan needed:

1 A strategy to 'shift' paradigm and change attitudes.

2 Resource allocation, both staff and Inset needs and physical resources.

3 Clear objectives, and targets for all concerned.

Paradigm shift

Indicators from all the diagnostic measures showed a positive response was possible. One member of staff, the deputy, was clearly identified as a potential facilitator. Her help was therefore enlisted to enable a more effective attack on 'changing the way we do things around here'. Working closely with this member of staff, a strategy for changing the paradigm was agreed. It was a two-pronged approach.

1 *A doom scenario*—continuing falling roll, if parents did not feel satisfied. The parents' questionnaire had indicated that the majority of negative feeling about the school was concerned with the extent to which parents' views were considered. Of the 39 returns, ten indicated that considering the parents' views fell in the range of poor to satisfactory. It was stressed that this might pose a threat to job security.

2 *The benefits to staff of sharing with parents the responsibility of educating children*—we agreed to lead by example, with myself, being highly visible at all times parents were on site, and another member of staff, organising class initiatives. We had now reached the stage where new targets needed to be identified in order to move towards fulfilling the objectives set out in the new mission statement.

New targets

Three staff meetings were taken to discuss moving towards more parental involvement and to set targets. It was agreed that no more than six targets should be set, and for the first year the following five were agreed upon.

1 Interacting more extensively and effectively with class representatives.

2 The setting up of an area in school for which parents could take responsibility.

3 Providing an opportunity for all Year 2 and 3 children to have at least one club activity a week.

4 Governors to take a more active role in the promoting of the school through press releases and written communication with parents.

5 Review of RE and the school behaviour policy. (RE already identified as an initiative in previous year's development plan.)

The five targets were written into the plan. £1,000 was allocated to meet additional resource needs for Year 1, as follows:

£600—staff development
£250—club/playgroup equipment
£150—parent facilities

For each of the five targets, specific objectives were necessary. These were worked out in meetings with the groups concerned. It meant that planning the change involved all key stakeholders. There was no opportunity to take a passive role.

Children were consulted in assemblies about the types of club they would like to have, and the playgroup equipment they wanted most.

All teachers were timetabled to have a staff development interview, and new job descriptions were negotiated. The new job description included a section relating specifically to parents. This brought an element of 'having to comply'.

For each of the five targets and the appropriate user groups, objectives needed to be set. This would reinforce the nature of the task to be completed and provide a yardstick by which progress could be measured and a sense of satisfaction achieved (see Appendix 7.1). Meetings with each of the relevant groups were arranged to agree objectives and clarify the precise nature of any change in job performance.

Implementation

In order to prevent drifting away from the identified new targets, time-scales were allocated to each. These were clearly identified in the development plan and responsibility for each was linked to a key person.

The implementation phase also required positive leadership. The Grundy model of strategic change places a great emphasis and importance on leadership. Undertaking the strategic analysis and adopting a strategic plan called for me to take a high profile and give a strong lead.

I had to consider my leadership style and take positive steps to promote the most effective way to motivate staff. I felt I needed to adopt a 'selling' style, which meant I needed to be able to clarify, coach, support, sell, explain and encourage staff in the task ahead.

I also needed to be successful in institutionalising my 'vision' for the four years ahead. I needed to be able to articulate the vision in such a way that everyone in the school became committed to it and day-to-day activities reflected its values. This meant almost daily positive reinforcement of some aspect of the plan.

Control

Control required checking to ensure that the change process was on course in terms of benefits to the school in relation to the cost. It needed to be a continuous process, so that problems where they occurred could be identified and remedied. It hopefully guarded against implementing change at all costs. Control measures were built into the implementation phase, in that each target identified has an element of re-consultation of the client-group to test the response (see Appendix 7.2).

Learning

Learning is the final stage in Grundy's 'implementing strategic change'. It is related to a summative assessment of the lessons gained from the change rationale and the effectiveness of the change process. This process does not exclude formative assessments being made and the intention has been to build in formative measures all the way through.

Grundy's (1993) five-point checklist for implementing strategic change (p. 125) forms the basis of how change will ultimately be judged:

1 Did change actually meet its key objectives and if not why not?

2 What should we do now therefore to secure the intended benefits of the change?

3 How might we influence key stakeholders to commit to any further necessary or appropriate change?

4 What lessons can now be drawn on:
   – how we diagnose, plan, implement and control change generally?
   – our overall capacity for and capability to implement change?

5 How can we disseminate these 'learning lessons' in an open way, and without embarrassment?

Where are we now?

The school has now completed one year of the four-year plan and has just set the targets for Year 2. It is too early in the cycle to assess the long-term benefits of planning in this way, but it is possible to discern several positive features which are directly attributable to strategic thinking and planning.

There is a much more clearly articulated view of 'what the school is about' and 'how we do things around here'. All staff, teaching and non-teaching, governors, children and parents, know and understand what has been named 'the school code' and refer to it frequently when talking about the school. There is also an expectation on the part of staff, governors and parents that there will be regular updates on all initiatives in which the school has become involved.

This has placed heavy demands on me and I feel my leadership is very much more in the public domain. It is no longer very easy to implement anything without consultation. The setting of targets related to the strategic plan and specific objectives for all staff have made the organisation more effective and allowed us to move forward in a purposeful way. There is less 'muddling through'. There is also less danger of jumping on a popular bandwagon in the hope of gaining public support or recognition. The school is much more focused. It remains to be seen whether this will help us to more easily meet our long-term objectives.

Planning in this way for school improvement has led to other initiatives. The strategic plan called for changes in the way staff were expected to operate and required them to acquire skills. Meeting these needs had far-reaching implications for staff training and development. The school is now committed to attaining the 'Investors In People' recognition for staff training and development.

Staff development has become the key factor in the Year 2 targets.

This chapter has been concerned with documenting the key element of the strategic plan, i.e. client orientation, but there were other aspects included in the finished document, such as personnel, curriculum development and premises, and the relevant governors' committees were heavily involved in producing a four-year forecast. Having a four-year plan for these aspects has been extremely beneficial. It has made the school more proactive in these areas. Regardless of the budget, we now have a priority list for such things as improving the school premises and a long-term staff development plan. Within the last year there has been spending on tangible benefits rather than holding back in case of unanticipated expenditure. This has had a very positive effect on staff morale and has helped to foster a much more committed approach.

It seems likely that for the foreseeable future the school will carry on adopting a strategic planning approach. The next four-year planning cycle will, however, need to have an input from personnel who are more experienced in data-handling techniques. The strategic analysis was the most important factor affecting the formulation of the strategic plan, yet it was the area where all concerned felt they had the least knowledge and expertise. It was the part of the process that generated the most doubts about the validity of what we were doing.

Hatten (1982) suggests 'Strategic management has improved the management practice in profit-making organisations, so, too, it can enhance management of resources in not-for-profit organisations'.

A strategic planning approach has helped this school to move forward and will, I believe, have even greater advantages when the teaching profession is more skilled at adapting business strategies and techniques for use in schools.

Appendix 7.1

Teaching staff objectives

1 Having a personal approach to all parents, using their name (headteacher on playground before 9.00 a.m. each day).

2 Establishing a close link with the parent who is the class representative and having regular meetings for the exchange of information and ideas.

3 Hosting a termly coffee afternoon with class representative for parents to talk informally about the school.

4 Providing a club activity for children.

5 Speaking to at least one parent a day on a 'social' level.

6 Paying attention to, and showing interest in, a child's non-academic progress and interests.

School resource objectives

1 Providing a coffee shop area for parents to meet informally.

2 Having clear signs for visitors around the school and a written welcome.

3 Enhancing playground play provision with purchase of equipment.

4 Providing a Friends of the School notice-board with up-to-date information about Parents' Association events.

Objective for governors' 'promote the school' working party

1 Appointing a press liaison officer to keep the press informed of school events, with an expectation of at least one article per month in the paper.

2 Arranging a rota of governors to attend coffee sessions.

3 Keeping in touch with parents through articles in the school newsletter.

4 Constructing an interim questionnaire to go out to parents in the summer half-term (May 1994) regarding parental satisfaction.

Headteacher objectives

1 Keeping a high profile by daily appearance at gate to talk informally to parents and listen to their comments/suggestions.

2 Writing a monthly newsletter which goes beyond informing parents of events and focuses on a positive aspect of the school in each monthly issue.

3 Demonstrating at all times the level of courtesy, care and interest expected in the school by and for everyone connected with the school—staff, children, parents, governors, visitors.

4 Planning in order to provide the opportunities and resources for staff development needs.

Non-teaching staff objectives

1 Having a personal approach to all parents, using their names.

2 Providing a club activity for children.

3 Speaking to one parent and one child a day at a social level.

4 Greeting all visitors to the school in a friendly manner.

Appendix 7.2

Target 1

1 Regular meeting between teachers and class representatives.

Target 2

1 Regular appearances by headteacher in the coffee shop to chat informally with parents.

2 Newsletter which invites parents to put forward their views.

3 Monitoring of use made of the coffee shop by parents.

Target 3

1 Feedback from children's survey and governors' second questionnaire, which will invite comments on recent changes, e.g. introduction of clubs.

Target 4

1 Governors' questionnaire to be sent to parents at the end of Term 1.

2 Open Day to measure level of support.

Target 5

1 Talk in the coffee shop re: behaviour/discipline.

2 Provide copy of the policy to parents, inviting comment which should establish the general response.

Staff feedback, staff morale and staff development are all continuously monitored at weekly staff meetings. Here agenda items include progress reports from target co-ordinators and general discussion of any matters arising.

'Where Are We Now', therefore, is continually assessed. Staff Development is established in this way and, where appropriate, courses attended. In Term 2, a school Inset Day, working with a County Advisor on the theme 'Working with Parents and Governors', further gauged the 'state of play'.

8 Primary school case study 2

Improving quality in a primary school

Philip Mann

Introduction

Education has undergone one of the most turbulent periods of change since the 1944 Education Act. Moreover, all the indicators point to yet another period of change following the Government's White Paper *Choice and Diversity: A New Framework for Schools* (House of Commons, 1992), the 1994 Education Act and the National Curriculum Review following the publication of the Dearing Report (SCAA, 1993). The education world is searching for a period of stability, and the promise of a *new* National Curriculum that is to remain unchanged for at least five years may give schools just that. With a rapidly changing technological world now upon us all, I think that this stability may be short-lived.

Coping with this speed of change is no easy task for senior managers in schools. Many headteachers are becoming increasingly aware that models of corporate strategy extensively used in industry need to be incorporated into the developmental planning processes of their schools, if they are to remain financially healthy and be successful.

This chapter is a record of one headteacher's attempt to achieve just that. It is an honest account of the pitfalls and high points that have been experienced to date in an attempt to improve quality in a primary school as we move closer to the year 2000!

Forming the strategic view

The distinction between strategic decisions and strategy is of great importance to any organisation that is in the process of planning its overall strategy, and the distinctions must be clearly understood by its senior managers. Johnson and Scholes (1984) reflect that 'Strategy is to do with matching of the activities of an organisation to the environment in which it operates' (p. 6). They also suggest '... that strategy is to do with matching of the organisation's activities to its resource capability and that ... strategic decisions often have major resource implications for an organisation' (p. 7). Furthermore they hypothesise that the '... strategy of an organisation will be affected not only by environmental forces and resource availability but also by the values and expectations of those who influence strategy' (p. 8).

The resources, environment, values, expectations, and objectives of the organisation are the sub-headings of Johnson and Scholes' framework for strategic analysis that must be considered in detail if an organisation is to make informed strategic choices. Johnson and Scholes suggest that the environment provides opportunities and threats that operate through a variety of variables and that '... the ability to sense changes in environmental influence signal the possible need for changes in strategy' (p. 61). Factors affecting an organisation's environment can be the state of the economy, political trends, rapidly-changing technology, fellow competitors, the local community and customer relations. They maintain that '... the evidence is that organisations which are better at sensing the environment perform better than those which are weak at it' (p. 61).

An understanding of the power relationships operating between the various stakeholders that influence the values and objectives of that organisation is also essential if a comprehensive analysis is to be undertaken. This is because, as with all human resources, there is always potential for conflict.

Resources can be seen as the organisation's capabilities. They can take the form of land, buildings, machinery, people, money and systems. They are seen as a strength or a weakness and form a very important part in determining the feasibility of any strategic choice.

As stated earlier in this book, Johnson and Scholes envisage three distinct aspects of strategic choice once a comprehensive analysis of an organisation's strategic situation has been achieved. The generation of options is the first step, with a selection of alternatives put forward. The next step is to evaluate these options, but difficulties are found because a number of criteria need to be satisfied simultaneously. Johnson and Scholes suggest three main criteria that can be used, those of:

(a) suitability—do they capitalise on strengths?

(b) feasibility—is it achievable in resource terms?

(c) acceptability—are consequences acceptable?

and they state that each criterion should be used objectively to test the options available before selection of the most appropriate strategy is made.

Once choices have been made the process of implementation can take place. Key tasks, plans and priorities must be carefully chosen that will enable things to happen. The identification of key tasks and priorities will help to form the basis of a resource plan which can help to monitor and control the whole implementation of the strategic change. Johnson and Scholes define key tasks which are concomitant with the major areas of attention on which strategic change depends. Priorities are concerned with timing, and there are actions that need to be tackled to get the project under way. People and systems are identified and together with these key tasks and priorities should form the framework for a complete strategic plan. This is a plan of action that will provide the basis for understanding the impact of changes in the sequencing of activities. The plan can also help to identify points in the programme at which certain key stages should be completed. Changes may need to be made to the organisational structure in order to make the plan successful. Johnson and Scholes consider the problems associated with strategic implementation when they state that:

> Underlying the whole area of resource planning is perhaps the single most complex issue in the implementation of strategy, the management of people. In the end, successful strategy implementation depends on the organisation, motivation and control of those who have to make strategies work at management and operational levels. (p. 267)

Undertaking a strategic analysis

Many of the educational changes in the last five years have driven school development plans and made them, as a result, reactive rather than proactive. The establishment of Local Management of Schools has created a market-place for parents to exercise a choice regarding the quality of education available for their children. The formation of a strategic plan enables schools to be proactive by developing a coherent approach to raising levels of quality. The success of such plans is reliant on how thorough the strategic analysis has been. In order to develop a strategic plan that is suitable, feasible and acceptable to all who have a stake in the school it must be comprehensive in its approach.

Strategic analysis is primarily concerned with providing an understanding of the strategic situation which an organisation faces. Managers will therefore need to develop a facility that takes a holistic view of the situation, concentrating on major and overall problems rather than dwelling on the difficulties which are of no strategic importance. It therefore follows that if sensible choices of future strategy are to be made, then a comprehensive resource analysis must be undertaken as a means of assessing an organisation's strategic capability. We will observe later how this might be achieved.

Context of the school

As stated earlier, this chapter is intended to give the reader an insight into the development of such a strategic view within the context of a group 2 primary school in the county of Berkshire. I am now in my fourth year of office as headteacher of Bearwood Primary School. The school is LEA-controlled and is situated in a semi-suburban environment on the outskirts of Wokingham. It has a teaching complement of eight full-time class teachers, of which five are at the top of the salary scale. It also has a part-time teacher working on average 0.3 full-time equivalent per week. The school also employs the following within its budget:

	hours/week
Bursar	30
Infant helper	15
Clerical assistant	10
Classroom assistants	30
Caretaker/cleaners	64

The current budget for 1995/96 is fixed at £314,983 and determined by a January Form 7 figure of 236 pupils on roll. The school was identified as an LMS pilot school and received its first delegated budget during the 1989/90 financial year. Table 8.1 gives the reader an insight into the school's recent budget history since 1991/92.

The teachers are divided into three teams, that of infants, lower juniors and upper juniors. Each team is led by a team leader who receives extra salary points for the responsibility.

Financial year	Form 7 roll	Gross budget allocation £	Employee costs as a % of budget
1991/92	240	292,002	87
1992/93	233	300,375	86
1993/94	226	322,199	86
1994/95	224	328,171	89
1995/96	236	314,983	90

Table 8.1   The variation in pupil numbers and relative staffing cost for Bearwood Primary School

Previous school development planning

Following my appointment to the position of headteacher of Bearwood Primary School I continued to use the established system of development planning. The LEA provides a framework for the school development plan (SDP) to be formulated on an annual basis. In the past, this has been a management tool designed by the Local Education Authority for monitoring the implementation of the National Curriculum and grants made available for training and educational support (GEST). An annual SDP has some shortcomings; it is both short-term and often piecemeal in design. It has therefore been my desire that the annual SDP should be considered as part of a whole-school strategic plan that covers a three to five-year period. For various reasons the construction of such a plan has proved difficult to complete. The following are just some of the obstacles experienced:

- the complex nature of the task
- where to start
- how to find the time
- developing full ownership amongst key stakeholders
- coping with resistance to change
- visualising what the final document might look like

As with many experiences in life, circumstances often overtake the situation and force the issue. This is exactly what happened at Bearwood.

Reasons for considering a strategic plan

Bearwood had steadily been suffering from a period of fluctuating pupil numbers and was expecting a fall in roll in January 1995 to 210. This assumption had been based on the careful interpretation of data gathered on the past annual pupil intake figures. It was of some concern, to both myself and the governing body's finance committee, that these data were beginning to show a trend for the annual intake of approximately 30. When compared to the current Standard Admission Number of 41 it could be seen that the school budget would not be able to sustain the current staffing allocation and that redundancies could well be a certainty for the 1995/96 financial year. The number of children on roll each January for the previous six years had been as follows:

1989	1990	1991	1992	1993	1994
236	231	240	233	226	224

Table 8.2   Form 7 pupil numbers

It was therefore felt by the governing body and myself that the immediate overall strategic decision must be to increase and maintain pupil numbers at the most efficient operating level, thus ensuring the effective use of limited financial resources. This would be achieved by raising the levels of quality of provision in all aspects of the school. It was perceived by myself as leader of the school that considerable scope existed for improvement in many aspects of the school, associated with both the children's learning experiences and the internal and external environment of the building. Any improvements to the former would take some time to be recognised, but there was considerable scope for the latter at minimal cost to the budget.

I had calculated that a pupil roll number for each January Form 7 Census should be as close as possible to 245. Reasons for this are not purely financial but are linked with the available accommodation. This number would provide a budget for the school that would maintain the existing teaching staff complement with full classes of 30, giving a considerable surplus for investment in resources within the school. These would include extra classroom assistants, minor works development, more non-contact time for staff and extra IT equipment. To date the roll has climbed to 236, but we still have a way to go before we reach the magic number.

Formulating the strategic analysis

A school with a falling pupil roll needs to take action quickly to prevent the snowballing effect of diseconomies of scale. Any development needs to be undertaken systematically in order that the predicted limited financial resources can be used as effectively as possible to reverse the effect of falling numbers. The need for a strategic plan was felt by myself to be essential but the construction of one is a complex task, especially in a school that operates a collegiate style of decision-making such as Bearwood.

As a starting point, a framework for a complete strategic analysis was therefore designed by myself. This involved the construction of a list for areas of strategic analysis for the whole school under the following headings:

- resources
- school environment and its wider community
- organisation and structure
- values and expectations of stakeholders
- marketing

This list of headings was formed by combining Johnson and Scholes' elements of strategic analysis discussed previously and the headings suggested by Fidler *et al.* (1991) for the sub-plans that inform a strategic plan for any school. The next step was to take a holistic 'snapshot view' of the school as I perceived it to be, and to develop a comprehensive list of areas to be analysed under each heading. The headings provided a structure under which items could be brainstormed over a period of about one hour at home. Unlike chief executives in industry it would be impossible to achieve this in a school environment! This task was completed and consideration was then given to the methods and processes of analysis, who would be involved and the problems that could be foreseen. A matrix was then constructed to facilitate the compilation of this data. Each area for analysis was then cross-referenced with what would be the headings for the detailed sub-plans for the final strategic plan for Bearwood. These headings were to be:

- organisation and structure
- curriculum
- staffing

- financing

- marketing

These areas for analysis were then collated under the five headings above to form a comprehensive plan of analysis for the school. Using this holistic approach has provided a good feel for the school's strategic position. The results of this activity can be found in Tables 8.3–8.7 at the end of this chapter.

The flow diagram contained in Figure 8.1 is an attempt to clarify this process for the benefit of the reader. It can be seen that some areas for strategic

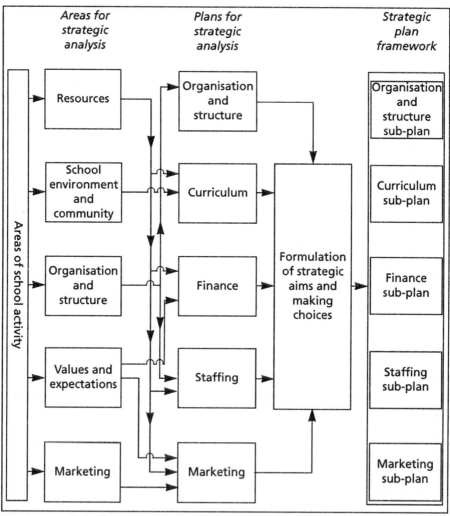

Figure 8.1   Flow diagram to illustrate the process of strategic analysis and strategic plan formulation

analysis, e.g. resources, would influence some if not all of the sub-plans and therefore these factors needed to be considered in each plan for the strategic analysis.

From such a comprehensive analysis, it was envisaged that key tasks would be identified and choices made based on informed decisions which would give direction and strategic fit to the school. These choices would be contained in a strategic plan, which would seek to maximise strengths, minimise weaknesses, take advantage of opportunities within the wider educational environment and seek to minimise threats. This plan for strategic analysis is very comprehensive, but by no means exhaustive. It was assumed that as the analysis progressed, further areas would need to be added. Once complete, possible areas could be identified for development which could be tested for suitability, assessed for feasibility and be acceptable to governors, parents and teachers alike.

After twenty-four months, the activities outlined in the plan for analysis are nearing completion. Some have been over-ambitious, some easy to complete, others are on-going, some have been overtaken by unforeseen events and not everything has progressed smoothly. The most difficult areas of the analysis have been experienced when change was perceived by established staff as unnecessary. Many colleagues in other schools will empathise with these difficulties. The following section illustrates a common problem experienced by many newly-appointed headteachers when faced with resistance to change.

Unfreezing the frozen

It is fairly common for headteachers newly appointed to primary schools of approximately 300 pupils to be leading an established team of ten teachers, 60 per cent of whom are likely to be very experienced primary-school practitioners who have been subjected to a period of considerable educational change which has been forced upon them over the last decade. In this context, staff can often feel more comfortable with established practices and might appear to the observer as inward-looking. In these circumstances any resistance to change can be considerable, especially if it is viewed as an extra burden on time. All inward-looking institutions, especially schools, often find review and evaluation yet another burden on time, but it is an essential part of the strategic analysis process.

Headteachers can feel frustrated by this resistance to change: is it only they who perceive weaknesses and room for improvement? Resistance to change has to be challenged if development is to take place. Strategies that utilise team building and management of change techniques amongst the staff need to be employed if the 'unfreezing' process is to begin. Several activities were undertaken with the staff at Bearwood Primary School that involved some standard management techniques. Brain-storming activities and SWOT analyses were used to crystallise views on a number of occasions. Achieving the right climate for change is one of the most difficult and complex tasks for managers in both industry and education alike. The plan for analysis was increasingly becoming an *aide mémoire* for developing this amongst the staff. Attempting too much too soon would often be met with resistance and so finding the opportunities to provide a further 'kick start for change' required skill in managerial timing that on reflection was sometimes lacking in myself.

Each area of strategic analysis within the plan was individually coded to facilitate the measuring and recording of progress. The five tables (see end of this chapter) were coded as follows:

1 Organisation and Structure (Table 8.3)

2 Curriculum (Table 8.4)

3 Finance (Table 8.5)

4 Staffing (Table 8.6)

5 Marketing (Table 8.7)

This has also made the task of monitoring and reporting progress easier. Useful input was provided in the early stages of the process through the involvement of the school's local LEA inspector. His position as a 'critical friend' was very helpful, especially when the plan for analysis was discussed at length. A review of the decision-making processes within the school was discussed in detail during a regular support meeting with me and it was agreed that the management structure and decision-making processes should remain unaltered as they were working quite adequately for the size of school. The chairman of governors was also involved in several meetings with me in order to determine possible ways forward, especially with reference to the structures of governors' sub-committees. Even though it was hard to be objective in their assessment, few difficulties have been experienced with these analysis factors. Where problems were experienced was in understanding the decision-making dynamics within the staff. Things came to a hiatus when it became necessary to make some fundamental changes to the entrance to the school and the administration area. An inadequate understanding of political systems within the staff meant that not enough consultation took place before the governing body's property committee proposed its options for change to these areas. The ensuing discussions, however, were healthy and now that the changes have taken place, the benefits are more obvious to all concerned.

Activity on reviewing the communication systems has been undertaken. The trialling of different SMT and whole-staff meeting structures has taken place during the last two academic years and as a result the following system is now in operation:

1 Daily five-minute briefings before school

2 Whole-staff meetings take place fortnightly at lunchtime

3 Teaching staff meetings/workshops weekly after school

4 Senior management team meetings fortnightly in school time

Changes have been made following the experiences associated with the changes to the entrance area just described. This level of communication now ensures that everybody in the school is more fully involved in the day-to-day as well as the strategic decision-making process.

Several meetings were held with the teaching staff to consider the introduction of a generic job description with additions to cover individual responsibilities. This activity coincided with the introduction of teacher appraisal and has proved very beneficial to all.

A curriculum review had already been undertaken before the design of this plan as a method of systematically planning curriculum development. The GRIDS curriculum review (McMahon *et al.*, 1984) package was used and questionnaires were completed by all the teaching staff. The information gathered has been extremely useful in deciding priorities and the findings have driven the curriculum school development plan for the last three years. Currently audits are being undertaken and inventories are being compiled of equipment and materials for each curriculum subject. A survey of available space was undertaken and new storage areas have been allocated. Systems for storage and retrieval now need to be designed in order that the efficient use of teaching resources can take place. Specific needs will then be identified, costings formulated and the necessary financial resources allocated within the strategic plan.

A teaching and learning policy statement was constructed by the staff at an early stage in the analysis, as part of the team-building and unfreezing process. The problems that were foreseen did not materialise and the published document assisted in the design of a statement on policy on classroom observation within the appraisal scheme at the school.

Awareness-raising is an important part of the unfreezing process. For example, established staff can at times find the process of LMS bewildering. This was the case at Bearwood and an LMS school budget workshop was provided for the teaching staff by the headteacher and the school bursar. This session was particularly successful in that it has developed a greater sense of shared responsibility. The consequences of falling pupil numbers were discussed at length and staff were then given time to reflect on the probable implications of a further drop in numbers.

An internal decoration and condition survey was undertaken by the governing body's property sub-committee and completed at an early stage in the process. This has been of great benefit in raising the quality of internal decoration and floor finishings. Visits have been undertaken to other local schools and comparisons have been made. Contacts are now being made with more local companies in an attempt to obtain sponsorship and other forms of assistance.

Through the consideration of a generic job description a policy on the use of non-teaching assistants was created. It has been shared with parents and staff alike and proved extremely useful during interviews for new personnel. An objective assessment of their impact in the classroom has yet to be completed, but initial observations indicate that further investment would be of great benefit to the children's education. Appraisal has assisted with the process of assessing the needs of the individual staff and those of the school. In meeting the staff's needs, the problem has been that of a contracting GEST budget, year upon year, that has hindered progress.

It is through the activities identified in the analysis for marketing that the greatest amount of unfreezing has taken place. A complete graphic audit has taken place and this provided a springboard for a number of innovations, notably a new format for the school newsletter, produced using desktop publishing techniques.

A questionnaire was designed by myself in consultation with the teaching staff and governing body. It is included for reference on pp. 184–185. I felt that it was important that it should appeal to as many parents as possible and that the majority of the questions should be of the open type in design. Parents were also given an opportunity to express their views on future development within the school and the resulting suggestions were fed into the strategic aims and choices phase of the process. Over sixty completed questionnaires were returned, representing a response rate of 47 per cent.

Many, if not all of these unfreezing activities are essential if the right climate for change and improvement is to be developed within a school. Once the appropriate climate is established, an understanding of the staff culture is a prerequisite for success. Levels of quality will only be raised if the staff perceive that there is a need for this to happen. Therefore systems need to be developed that assist with this process. The following section will give the reader an insight into my attempts to determine the right climate and culture for the improvement of quality at Bearwood Primary School.

Sharing cultural goals

Headteachers continually manage people as they strive to develop a quality environment in which children can learn. One of the most significant elements of this process is the understanding of their school's culture. If there exists a mismatch between cultures, then attempts to improve aspects of quality will have limited impact. School cultures vary considerably and have a direct influence on schools' success. They are the sum of the shared beliefs and values, in short the character and personality of the school. Techniques and mechanisms need to be employed that can be used to develop a shared culture within a school. John West-Burnham (1992b) observes that:

> Culture only has meaning when it is given expression, when it is expressed in tangible forms. The critical difference about culture is that it is those abstractions which are shared, those which are widely held and dominant. (p. 84)

Without this understanding, school improvement can be hindered. The expression of shared values and beliefs needs time to evolve. It cannot and should not happen overnight but once it does, the improvement of quality through sharing cultural goals can become a reality.

At Bearwood Primary School, some efforts were made to develop systems for school cultural development before the strategic analysis had begun. In order of implementation they were:

- the publication of a staff handbook
- a clearly defined meeting structure to improve communications
- the development of a team planning approach to the delivery of the curriculum
- the development and publication of a Teaching and Learning Policy statement
- the formation of a system to be used by all staff for monitoring pupil behaviour

The creation of these systems and procedures has provided a framework within which cultural changes could occur. The rate of change has of course been influenced by the degree of successful incorporation into the working systems of the school and staff.

During the period of strategic analysis I have developed an understanding of the hurdles one has to face if improvements in quality are to be made. As stated in earlier chapters in this book, the issues of change related to organisational culture need to be thought through very carefully. Managerial skills of the highest order need to be utilised in order to both minimise the effects of what will inevitably result in conflict amongst staff and yet at the same time take the school forward. Hersey and Blanchard's Situational Leadership model (1988) has been of great assistance to myself in utilising strengths of individual staff members during the process.

Another key aspect is the need to generate a genuine shared vision amongst the whole school community. Achievement of this takes time, for this shared vision needs to evolve. Factors such as recruitment can help speed up the process, providing that any newly appointed staff are inducted within a framework of the desired shared vision. Failure to induct correctly would quickly result in them being absorbed by the existing culture of 'the way we do things round here'.

As is the case in many schools, opportunities for recruitment are minimal and therefore other strategies need to be employed. However, external factors outside the control of the school can help focus attention on the need for change and improvements as in the case at Bearwood.

A fall in pupil numbers was expected during the years 1992/93 and 1993/94, and so the governing body formulated a small Marketing Working Group to look specifically at promoting the school. This group used the Marketing Plan Analysis sheet (see Table 8.7, pp. 182–183) as a framework for action. It met on four occasions and its members consisted of the head and deputy together with four or five governors who had an interest in the subject. Recommendations were made to the governing body regarding the production of a variety of enhanced graphic material for promoting the school. The most significant of these was the production of a half-termly newsletter using sophisticated desktop publishing techniques. The necessity for a mission statement was also proposed. This generated much useful dialogue between the staff and governing body. Values, beliefs and expectations were discussed in an open forum and the format of wording was finally agreed upon. It is now displayed in a prominent position at the entrance to the school. It reads as follows:

At Bearwood, the staff, parents and governors work in partnership to provide a lively, stimulating and caring environment. All children are encouraged to develop socially, emotionally and intellectually to the best of their ability.

The mission statement has provided the main focus for the development of a shared vision amongst the school staff. The four key elements of *partnership, child, caring environment* and *quality* have been identified. By using brain-storming techniques with the teachers, non-teaching staff, governors and parents separately, each group has been able to generate lists of suggestions for future development for each key element.

All information gathered through the analysis has now been collated under each appropriate heading ready for the next stage of the strategic planning process. At that stage, choices will be made for the school that will influence its direction and development over the next five years, taking its school community with it into the next century and an ever-changing world.

Making choices

A strategic plan working group was formed at the beginning of 1995, composed of the chairman of governors, the chairman of each governing body sub-committee, any further governors with an interest and the senior management team of the school. Its terms of reference were to assist the head in producing a draft strategic plan for Bearwood in readiness for consultation within the school community. Its first task was to assimilate all of the proposed suggestions for development, including the views and suggestions of parents that were gathered through the feedback questionnaire, into a more manageable format for further discussion. In order to undertake this difficult task it was decided by the working group that staff, governors and the parent-teacher association committee members should be invited to an evening workshop to complete the task.

Lists of suggested areas of school development were compiled for the identified key elements of *partnership, child, caring environment* and *quality* and checked by the working party for duplication and ambiguity. Once completed, five duplicate sets of lists were then prepared for the workshop and, to facilitate collation at a later date, each list for each key element was printed on a different coloured paper.

On the evening, the representatives of the school community were given refreshment and then asked to organise themselves into five representative groups. They were then set the task of allocating all the suggestions into a time-frame of:

- short (within one year)

- medium (one to two years), and

- long-term (three to five years).

Considerable debate ensued regarding each suggestion and it soon became obvious that variations existed in priorities between the representative groups. There were, however, a number of similarities and more refreshment helped the evening to progress to a very successful conclusion.

The time-frame sheet from each group was then compared with those of the other groups and by giving a point to each suggestion a shared list was created. This has now provided a comprehensive list of democratically chosen options that carry with them a high degree of consensus. It now only remains for the working group to cross-reference these lists of options with the strategic analysis tables (Tables 8.3–8.7) at the end of this chapter. The group will then review its strategic aim and direction for the school in the light of any local and national developments. Options will then be prioritised and costings will be sought in order that financial decisions can be made in the context of funds available and allocated over the time period of the plan.

Summary

The plan for strategic analysis at Bearwood Primary School has provided me with a very useful mechanism by which I can guide and direct the development of the final strategic plan for the school. Contained within the analysis have been several elements that have required a contribution by the staff in time and energy. The advantage of undertaking such a comprehensive analysis is that the governing body is now in a very good position to make strategic choices based on informed decisions in the knowledge that the views of all those who have a stake in the school have had an input into the process. Following the identification of these key tasks and formulation of the necessary strategic choices, a draft plan will be made ready for consultation. The group will then assist the headteacher in the compilation and publication of the strategic plan to the wider school community during the academic year 1995/96 in readiness for implementation at the beginning of the next financial year.

There is still a great deal to do before a strategic plan for Bearwood Primary School becomes a reality, and then the process of implementation and monitoring will begin in earnest. During the process of strategic analysis there have been problems and pitfalls on the way, but hopefully the correct climate for the improvement of quality will have been established. Already the pupil numbers are rising close to the total identified as strategically cost-effective. A new strategic aim can be formulated, but the plan for analysis will provide the necessary framework within which to work. It has given me a greater understanding of the resources available in readiness for the construction of the final strategic plan. It has meant that the staff and governors at Bearwood Primary now have the ability to sense the strategic environment of the school with greater clarity than ever before. This in turn will assist them in providing a higher quality education to all of the school's pupils, in full partnership with their parents and the community in which they live, into the next century.

Table 8.3 Areas of analysis for organisation and structure plan

Analysis factors / Area of strategic analysis	Area for analysis	Methods and processes to be employed	Staff involved	Foreseen problems
Organisation & structure	1.1 decision-making process	a review formal decision-making network b analyse 'political' systems within staff and construct organigram c review of governing body sub-committee structure	– Head & 'critical friend' – Head & Deputy – Head & chair of governors	– potentially difficult to determine with objectivity and efficiency – possibly difficult to obtain a true picture
Organisation & structure	1.2 communication systems	a review system of communication b determine overlap by consulting with staff	– Head & Deputy	
Organisation & structure	1.3 review of job description	a consultation with whole staff re: generic job description b consultation with staff re: additions to generic job description to cover individual responsibilities	– Head & Staff	– lengthy process but could be combined with initial meetings for appraisal training

Analysis factors / Area of strategic analysis	Area for analysis	Methods and processes to be employed	Staff involved	Foreseen problems
resources	2.1 curriculum	a strengths & weaknesses review with GRIDS survey b curriculum materials audit & inventory c assessment of storage and retrieval facilities	– whole staff & governing body – curriculum postholders – all staff	– time-consuming – limitations re: building and storage facilities
		d assessment of match/mismatch and teaching and learning statement & curriculum planning e.g. 'Gender Watch' & 'Book Watch'	– Head, Deputy and team leaders	– possible difficulties with historical 'ownership' of materials
resources	2.2 diversification	a searching for alternatives and matching of options with strategic plan	– SMT & governing body	– implication for other schools and LEA etc.
values & expectations	2.3 teaching and learning styles	a creation of teaching and learning policy statement	– whole staff (incl. NTAs)	– possibility of conflict from Governors over ratification of policy statement
environment	2.4 liaison with secondary schools	a review of liaison events	– SMT	
environment	2.5 liaison with playgroups	a review of liaison events b determine playgroup needs	– Head, Deputy & infant team leader	– staff resource implications re: supply cover – maintaining a balanced involvement with both playgroups

Table 8.5 Areas of analysis for finance plan

Analysis factors / Area of strategic analysis	Area for analysis	Methods and processes to be employed	Staff involved	Foreseen problems
resources	3.1 current budgets	a review of effective use of available resources b review of budget building process c pupil number projection d complete inventories of all curriculum areas	– Head, Deputy, finance officer & finance committee – Head – Head, finance & clerical officers – all staff	– possible values, expectations and power – time-consuming
resources	3.2 structural resources	a internal decoration condition survey	– Head & committee	– possibly subjective cash limited and potential for conflict re: values and expectations
environment	3.4 review of other adjacent primary schools	a visit other schools	– Head & Deputy	
environment	3.5 local industrial community	a construct an inventory of all local industry in catchment b establish regular contact with local businesses	– Head & governing body – Head & staff	– time-consuming but potentially very useful

Table 8.6 Areas of analysis for staffing plan

Area of strategic analysis / Analysis factors	Area for analysis	Methods and processes to be employed	Staff involved	Foreseen problems
resources	4.1 use of non-teaching staff	a review of job description b shadowing to determine impact on children's learning	– Head & Deputy	
staffing	4.2 staff training	a staff development review	– Inset co-ordinator	– possible mismatch with individual school needs

181

Table 8.7 Areas of analysis for marketing plan

Area of strategic analysis \ Analysis factors	Area for analysis	Methods and processes to be employed	Staff involved	Foreseen problems
marketing	5.1 all graphic material to external agents	a complete graphic audit of all distributed material	– Head, SMT, governing body & consultant designer	– large surface area
resources	5.2 administrative resources	a complete review of equipment b technology and IT review	– Head, finance officer, clerical officer & governing body	– time-consuming
values & expectations	5.3 parents' views of school effectiveness	a parent feedback questionnaire using 'open' style questions b open meeting	– all staff	– skills required by staff and unwillingness by some parents – need to be confident of outcome
values & expectations	5.4 school booklet	a complete review	– Head & governing body	– consultation could be lengthy
values & expectations	5.5 mission statement	a review & modification of mission statement	– whole staff & governing body	– there could be difficulties in obtaining a balance
environment	5.6 church group liaison	a consultation with church leaders about improved liaison	– whole staff & governing body – Head & Deputy	

Table 8.7 Areas of analysis for marketing plan—*continued*

Area of strategic analysis	Area for analysis	Methods and processes to be employed	Staff involved	Foreseen problems
environment	5.7 liaison with independent/GM sector	a review existing links b assess methods of recommendation process to parents	– Head & Deputy	– possibly contentious
environment	5.8 relationship with existing parents	a review feedback-gathering systems	– Head, Deputy and parent representatives	
environment	5.9 relationship with press	a media audit of previous press coverage to determine educational balance	– Head and SMT	

BEARWOOD PRIMARY SCHOOL
PARENT FEEDBACK QUESTIONNAIRE

The Governing Body and Staff are currently undertaking a review of the school. Information from this questionnaire will be used to help formulate a progressive plan that will cover all aspects of school life in Bearwood.

1. Would you feel that you could recommend the school to others?

   Please tick   YES ☐   NO ☐   DON'T KNOW ☐

2. Do you feel that you are fully involved and informed about your child's education at Bearwood?

   Please tick   YES ☐   NO ☐

   If your answer is NO please state why.

   _____

   _____

3. Please tick aspects of school life at Bearwood that you consider to be a strength.

   - curriculum content   ☐
   - learning methods   ☐
   - linking with the community   ☐
   - our 'open door' policy   ☐
   - extra-curricular activities   ☐
   - reporting to parents   ☐
   - display   ☐
   - reading programme   ☐
   - parent information   ☐
   - pupil behaviour   ☐
   - school uniform   ☐
   - homework   ☐

   Anything else not featured?

   _____

   _____

4. Are you satisfied with the management of pupil behaviour within the school?

    Please tick　　　　YES ☐　　　　　　NO ☐

    State any improvements you would like to see.

    _____

    _____

    _____

    _____

5. Which of the following would you like to see at Bearwood?
    Please tick as many as you like

    - a nursery　　　　　　　　　　☐
    - an after-school childcare club　☐
    - a holiday playscheme　　　　　☐
    - extra sports facilities　　　　　☐
    - adult classes　　　　　　　　　☐

    Please state any others.

    _____

    _____

    _____

6. What future developments would you like to see happen within the school?

    _____

    _____

    _____

    _____

    Please give your completed questionnaire to your child's class teacher or place it in the box in the entrance area.

    Thank you for completing this questionnaire,

    Philip Mann

9 Secondary school case study 1

A sixth-form strategy for a comprehensive school

Peter Thomas

Context of the school

The school in this case study is an LEA, mixed, group 6, 11–18 comprehensive school of 1,400 pupils with a sixth form of 230 students. It is fully established as a comprehensive school, having received its first all-ability intake in 1971. The roll is stable and is usually oversubscribed, despite the local demographic downturn. The school is operating in a dynamic, turbulent and complex local environment: the nearby grammar schools are flourishing and the College of Technology is expanding rapidly; there are several grant-maintained schools and two of the five local comprehensive schools have received TSI (technology college initiative, DFEE, 1995c) funding; there are falling rolls in all the putative 'catchment areas' and few signs of recovery yet from the recession in the job market.

The growth of some of the sixth forms (and both Colleges of Technology) in the area has been caused by the recession, obliging youngsters to stay on in post-16 education given the few traineeships or jobs. Research and intelligence data from the LEA, however, confirm that the demographic downturn will persist for several years. As a direct result of this downturn there is competition for pupils at age 11 (and increasingly at age 16). There is also considerable uncertainty concerning the Commissioners' proposals for the four unitary authorities in the county and the implications for the school. Such 'environmental turbulence' (Hoy and Miskel, 1991) in the external environment has caused the senior management team to review its mission statement and curricular provision. This 'zero-based' approach to the entire scope of the school's activities has raised fundamental questions about the markets it should be serving and the services it ought to be offering. The matching of organisational activities to services has focused the senior management team's attention not solely on curricular provision but also on the issue of competitive advantage and on strategies to maintain this advantage. Strategic management has implied a colder, clearer eye descending on the school's activities in order to reposition the school in relation to the local environmental challenges.

The school development plan before introducing the strategy

In the mid-1980s the school started to use the review and evaluation approaches suggested by the ILEA Inspectorate (1977). Here there were a series of small-scale curriculum improvement efforts carried out by teams of three or four interested staff. This pathfinding work was augmented and strengthened by the LEA publications on school development planning by Straker (1988), who broadened the scope of initiatives to include whole-school development. The school development plan in 1988 was derived from staff priorities for development and from perceived needs arising from evaluating the Inset Grant cycle at the school. The plan used inter-related elements of statutory INSET days and work teams with detailed action plans for achieving the annual targets (many of which were framed by the LEA). In retrospect it is interesting to note how the actual format of the LEA document created an institutional 'mindset' for schools and obliged them to focus on incremental and internal development issues.

By 1989/90 the school had refined its institutional development plan drawing from DES (1989), Caldwell and Spinks (1988), Fidler and Bowles (1989), the start of the five-year developmental TVEI-extension programme and the pilot experience of LMS. What distinguished this phase was that the composite school development plan became the focus for a range of interconnected goals exploring 'where the school is now and where it wants to grow towards' (DES, 1989, p. 12) and now included action plans to achieve these goals over a one to three-year period with clear line managers for task groups. The plan was managed by a steering group of staff drawn from standard scale teachers, middle managers and a deputy head. During this phase, however, development planning was still largely incremental rather than part of a coherent strategy—'a disciplined effort to produce fundamental decisions that shape what an organisation does' (Olsen and Eadie, 1982, p. 4). The next section exemplifies and elucidates the largely reactive nature of development in the sixth form at this time.

The recommendation to adopt a more forward and outward-looking strategy which took cognisance of external environmental factors as well as local contextual factors was made by the school development plan steering group.

This group recommended that the school should move beyond traditional planning to a rather more strategic approach which emphasised Johnson and Scholes' key principles (1988, pp. 5–6):

- the long-term direction of the organisation
- the entire scope of the organisation's activities
- the matching of the organisation's activities to the environment which it serves
- the matching of the organisation's activities to its resource capability
- the expectations and values of the stakeholders in the organisation
- attention to the external threats and opportunities and internal strengths and weaknesses

The reasons for considering a strategic analysis of the sixth form

There had been a tacit realisation for several years amongst most of the senior management team, the school development plan steering group and many of the staff, that the post-16 curriculum at the school was not properly matched to students' needs, and that the existing curricular routes were not really tenable. However, whilst colleagues agreed, for the most part, that some realignment of the post-16 curriculum might be necessary, they did not all agree on the focus of that realignment, nor on the scale of the realignment. This felt need was the main prompt for a strategic analysis of 16–19 provision at the school together with the senior management team's aim to create a vision of long-term success for the school as a whole.

Another trigger for a strategic analysis of the 16–19 span was the demise of TVEI-extension funding. For whilst the TVEI-funded enhancement to the post-16 curriculum had strengthened the post-16 span at the school by the provision of compulsory 'entitlement' modules, it had done little to alter actual curricular routes for students. The ending of TVEI funding forced the school to make a decision about whether to continue to fund the post-16 entitlement modules or revert to the pre-TVEI curriculum structure. This enforced decision coincided with rapid developments within the wider context of post-16 education and training (National Education Training Targets; the piloting of BTEC First Diplomas in schools and preparatory work on NVQs—National Vocational Qualifications; and GNVQs—General National Vocational Qualifications), which obliged the school to reconsider its somewhat Procrustean A level or GCSE re-take or secretarial course curricular routes.

In terms of the analysis presented in Chapter 4, this may be seen as an attempt by the SMT to provide instructional leadership—to influence what teachers actually do in the classroom. There were also local contextual factors which prompted the need for a strategic analysis. The first was that the school franchised a BTEC First Diploma from the local College of Technology as a replacement for the moribund CPVE (Certificate in Pre-Vocational Education) course. This pilot course however was very much a stop-gap measure rather than a component part of a deliberate long-term strategy. Quinn (1980) refers to this kind of measure as logical incrementalism (see Chapter 3 for fuller details). Similarly, the decision to apply to become an accredited BTEC centre was not a strategic one, but was rather another incremental decision taken simply to replace the dated City and Guilds secretarial course with a more modern BTEC Business Studies course which had a broader appeal to prospective students. These short-term measures could be seen as a provisional strategy or holding phase whilst a strategic analysis was carried out. At this time the provisional BTEC strategy could easily have been reversed. It was at this time that most of the senior management team agreed that such additions were piecemeal and too short-term and that what the school really needed was a planned and systematic sixth-form strategy which had time horizons of a different order.

Another reason for considering a strategic analysis of the 16–19 curriculum was prompted by the collection and interpretation of value-added data for several A level cohorts at the school. The value-added calculations were carried out because the SMT wanted an evaluation of present operations. It was felt that the data would provide empirical evidence on exactly how our students were performing in relation to national norms.

These, then, were the main reasons for considering a strategic analysis of the post-16 provision at the school.

Carrying out a strategic analysis

Context

The intention of the 1988 Education Reform Act has been to change schools and colleges from 'domesticated' organisations which do not have to struggle for their survival, since their environment guarantees them a steady flow of resources and clients, to 'wild' organisations which are not protected and whose very survival depends on maintaining quality of performance and attracting enough clients (Carlson, 1975, locates organisations on this spectrum).

Under the combined impact of more open enrolment, LMS, falling rolls, financial stringencies and LEA reorganisation, the condition of schools and colleges has shifted deliberately and significantly from 'domestication' to 'wildness'. And because schools and colleges are now self-governing, and are wholly responsible for their own futures, so their survival depends upon their own individual efforts.

The next section is concerned with describing how a strategic analysis was carried out in order to decide upon a sixth-form strategy which would contribute to the long-term success of the school.

Strategic analysis

Strategic management is concerned with 'deciding a strategy and planning how that strategy is to be put into effect' (Johnson and Scholes, 1984, p. 10). The strategic analysis component requires an organisation to systematically evaluate its position first within its environment and to constantly adapt in order to achieve a 'best fit' (Chapter 5 provides fuller elucidation of the three components of strategic analysis).

First it was necessary for the school to assess the precise nature of the environment in which it would be operating—was it simple and stable, or dynamic and complex? Johnson and Scholes suggest that 'in dynamic conditions it makes more sense to consider the future than rely on the past' (Johnson and Scholes, 1984, p. 66). In the present turbulent conditions in education it was clear that the school could not afford to be complacent and had to be forward-looking and attempt to position itself so as to achieve a 'best fit' with the environment whilst taking cognisance of economic, political, social and legal environmental influences and the perceptions of stakeholders. It was felt that such a framework for strategic thinking would enable the school to see such influences as possible opportunities for the school's current strategic standing and others as threats (strategic mismatch with the environment).

Secondly, the strategic analysis required the school to plan its responses to these opportunities and threats in line with its resource capabilities. The school needed to form a view of its resource capability by means of an audit of the efficacy of the curriculum and existing plant, management structures, personnel, finance, reputation, ethos and clients' perceptions. The analysis of the effectiveness of resource management revealed particular strengths and weaknesses (the internal strategic position) which the school needed to consider when deriving future strategic direction.

Quality audit of resources—the collection of evidence for strategic analysis

A. Value-added data

(a) A comparative analysis of the whole-school A level performance in relation to Audit Commission (1991b, 1993) value-added archive data.

(b) An analysis of A level performance by subject department using Conway's (1992) value-added system to focus down on departmental performance.

The analyses were intended to provide at-a-glance management information on school and departmental performance. The Audit Commission's GCSE points score was worked out using A=7, B=6 ... G=1. A level points were scored A=10, B=8 ... E=2. Plotting a graph of total GCSE points score against average A level points score, the Audit Commission found a correlation of 0.62. It was felt that this was a moderately strong correlation when the nature of the data was considered and was a system worth trialling.

Conway (1992) used a different system of points scoring for GCSE: A=5, B=3, C=1. Conway used this particular system to enable him to monitor the progress of the students at his college. Conway's system was also trialled because it increased the correlation coefficient from 0.65 using the Audit Commission scoring to 0.8. There were also subtle differences between the two systems. It was clear that the F grade was worth little if anything more than a G at GCSE when considering a pupil's suitability for A level study, and so it was thought reasonable (as Conway suggested) to give both those scores zero. Furthermore, if two students were scored using the Audit Commission's system, one with nine As and the other with nine Bs at GCSE, they would receive 63 points and 54 points respectively. Using Conway's scoring system, however, they would score 45 and 27—a difference of 40 per cent. The second set of figures tallied more closely with the school's experience of A level candidates.

Results

The results of the value-added data were unsurprising. They showed that students appeared to be performing below the national average in some areas with a slight convergence towards the higher grade end. The convergence was more marked for the second cohort's results. Here, low-achieving students seemed to be performing below the national average and more able students at or above the national average. There were a number of problems in interpreting the data. The school's 16–19 Co-ordinator posed the following explanations:

1 One explanation would seem to be that the students were under-performing and that the reason for this was the sixth-year teaching experience which they were receiving. But this was far too glib.

2 The Audit Commission data was for students who took A levels in 1988, i.e. an *O level* cohort. It could well be that the relative under-performance of the students is not specific to this one school, but rather reveals something about the difference between GCSE and O level as a preparation for A level. In fact this would seem to be quite a likely explanation considering the relatively high rate of improvement in national GCSE grades compared to the improvement in national A level grades.

3 It could be the direct result of over-performance at GCSE followed by average performance at A level. This is the most difficult to identify and, more importantly, if this is the case then the validity of the system is brought into question for some schools.

Despite the problems of interpreting the data, there was broad agreement nonetheless that the school's liberal admissions policy for entry to A level study needed overhauling and that more appropriate routes and pathways were needed.

B. Routes and pathways

The 16–19 team presented a costed option for the development of the post-16 curriculum which outlined the staffing costs and advantages and disadvantages of the current provision, together with a rationale for change.

1 Costs of current one-year provision

The costs for the development of the sixth-form curriculum were worked out on the basis of total teacher periods and proposals were made initially within existing resources, i.e. from the total staffing from existing GCSE re-take courses and franchised BTEC courses.

2 Advantages of the current provision

- The pilot franchised vocational programmes allowed students who had 'failed' at GCSE to make a fresh start with a different approach to learning and permitted students with a clear idea of their career plans to get started on a relevant course.

- The existing GCSE re-take programme was flexible and accommodated students who did not have clear career ideas.

- It was also popular with parents and delivered an accepted qualification.

3 Disadvantages of the current provision

- The track record of the re-take course was poor in terms of the results achieved by the students. It lacked credibility in the eyes of students who felt that it merely gave them another chance to fail their GCSEs.
- The pattern of the modest vocational provision was too restrictive and needed far more flexibility to tie in with students' aspirations.
- The franchised vocational course with the college was not of merchantable quality.

4 Rationale for proposal

At the heart of the rationale for the development of the post-16 curriculum was a commitment to a wider range of one, two and three-year curricular pathways which ensured meaningful progression to further or higher education, together with the removal of moribund GCSEs (Biology, Humanities etc.), but with the retention of the option for core GCSEs (English and Mathematics) with A levels or GNVQs. The proposal was also based on market research.

Market research suggested that students would be interested in a wider range of post-16 courses, especially those whose teachers forecast that they were likely to score no better than an 'E' at A level. There was also a new market for a range of vocational courses which offered planned progression from foundation to intermediate and then to advanced courses within the sixth form. The proposal took cognisance of this new market and included the possibility of students remaining at school in the sixth form for three years if they wished to stagger their programme. The evidence suggested that the one-year courses which were likely to be the most popular were GNVQs in Leisure and Tourism and in Business and Finance. Market research amongst Year 11 students showed that the two-year advanced GNVQ courses in Business and Science would be the most attractive.

A close reading of the syllabus for GNVQ Intermediate Leisure and Tourism suggested that half of the modules could be co-taught with modules in GNVQ Intermediate Business and Finance. A similar saving could be achieved in the GNVQ Advanced Science course, where half of the modules could be co-taught with modular A level Science courses.

The 16–19 team presented these costed proposals to the SMT, which accepted them with a few minor modifications. The 16–19 team was then tasked to research the feasibility and acceptability of other GNVQ courses for a possible phased introduction and to prepare a paper identifying the other main resource implications of the strategy.

5 Management structure for possible new courses

The range of new and upgraded GNVQ courses implied a new management structure with individual GNVQ team leaders for each course together with a whole-school GNVQ Co-ordinator for quality assurance, assessment and training. The recommendation was that team leaders were not to be given incentive allowances but extensive training and opportunities to augment their management experience. The GNVQ Co-ordinator post would be a key appointment for driving the new strategy and this would need to be reflected in the status afforded to it. The SMT accepted these recommendations and the governing body approved the new post and funding for the staff training.

6 Accommodation and equipment

Background: following deliberations by the governors' sites and buildings sub-committee, the governing body endorsed the recommendation of the head to buy a new building to act as an additional sixth-form common room. The head, the site manager and governors then prepared a phased accommodation development plan with the officers of the LEA for new and replacement buildings, including a purpose-built Business Centre.

Audit: the 16–19 team carried out an accommodation and equipment audit in respect of the range of proposed courses and presented a series of papers to the SMT, identifying precise accommodation requirements and equipment (including the provision of an IT suite in the library). The team then met with the SMT to consider the detailed rooming implications of possible new courses together with the co-teachability of GNVQ modules and modular A levels, and in relation to the two phases of the accommodation development plan agreed with the LEA.

7 Analysis of organisational culture and stakeholder survey

Thirdly, the strategic analysis required the school to analyse its culture and stakeholders. The team took soundings from a range of stakeholders about their perceptions and feelings concerning a possible realigned post-16 curriculum. An attempt was made to gauge stakeholders' feelings about 'the way we do things round here' (the organisational culture) and how they felt about the 'goodness of fit' of this culture with the challenges facing the school. The survey used questionnaires and interviews in order to determine opinions and feelings about the character of the sixth form, existing provision, deficiencies/strengths, and to locate stakeholders on force-field and commitment charts (see Tables 9.1 and 9.2). The detailed analysis of stakeholders' perceptions in the commitment chart (Table 9.2) revealed that there was much work to be done by the 16–19 team and the SMT to win the hearts and minds of those resistant to change in the sixth form. In order to gain commitment to change so as to avoid alienating key stakeholders it was necessary to prepare a commitment plan which would deliberately and systematically achieve a critical mass of commitment to change.

Driving forces	Resisting forces
16–19 team	the climate created by the 2.9% pay award
most of the SMT	one deputy head concerned about GNVQs and the possible change to the character of the sixth form
many staff	
most governors	
parents of prospective one-year students	head of sixth form concerned about the effects on recruitment to A level
better progression	some students on A level courses
better routes and pathways	some prospective A level students
availability of GNVQs	some parents apprehensive about possible change in the character of the sixth form
shifts in 16–19 curriculum development nationally	
local competition	resistance to change from some staff

Table 9.1 Force-field analysis derived from stakeholders' perceptions of a possible realigned post-16 curriculum

Individual	Opposition	Let	Help	Make
SMT 1				XO
SMT 2	X			O
SMT 3				XO
SMT 4		X		O
SMT 5				XO
SMT 6				XO
Ho6	X			O
HoD1	X	O		
HoD2		X	O	
HoD3		X	O	
HoD4		XO		
HoD5		XO		
HoD6	X	O		
HoD7			XO	
HoD8	X		O	
HoD9		XO		
HoD10	X		O	
HoD11			XO	
HoD12		XO		

Existing position=X
Desired position=O

Table 9.2 Commitment chart of stakeholders' perceptions of a realigned post-16 curriculum

A subsequent evaluation of the commitment chart expectations suggested that it placed too stringent demands on staff to *make* things happen rather than simply *letting* them happen. As a result of the evaluation the commitment expectations were modified along more realistic lines.

Questionnaires

There were four questionnaires:

1 A Year 11 questionnaire completed by pupils who said they would be taking A levels and by pupils who said they would be taking one-year courses.

2 A Year 12 questionnaire completed by Year 12 students on two-year A level courses.

3 A Year 12 questionnaire completed by students on one-year sixth-form courses.

4 A staff questionnaire on existing provision, the match with students' needs, areas of deficiency and strength, and an evaluation of the TVEIE post-16 entitlement provision (General Studies and IT etc.).

In addition to these questionnaires, parents and governors were asked at parents' evenings about new courses in the sixth form.

Synthesis of evidence for strategic analysis

Johnson and Scholes suggest that when an organisation has formed an empirical view of its environment, its resource capability and its organisational culture, it must then prioritise its strategic issues. Bryson (1988, p. 5) refers to this as the 'vital step between strategic analysis and the development of strategy' and suggests that strategic issues are the fundamental policy questions affecting the organisation's mission and values (see chapter 4).

The end-process of strategic analysis was the compilation of a SWOT analysis which derived from the data in the systematic analysis above. The SWOT analysis was a useful at-a-glance chart against which to test choices.

The SWOT analysis (drawing upon the approach suggested in Johnson and Scholes, 1993) was conducted in order to form a view of the school's internal strategic position with regard to its resource capability. The analysis set out in Table 9.3 represents the distillation of the views of the school development plan team and the post-16 development team. The major practical difficulties of carrying out the SWOT analysis were those of the scale and depth of the analysis and what was practicable for a small team with limited time.

Evaluation of the SWOT analysis

The evidence from the SWOT analysis was very important to the overall impact of the final strategic recommendations made to the senior management team and proved a useful *aide mémoire* in briefing sessions.

The SMT used the SWOT analysis and the evidence presented above to highlight fundamental policy issues.

Strengths	Weaknesses	Opportunities	Threats
budget surplus to fund development	variable results and value-added at A level	the strategic plan new curriculum pathways available	environmental turbulence caused by the ERA
Expertise in 14–18 curriculum development	limited 16+ curriculum routes	greater flexibility available	predatory local schools
high quality staff	marketing	growth of sixth form because of new routes	losing A level pupils to grammar schools
general support for GNVQ	study facilities at 16+	restructuring of 14–18 span and roles and responsibilities	social cachet of GMS and Technology schools
oversubscribed school	fixity of attitude of some stakeholders	good parental support for new GNVQ courses	college expansion
good reputation	resistance to change of some stakeholders who favour incrementalism rather than zero-based approaches	pupil interest and broad-based support	'exit' of M/C parents
experience of drafting submissions		better progression 16–19	'exit' of A level staff
BTEC pilot experience			changing nature of intake
proactive SMT			
large sixth form yielding a healthy budget and bonus	existing admissions policy		

Table 9.3 SWOT analysis

Strategic issues

1 Should the school opt for a sixth-form strategy based on differentiation and focus with an overly academic A level sixth as its 'flagship'?
   If so, it should eschew 'open access' to the sixth form and focus instead on A level.

2 Should the school deliberately make use of the emerging and flexible post-16 framework? If so, it should plan for the phased introduction of GNVQ at Intermediate and Advanced level in a range of programmes.

The next stage involved the synthesis of the evidence and building it together into a series of possible courses of action.

Generating and evaluating options

The series of meetings on these fundamental policy issues triggered strategic choice which set in train the planning stage for the implementation of the chosen strategy.

Sixth form strategic options

Option 1—do nothing and wait for the Government to rationalise 16–19 accreditation patterns: in the light of GCSE and National Curriculum planning this was a tempting option, though strategically dangerous because many prospective students fell outside of the traditional A level or GCSE re-take routes and could well be forced to go elsewhere for their post-16 education. Several HoDs and a number of staff favoured this 'wait and see' option.

Option 2—provide a wider variety of new A and A/S levels to deliberately expand the 'academic' sixth form ethos: this had an initial appeal for some staff, though it would be prohibitively expensive both in terms of staffing 'loss-leader' courses and in terms of lost AWPU income from those 'existing' students for whom A level is not appropriate.

Option 3—provide an overtly vocational sixth form with a wide variety of GNVQs and restricting the range of A levels: this option would undoubtedly cost the school dearly in the long term because if it is not to become a large secondary modern school in the eyes of the parents then it must keep its academic pupils, especially post-16. In the era of league tables and open enrolment, an overtly vocational sixth form might well drive away academic pupils at age 11. The option would send the wrong marketing images to prospective academic students whose understanding of post-16 provision may well lag far behind recent developments. It is likely that a unifying vocational education framework would alienate A level students and their parents who expressed concern about a possible change of character in the sixth form.

Option 4—provide a balance of courses at 16+ with a range of GNVQ courses, a few new A levels, a more restricted range of 16+ GCSE and A/S courses, together with a thorough-going review of the existing 16+ entitlement core: this was an attractive option (though potentially expensive in the start-up period for new A levels and equipment costs for GNVQs), because it retained a broad student base whilst consciously maintaining the academic character of the sixth form. It was felt that this compromise position would allay the fears of many stakeholders resistant to change but would imply committing new buildings for sixth-form use to accommodate the planned expansion. This in turn would have knock-on implications for set sizes and accommodation in the rest of the school. Some staff warned of the dangers of 'drum tight' timetabling in the middle and lower school and how this could well backfire at KS3 and KS4 with depressed test scores and examination results.

Strategic choice

Next, the SMT evaluated each option and considered which course of action would be most viable using stakeholders' perceptions to gauge Johnson and Scholes' three broad criteria: suitability, feasibility and acceptability, i.e. does the chosen course of action maximise the SWOT analysis; is it feasible given the school's resources and the nature of the required changes; and is it acceptable to the internal and external stakeholders?

The view was taken by the SMT that the school could not simply be reactive or it would lose tempo and competitive advantage. It had, therefore, to reject option 1. Second, it was felt that the school ought not to appear extreme in the eyes of its key stakeholders or it might alienate its majority student body (by choosing option 2), or its minority A-level student body (by choosing option 3). Options 2 and 3 were, therefore, high-risk strategic options and could not be entertained. Option 3 also signalled a marked culture change for the school and was felt to be unacceptable to prospective A-level students and their parents, and might be perceived to be a reckless change by other parents. Thus it could not be considered as a 'best fit' strategic option. The vision of the future was for a fully comprehensive, all-ability sixth form. Thus option 4 was seen to provide the most viable and acceptable option because it moved the curriculum forward appropriately and was a cautious option which would not alienate stakeholders. It preserved the best of the school's existing tradition and avoided the worst excesses of reckless change. Some felt that it lacked distinctiveness and focus, though there was broad agreement that the school would do well at this time to address educational, revenue and differentiation issues simultaneously.

In terms of Johnson and Scholes' criteria for making the strategic choice, option 4 was the most suitable because it maximised the strengths and opportunities in the SWOT analysis and provided practicable measures to address weaknesses and threats. It was feasible though likely to be expensive in the start-up period, and would require changes elsewhere in the school. Finally, it was acceptable in respect of the internal school culture and to the range of external stakeholders. Option 4 was not, however, without its operational problems and these are discussed in the section on planning implementation below. The key issues arising from option 4 are as follows:

1 Re-directing resources to new A levels (RE etc.) and to new GNVQs throughout the course of the phasing plan. (In the short term, the recommended GNVQ courses could be provided largely within existing staffing.)

2 Avoiding expensive GNVQs such as engineering, manufacturing and construction. These are best taken at the college.

3 Researching the possibility of GNVQ level 1 courses in the 14–16 span to assist progression.

4 Accommodation needs for new courses.

5 Training needs.

6 Reassuring parents about the strategy.

7 Devising ways to counsel students and their parents about the appropriateness of GNVQ advanced courses rather than A level courses.

8 Marketing of new courses.

9 Evaluating the advantages and disadvantages of franchising arrangements for GNVQs.

10 Writing submissions and new course modules.

11 The management of the co-teachability of GNVQ Advanced modules and modular A levels.

12 Seeking commercial investment for the new courses.

Consultation on the strategy

The 16–19 team discussed the options with the SMT and managed to convince the Head of the Sixth Form and the Deputy Head, who were doubtful about the development of GNVQs at the school, that the proposed course of action (option 4) was necessary for the long-term health of the sixth form. The SMT and the 16–19 team then drafted a sixth-form strategy briefing paper to present to the full staff and to the governing body, which explained the reasons for the strategy. The strategy was then discussed with the whole staff. Presentations were then made to the governing body to work through the possible strategic options and to seek its endorsement for the recommended course of action. Once the selection of strategy had been approved then the SMT presented the detailed implications of the chosen strategy to staff at the level of the general changes to organisational structure, systems, and resource commitments. The 16–19 team held a rational model of management and used the school's formal bureaucratic structure (SMT meetings and governors' meetings) to seek approval for the recommended option. Consultation rather than participation was the mode of wider staff involvement. The final stage was to devise an implementation plan in order to effect change in a planned and seemly manner.

Planning and implementing the chosen strategic option

The stage of planning and implementing the chosen strategic option raised the problems implicit in managing change. The problems concerned changing the organisational structure, resource planning and the management of commitment.

Organisational structure

The SMT accepted the recommendations from the 16–19 team that the organisational structure of the sixth-form curriculum would need to be re-thought in the light of the chosen strategy. It sought to use this restructuring as an opportunity to enhance staff retention and contribute to the development of improved teacher motivation, morale and expertise. A range of measures (largely within existing resources) were suggested to support retention whilst meeting the requirements of the new organisational structure. These measures included: combination job rotations to retain the services of several key staff; the provision of flexible part-time contract arrangements; new professional development opportunities as team leaders for staff who sought new challenges in the GNVQ teams; and the renegotiation of job descriptions with staff whose existing short-term targets had now been met (see Table 9.4). At an early stage it was necessary to secure the governors' formal approval to hire an additional specialist full-time Business Studies teacher with BTEC experience instead of hiring non-specialist temporary staff.

In terms of the Bolman and Deal (1991) typology of leadership types explained in Chapter 4, the SMT's dominant style was structural, based on a rational view of management. However, the SMT had to recognise and manage the political consequences of creating the new framework. The practical difficulties associated with creating the new organisational structure were those typically found in setting up new initiatives. The promotion of some staff and the new career development opportunities/job rotations afforded to others undoubtedly created resentment amongst some of the staff who felt that their work was undervalued and expressed concern that they

Line manager	Deputy Head
GNVQ Co-ordinator	Ex BTEC leader
GNVQ team leaders	New professional development opportunities
16–19 IT Manager	Renegotiated job description

Additional staffing in Year 1

GNVQ Advanced Business	Year 1: 1 FTE (0.5 Business for the balance of the new P/T GNVQ Business contract, and 0.5 IT to deploy) Year 2: double groups of BIS and GNVQ Advanced and so the 0.5 will be needed for Business

New contract

0.5 GNVQ Business	Ex F/T Business Studies teacher with BTEC expertise

Table 9.4   Possible new roles and responsibilities for the new management structure

had less opportunity to show what they could do. In addition to the management of resentment it was also necessary to assuage the fears of those few staff who disliked what they saw as the proliferation of GNVQ courses 'contaminating' the academic character of the sixth form and objected to the deployment of resources to GNVQ development. Second, there were 'boundary management' problems which emerged as a result of the new organisational structure. Here some heads of department objected to their staff assuming new roles and responsibilities outside of their departments and voiced their concerns about the likely deleterious effect of GNVQ—the loss of 'specialist' teacher periods in their departments, and the effects of GNVQ training and curriculum development on continuity in their departments. There were other boundary issues which needed clarification, such as the new sixth-form IT manager's role in the refurbished library/resources centre, and day-to-day practical demarcation matters such as responsibility for the care of new IT equipment located in the library/resource area.

Resource planning

The governors agreed to provide optimum levels of teaching materials and equipment for the new courses and asked the GNVQ Co-ordinator to submit a series of programme budgets estimating individual GNVQ costs. The co-ordinator established the projected costs with each GNVQ team to allow for a year's lead time for all new courses except for GNVQ Business (Intermediate) which was to start immediately. Each budget identified the following costs: rooms required, equipment, teacher periods, non-teaching staff time, teaching materials and consumables, overheads (telephone, examination/module fees), reprographics and training. The short-term budgets were submitted to the

SMT together with a long-term budget request for an upgraded IT suite in the Business Centre and upgraded computer facilities in the library/resource centre to strengthen IT in the sixth form.

The SMT accepted the GNVQ budgets with a few minor alterations, then set up a special IT project group to report on the relative educational merits of the IT upgrades and a timetabling team was also tasked to report back on the accommodation and timetable implications of the courses.

The main problem with the new courses was their impact on the resource of space because teaching space was at a premium in the school. The proposal for new GCSE courses was initially costed within existing teaching accommodation resources by removing outmoded GCSE courses, by co-teaching of GNVQ/A levels, but this proved impossible given the incompatibility of some of the GNVQ Advanced modular elements and A levels.

The head and site manager presented the 16–19 team's accommodation development plans to the governors' sub-committee on sites and buildings and, following their approval, the SMT explained the plans at a meeting of HoDs. The SMT team accepted the recommendation of the 16–19 team that the school should not become involved in franchising arrangements again, but should apply to become an accredited centre.

Following the governing body's approval of the sixth-form strategy, the 16–19 team began preparing the voluminous documentation for the various submissions. The GNVQ Co-ordinator then worked with the school's Inset Co-ordinator to identify and cost GNVQ training needs, to decide arrangements and personnel for assessor and verifier training and to apply for earmarked vocational training funds from the LEA. The prospective team members for the GNVQ courses had been selected and approached in the early stages of planning implementation in order to ensure that there would be a good balance of flexible staff with a willingness to teach outside of their professional 'comfort zones' on the new GNVQ modules. All the staff who were approached were keen to join the teams and were also prepared to undertake extensive training during the planning phase.

The management of commitment

Johnson and Scholes suggest that:

> Strategic changes are seldom made as a result of senior management decisions alone. It is much more usual for strategy to evolve as a result of the activities, perceptions and influence of many other individuals including the different levels of management.

Furthermore, when it comes to the implementation of strategy, the chances of achieving success without all levels of management understanding the strategic issues involved is a formula for disaster. (1988, p. 21)

Handy, too, reinforces the imperative for whole-school involvement: 'The solution is to ... drench the organisation in a common set of values' (1985, p. 246).

The SMT wanted broad-based staff involvement in the planning, teaching, assessment and management of the sixth-form strategy and involved thirty staff in the planning for implementation teams. The individual GNVQ team leaders nominated by the GNVQ Co-ordinator were accepted at an early stage in the planning process, as the SMT wanted to establish a consultative and democratic approach to GNVQ team management and decision-making. A 'tight-loose' model of accountability was agreed with the GNVQ teams where tight control was to be kept over the achievement of key tasks (deadlines for submissions, training budgets, and the writing of modules); but loose decentralisation was also to be provided to give flexibility and scope for team initiative. In this way the teams were given a measure of autonomy about how to achieve these goals.

To ensure that the whole staff understood the post-16 strategic issues facing the school, the 16–19 team circulated briefing papers to all staff and mounted displays to explain 16–19 developments locally and nationally and gave a series of brief presentations to staff and governors. At this point the school also committed formally to work toward the national standard for staff development (Investors in People) and felt that it would be appropriate if all the staff (teaching and support staff) who worked at the school were told of the strategic challenges facing the school and the reasons for the sixth-form strategy. Whilst the presentations did not entirely succeed in 'drenching the organisation in a common set of values', they were nonetheless symbolically important because they reinforced the kind of common culture that would be appropriate in the future and elevated the primacy of GNVQs in that vision of success for the school. It was also the first time in the history of the school that the *entire* staff had been gathered together for a training session.

Johnson and Scholes suggest three broad criteria for courses of strategic action: suitability, feasibility and acceptability. The sixth-form strategy was suitable in that it maximised the SWOT analysis. It was feasible given the school's resources and the nature of the required changes. But was it acceptable by the internal and external stakeholders?

The acceptability of the planned strategy to stakeholders

The governing body felt that the sixth-form strategy was broadly acceptable to them because it would retain the essential character of the school's sixth form whilst helping to create a vision of long-term success for *all* those who wished to stay on beyond 16. Several governors, however, were concerned (along with a few of the senior staff) about the numbers who would be taking the courses and the viability of group sizes in the start-up year. Most of the staff found the strategy realistic, rational and necessary. Some criticised the 16–19 team and the SMT for not 'preparing the ground' properly—with not keeping them up-to-date with developments—and felt a lack of ownership of the strategy. A few doubted the wisdom of broadening one-year courses in the school and felt that it threatened to introduce a dissonant culture in the sixth form.

A concern of the SMT and the several 16–19 teams was the acceptability of the new courses to pupils at a time when the local college would be offering the full range of GNVQ courses without the strictures of a school sixth form and with the likelihood of rather more flexible entry qualifications.

The 16–19 team agreed that the internal and external marketing of new courses was essential during the planning year. First, members of the team talked with pupils in tutor periods, social education sessions and in assemblies about the range of new courses available and to acquaint youngsters with the new nomenclature. The team, together with senior staff, then met with parents at 'What Next?' evenings and parents' consultation evenings. In this way the team provided an increased awareness of the importance of the new pathways, the structure of GNVQ, progression, assessment, the phased introduction of courses and why GNVQ would be an attractive alternative to GCSE re-take courses and an alternative route to Higher Education. The GNVQ Co-ordinator produced a GNVQ 'flyer' to explain to the community the kind of courses that would be available and the projected phasing plan. Another challenge was the internal marketing of courses to staff to improve understanding and acceptability. The intention here was to allay the fears of those staff who expressed concerns about planning on 'shifting sands' for GNVQ (the late revisions to Advanced GNVQ Science for example) and what they perceived to be the uncertainty of status of GNVQ. The team contacted admissions tutors in a variety of higher education institutions and sought confirmation about the acceptability of GNVQs as a legitimate route to higher education. Most institutions confirmed that they would look favourably at GNVQs as acceptable entry requirements.

The satisfactory completion of the major building programme and the opening of the Business Centre during the year of planning implementation certainly helped to boost confidence in the strategy. However, the SMT had to remind all staff about the fragility of confidence in the new pathways and how this confidence could easily be undermined by careless derogatory comments.

Relationships with future school development planning

1 Achieving the next stage of the strategy

Fullan (1989) suggests that there are three phases to the change process. Phase 1 is initiation, mobilisation and adoption; phase 2 is implementation or initial use, and phase 3 is continuation, incorporation, routinisation or institutionalisation. The school is largely in Fullan's phase 1, though with some initial use (GNVQ Business pilot) from phase 2. The challenge for the 16–19 team and the SMT is to devise a clear model for proceeding beyond phase 2 and to the incorporation and eventual institutionalisation of more GNVQ courses from all the five vocational areas. What was clear from staff reaction when the 16–19 team explained the possible planned introduction of GNVQs in these other vocational areas (Catering, Care, IT, Media and Performing Arts) was that many favoured a policy of 'wait and see' until there were enough examples of good practice to replicate. The 16–19 team and some of the SMT, however, argued that there was merit in being a pathfinder in the GNVQ field.

2 Relationships with modular A levels

Concurrent with the development of the post-16 vocational track (GNVQs and NVQs) there has also been the move towards the modularisation of A levels. There is now some possibility of credit accumulation and credit transfer over a longer period than the normal two-year duration of an A level course. There is, therefore, a clear convergence of A levels and GNVQ units which will be roughly of the same size as A level modules.

It is increasingly likely that GNVQs will be drafted with A levels in mind as has already happened with the Advanced GNVQ in Science, for instance. The trend to modular A levels in the future and their 'goodness-of-fit' with GNVQs will have enormous implications for 16–19 curriculum planning and delivery in schools. (The 16–19 team is currently mapping the possibility of co-teaching GNVQ units and A level modules in a range of courses.) It seems likely that the designers of A level syllabuses in the future will draft their syllabuses to facilitate this co-teaching in order to maintain their market share. There are considerable grounds for optimism that with so much convergence now taking place there may well be new combination routes for A levels and GNVQ which allow common modules for each track. And when the emerging framework permits, the school will then seek to implement such a unified credit accumulation system in its own post-16 curriculum if such a system is practicable. It seems likely that with a range of GNVQs and modular A levels already in place the school will be able to take advantage of this emerging framework without a major culture change in its sixth form.

10 Secondary school case study 2
A strategic plan for a comprehensive school

Barbara Evans

Context of the school

Richard Aldworth Community School is an 11–16 mixed comprehensive with 930 pupils on roll. It is situated in a highly competitive local environment being one of eight such LEA schools within the town, all of which could be regarded as competitors. Whilst two of these schools are oversubscribed, three others are severely affected by falling rolls. Richard Aldworth has seen a gradual but relatively small fall in roll over the past two years. A similarly small but significant fall in examination results has accompanied this trend. Subjective observation would suggest that this is attributable to the loss of the more able pupils to our competitors. Despite intake, the school has sustained a relatively high position within the league tables, suggesting a strong value-added factor, particularly within certain subject areas. Coupled with an excess of places within the town, this trend was an important factor in the school's decision to adopt a strategic approach to management.

Development planning at Richard Aldworth School: a historical perspective

Historically, development planning at Richard Aldworth School must be viewed in conjunction with a curriculum review initiated by the newly appointed headteacher in 1990. This sought to respond to changes emanating from the 1988 Education Act. Essentially, it resulted in the formation of a faculty system. This, it was envisaged, would better meet the challenges of the Act through a more cohesive grouping of subject areas which would better facilitate cross-curricular work within a National Curriculum and the creation of a smaller, more effective curriculum group. This was seen as a transposition within the school structure of the devolved style of Local Management of Schools (LMS) which has made schools more responsible for their own destiny within the context of increased accountability.

The first school development plan involving governors and teaching staff was produced for 1991/92. Global targets were set on a yearly basis. The senior management team considered proposals from staff. After extensive discussion, suggested priorities were then considered and invariably supported by governors. It was intended that the six newly formed faculty areas should produce similar annual plans modelled upon and responding to the format and targets identified within the school development plan. Subsequent years included an evaluation of the previous year's global targets (generally five). The development plan included the school's mission statement and related objectives (of which there were twenty-four), an evaluation of the previous year's global targets, an action plan for current global targets, proposals for use of statutory days, a staffing structure and curriculum analysis.

This represented a considerable improvement on past practice. However, whilst the mission statement was an accurate description of goals and associated beliefs and values, it failed to encapsulate anything distinctive. Neither were the twenty-four objectives either memorable or selective. Both were all-embracing and conceivably equally applicable to any of the other 11–16 community comprehensives within the town. The targets, whilst responding to external legislative requirements in some cases, tended to be inward-looking and short-term. Theoretically, they formed the basis of a holistic approach. In practice, faculty plans tended to divide into discrete as well as global targets. Furthermore, priorities for development were not based on any formal market research. Neither was there a marketing plan.

The process of school development planning thus described was a positive step in organising in a more purposeful and coherent way the school's aims and values and its development needs related to national and LEA initiatives. It also enhanced, to some degree, a shared sense of direction although it failed to provide a comprehensive rationale for decision-making and was limited in terms of the school's vision for the future.

Why adopt a strategic approach to management?

The last decade has seen increasing pressure on the Education Service for external accountability. New powers and responsibilities enforced by the 1988 Education Act relating to the National Curriculum, open enrolment, financial and staffing delegation, make for a market model of education.

Under formula funding the financial viability of schools is dependent on their success in responding to factors influencing client choice. This has to be balanced against a school's professional judgement of the needs of children and incorporated within a concept of marketing which sees public relations as a broad-based multifaceted approach to building public understanding.

Schools stand at the interface of a massive shift in the balance of power between central government, LEAs and themselves. LEAs have lost much direct control through the devolutionary philosophy implicit in LMS. By the same token, schools' decision-making is greatly enhanced. This makes them far more responsible for their own destiny and places far greater demands on the analytical, managerial and interpersonal skills of school managers. This calls for an approach to management which looks at the whole institution and its long-term direction in relation to the immediate local as well as national political, economic, social and technological environmental influences which may impinge upon it.

Against this background, the motive for evolving a strategic approach to planning at Richard Aldworth School was based upon a desire to be proactive rather than reactive. This was coupled with a realisation of the importance of attempting to establish some explicit overall direction for the school which would guide it through the plethora of change and uncertainty, thereby enabling it to operate more effectively without compromising its major aims and values.

Process of involvement

The first formal school discussion on strategic planning took place at a senior management team (SMT) meeting. Preliminary discussions sought to clarify concepts before addressing the logistics of implementation. It was recognised that all staff needed to be involved in this initiative if there was to be a positive response to change. This led to the formation of a strategic planning group (SPG) which, it was envisaged, should be comprised of a wide cross-section of staff. The emergent group of volunteers was, in fact, smaller (two members of the SMT and three others) and less representative than was desired.

At the first meeting of the SPG the head introduced the idea of a regular 'SPG Newsletter' which would keep all informed of the development of the school's strategic plan through the activities of this group and their plans for the future. This was also seen as a prompt for staff to feed back their comments, if they so wished.

This can be seen as a symbolic act on the part of the head insofar as it marked a change of management style and heralded a new way of working. Interestingly, the new 'chatty' tone of this communication met with some resentment from staff. Clearly they were not ready for such a change and initially reacted with cynicism. Lack of Inset time for the whole staff at the launch of this major new initiative was a serious omission which undermined attempts to change the culture and to empower staff to respond positively to a more participative way of working. Such change takes considerable time, skill and on-going attention.

Thus involvement may be shown diagramatically as in Figure 10.1, with the small SPG group of five steering the whole process and carrying out the major tasks of data collection for the 'Analysis' phase.

At this stage the remaining SMT members were kept informed of progress. The governing body also reviewed the work of the SPG at regular intervals. Their other major role was to provide evidence for analysis as one of the key stakeholder groups and ultimately to ratify the proposed plan. Similarly, the teaching staff were involved in providing evidence either as a whole staff or as members of the curriculum and guidance committees. The whole staff were consulted at key points, i.e. when draft documents were produced, and at the

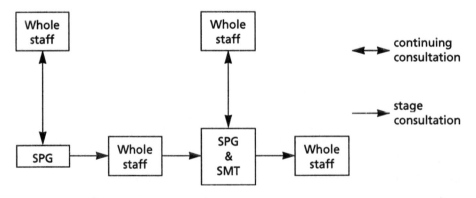

Figure 10.1   Staff involvement

final stage participated in drawing up faculty and guidance plans to implement the strategy. After the analysis phase this small SPG was expanded to include all members of the SMT.

Model for implementation

A model for implementation based upon that provided by Fidler and Bowles (1991, pp. 23 and 34) was adopted. This was accompanied by a revised process checklist incorporating the main elements of the Johnson and Scholes model, i.e. analysis, choice and implementation, within a linear format. A column was added for worksheet references with numbers corresponding to exercises from the *ELMS Workbook*. A code was drawn up to denote the school's response to the various aspects. Whilst it was deemed necessary to review all aspects within a designated area it seemed likely that the school would decide that it had already covered certain parts of the process in its own way, although it would be crucial to address other aspects, particularly those representing a departure from school development planning. A decision to postpone work on other areas might be taken. This is followed by a column used to indicate the group or individual responsible for carrying out work on a particular aspect. This then provided a comprehensive working document for our school which enabled us to map coverage of the whole process over a period of time.

Planning cycle and time-scale

The time-scale proposed by *ELMS* was adopted. This gives a basic repeat cycle of two years in the first instance with three months to devise the strategic plan. In practice the time-scale for devising the strategic plan proved to be inadequate. Approximately nine rather than three months were spent at this stage. Several contributory factors are worth citing here. First, any form of systematic analysis was a new undertaking for the school and required considerable time for explanation and discussion as well as for carrying out; secondly, there was an expressed commitment to collaborative and participative work, again representing a shift of management style. Feedback and consultation as each step of this phase was developed proved to be an immensely time-consuming but, it was conceded, necessary business. There was concern that communication should be seen to work effectively as a two-way process: any consciousness of an autocratic structure employing directive strategies, at any level within the school, needed to be dispelled in order to create the necessary climate for whole-staff ownership. The deadline for faculty and guidance plans was extended due to the imminence of the summer term. Finally, there was a desire to cover everything fully.

Since the first cycle was considered crucial to the success of the whole project it was felt that such extension of time was justified. Once methods of working have been established for a particular school and relevant concepts fully understood and accepted it is conceivable that the given time-scale for subsequent cycles at least, is realistic.

Carrying out a strategic analysis

Strategic analysis is informed by evidence relating to the three elements identified by Johnson and Scholes, namely, the environment, resources and values/culture. Whilst an audit and evaluation of the culture of the school and resource capability seeks to identify internal matters which give a view of the school's current position, scanning the external environment prepares the school for an assessment of issues which are separate from the school but which could have an influence upon it, e.g. the development of unitary authorities. Such matters are likely to be in the political, economic, sociological and technological domains. When the analysis is complete the school should be in a position to identify those influences and issues which need to be accommodated within its planning in order to secure its future well-being.

In order to complete an analysis it is necessary to consult with the major stakeholders in the school. Staff, pupils, parents and governors were identified as the main stakeholders and market research was carried out to determine their level of satisfaction.

Systematic data collection includes formal research methods such as questionnaires and the *ELMS Workbook* exercises as well as empirical research of a more subjective nature, e.g. keeping a diary of observations, feelings, reactions, interpretations, and reflections. The latter convey a feeling of what it was like to be participating in the action whilst the former attempt to give factual evidence to inform decisions and guide actions. A diary was kept throughout the analysis and subsequent phases of the strategic planning process. This complemented the 'bald facts' provided by minutes and other methods of data collection. It also collected together valuable, albeit subjective, insights into the culture of the school. Questionnaires and the *ELMS Workbook* exercises were used at two main points in the strategic planning process:

1 During the analysis phase in order to audit and evaluate the school's current activities, indicate the level of stakeholder satisfaction and to assess which external influences would be important in shaping the school's future.

2 As preparation for drawing up the more detailed 'sub-plans' for marketing, curriculum, staffing and finance.

In both instances a process checklist was devised. For the first analysis phase this was a revised version of the *ELMS Workbook* example already referred to. This checklist of components structured the entire process and proved invaluable as a monitoring tool. Further reconnaissance occurred after the major 'analysis' phase when the chosen strategic direction had been formulated. To be operationalised, detailed plans for the areas mentioned above, together with an 'Organisation Structure and Decision-Making' document, had to be devised. This resulted in a second, smaller cycle of data collection using exercises entirely drawn from *ELMS* to further inform the four specific sub-plans. Another checklist of similar format was therefore used in conjunction with the original checklist and indicated, predictably, that much of the analysis, particularly in three of the four areas, had already been covered.

This leads to a further purpose in carrying out some of the exercises. As has previously been stated, any formalised market research was a new idea to the school. Yet marketing had been identified by staff through *ELMS* exercise S7S as an area requiring particular attention. Our approach to marketing thus far could be described as being somewhat haphazard. Certainly there was a need for a coherent marketing strategy. In order that an effective marketing plan could be drawn up, further work of an educative kind was desirable. Thus the *ELMS* exercises were used at this stage as much to raise awareness amongst staff at all levels as to provide information on their views and opinions. MIS4 and MIS7 were used for the same purpose, in this case to prepare staff to use performance indicators with confidence when drawing up faculty and guidance plans.

Stakeholder analyses

(a) Staff

Whole-school involvement is a key issue when seeking the views of staff. Non-teaching as well as teaching staff need to be involved. On this point, a critical mistake was made at an early stage which was hard to rectify. This was partly the result of poor planning insofar as staff views, sought through *ELMS* exercise S7S on school performance, were collected at the end of a staff meeting. Whilst this guaranteed a high response and 'no conferring', the timing also placed pressure on staff to remain beyond directed time in order to complete the exercise, thereby undervaluing it somewhat, I feel. It was only after the meeting that we realised that other main sectors of non-teaching staff should have been similarly involved. Comments made afterwards indicated that staff welcomed being involved.

(b) Pupils and parents

Half the pupils in Year 7 (Y7) and Year 10 (Y10) were selected on a tutor group basis to complete a pupil questionnaire, giving a 20 per cent sample of the school. The parents of these same pupils completed a corresponding questionnaire. The two age groups were selected for different but complementary reasons. Having completed a term at the school we considered involving Y7 to be a positive step in establishing our partnership with new entrants who might be keen to volunteer first impressions. Y10, being more established, could provide a consolidated view, to include other areas of interest, e.g. options. Comparison between the two years might also be useful.

Information was sought on the following main areas:

Pupils

■ themselves—questions here were included partly to ease pupils into the questionnaire and partly to give a clue as to how positive they felt about themselves (correlation with their opinion about the school could be enlightening)

■ parental support

■ lessons—preferences for learning styles

■ care and support

■ buildings, facilities, equipment

■ extra-curricular activities

■ final recommendation

Parents

■ communication and partnership with the school

■ standard of education

- homework

- special needs provision

- extra-curricular activities

- care and support

- lunchtime arrangements

- facilities, equipment

- discipline and uniform

- transfer arrangements

- final recommendation

Again, where overlap exists, correlation between pupils' and parents' responses could be enlightening.

Draft copies of the questionnaires were trialled by the SPG. This resulted in minor adjustments. A more serious design fault was evident, however, when we received the results. Two parents had used the 'further comments' section to write about individual teachers. This highlighted the need to preclude such comment by a covering statement referring them to the usual channels for such matters. Such issues should have formed part of the ethical framework governing access and release of information which needs to be established at the outset.

Pupil questionnaires were completed during a set tutor period. This ensured 100 per cent response and facilitated a common approach. Enlisting the co-operation of heads of year was also a political move aimed at increasing their support for the initiative. In order to maintain anonymity yet ensure as full a response as possible, tutors were asked to make a note of pupils returning the enveloped replies so that they could pursue those outstanding.

(c) Governors

Whereas staff, pupils and parents provided us with quantitative data, governors provided data of a more qualitative nature. Open-ended questions were framed such that their views on the strengths and weaknesses and any distinctive features of the school could be combined with their considered opinion of external factors which the school needed to take account of, their vision for the school over the next five years and possible contribution to its achievement. This also served the purpose of focusing their attention on the sort of impending changes strategic planning would be likely to introduce. It seemed expedient for the head to provide governors with suggestions from the list given in *ELMS* exercise S7S of the sort of areas they might consider when assessing the school's current position. The list in S9 concerned with vision was used in a similar way.

The governors' questionnaire was designed such that their response could usefully be considered in conjunction with that of the SMT to the environmental scanning exercise (S3) they carried out.

Similarly, triangulation, whereby evidence from different sources collected by different methods is compared, was a planned feature of the other three stakeholder analyses.

Accommodation audit

The accommodation audit (S1) involving heads of department was quite straightforward and a good starting point for wider staff involvement in this respect. However, the culture survey (S4S) carried out by all members of the then separate SPG and SMT was predictably more problematic in terms of quantifying the results.

This concluded the first round of data collection. From this point, on the SPG operated in its expanded form (original SPG plus remaining SMT). Individual members drew on all data collection reports to date in carrying out the classic SWOT (Strengths, Weaknesses, Opportunities, Threats) analysis as a means of further convergence. Two more exercises were undertaken by this group as final preparation for production of the strategic plan. These related to 'vision of success' (S9) and 'strategic issues identification' (S10).

Analysis of evidence

Staff response to exercise S7S on school performance

The response to this exercise was 97 per cent, there being fifty-seven recorded responses and two incomplete. Items with the top six scores for 'present rating' were highlighted as areas in which the school should consider promoting its image. Items with a higher 'desired rating' than 'present rating' indicate possible areas for action in the school's strategic plan. Again, the top six highest 'desired rating' scores were recorded. It is pertinent that the four items which received the highest desired rating also had considerably the biggest difference in score, over one hundred in each case. These are, in order:

No. 14 behaviour and appearance of children

No. 1   academic standards and ethos

No. 21 buildings and physical environment

No. 20 promotion of the school

The other two highest desired rating items are the only two items which also featured on the high present rating table, namely, item 10 (special needs provision and attitudes) and item 3 (caring and supportive structures). This suggests that we do these things well, value them and need to promote them.

As the designated school for the disabled within the town, a high rating for item 10 is not surprising. Since the school does not attract a large percentage of the most able pupils, 'special needs' is likely to have been interpreted in a narrow sense to refer to low-ability pupils. (This conjecture was supported by parent comments in their questionnaire on provision for the most able. In effect they were unaware of the existence of any such provision.) However, a possible conflict exists between promoting this as the school's distinctiveness whilst desiring most strongly to achieve high academic standards and an academic ethos (item 1).

This part of the analysis also highlighted other areas warranting attention: although not scored as top desired rating items, high differences in score existed for items 4 (vocational courses and outlook) and 23 (staff development).

'Other attributes' listed (24) were so diverse as to be impossible to collate. This suggests a weak culture.

Response to pupils' questionnaire

There was 100 per cent response to the pupils' questionnaire, this being comprised of ninety-one from Y7 and seventy-six from Y10. Results were recorded separately for the two years and then combined. Not all pupils answered every question. Such problems can only be addressed by tutor reinforcement and reminders to pupils regarding checking completion. However, since the response to individual questions remained generally very high, results were recorded such that the percentage given is that of the total number of respondents overall. The top six strengths and weaknesses were as follows:

Top six strengths

No. 7   parents interested in how I do at school

No. 20   working with friends

No. 15   teachers make it clear how we should behave

No. 14   teachers make sure we do homework

No. 34   enough books and equipment

No. 9   parents make sure I do homework

Top six weaknesses

No. 31   school clean and tidy

No. 6   believing I will be successful in life

No. 21   lessons where I work on my own

No. 39   range of trips and visits

No. 36   things to do at break and lunchtime

No. 29   views on school can be heard

Of these, items 31, 39, and 29 lend themselves to direct action. All except the last item correlate with parent and/or staff views.

Item 28 on bullying receives a significant minority response (28 per cent), sufficient for concern in this particular area since it also correlates with parents' comments. Top six differences between Y7 and Y10 are relevant only insofar as they confirmed a more positive outlook from younger pupils.

Response to parents' questionnaire

Because response to the parents' questionnaire was 6 per cent less than that for the pupils and because 65 per cent of questions on the parent questionnaire did not receive a full response to a considerably larger degree, the lack of response to particular questions was more significant. Therefore the percentage recorded as satisfied/very satisfied is that of the total number answering each individual question. This necessitated individual calculations in the final Y7 or Y10 and combined summary. Again results were recorded separately for the two years and then combined.

Surprisingly, there was an 8 per cent lower response from parents of Y7 pupils. An anticipated low response to a question on special needs reduces the validity of the percentage result. An item referring to arrangements for the more able received a low response, with several comments to the effect of 'what arrangements?' Interpreted either as 'there are none' or 'we are not aware of any', such a response is disturbing but unremarkable, remembering the staff's high desired rating for academic standards and ethos together with their likely interpretation and rating of 'special needs'. Other comments, particularly from Y7 parents, were made to the effect that gaps are due to lack of knowledge or experience (poor communication on the school's part?). Whilst Y7 parents' final percentage scores are slightly higher overall, the relative scores are comparable. The top strengths and weaknesses were as follows:

Top strengths

Nos. 1 & 26 overall satisfaction/recommendation

No. 2   school's approachability

No. 3   amount of information provided about the school

No. 11   grouping or setting of pupils

No. 20   arrangements for transfer from primary school

No. 9   standard of education provided

No. 25   child's general happiness

Top weaknesses

No. 15   range of subjects offered as options

No. 6   frequency of parents' evenings

No. 13   range of trips and visits

No. 14   amount of homework provided

No. 23   lunchtime arrangements

No. 19   discipline

No. 10   examination results

Several items overlap, as was illustrated in the comments made, and all but the first two correlate with pupil and/or staff responses. Of these the following items emerged as areas of priority:

221

No. 15 arrangements for options

No. 6 frequency of parents' evenings

No. 13 range of trips and visits

No. 23 lunchtime arrangements

No. 19 discipline

There is an apparent contradiction in the listing of 'standard of education' as a strength yet 'examination results' as a weakness. The relatively low score for satisfaction with examination results was registered as an area for concern.

Response to governors' questionnaire

There appeared to be some contradiction in the responses from governors to their questionnaire, e.g. examination results were listed as both a strength and weakness. Closer examination through discussion with the head afterwards suggested that they were, in fact, concerned about the lack of *consistency* of academic standards across the curriculum. This was 'by far the most widely supported' concern, with condition of the buildings and general environment and the behaviour and appearance of children emerging as other main areas of weakness. The very diversity of response given to the question on distinctiveness suggested that the school did not possess strong distinguishing characteristics. (This was supported by a similar response as part of the culture survey.) Governors highlighted the need for good staff development and training. This correlates with staff response to exercise S7S.

With regard to other developments sought over the next five years and the contributions they could make to these, the response was unimaginative and disappointing, there being no references to influences in the external environment which could impinge on the work of the school. When asked directly what political, social or cultural developments are likely to impinge on the school over the next five years, those listed below were mentioned most often:

1 Increased governmental pressure to become grant maintained

2 Possible changes arising from the Local Government Review

3 Further parental pressure on schools

4 Continued under-investment in education

5 Continued high unemployment

It is interesting to compare this list with the SMT response to exercise S3S on environmental scanning. Parental pressure, under-investment in education and some form of pressure linked to grant-maintained status were all mentioned again. At the planning stage it was suggested that the list for S3S be updated to include local government reform. This was forgotten but the report does acknowledge that had it been included, it is likely that it would have been rated as being very important.

In carrying out data collection for this part of the 'analysis', it was rewarding to observe the existence of key correlations between all stakeholder groups in the following areas:

- quality of education

- care and support

- buildings, facilities and equipment

- extra-curricular activities

Such congruency made a significant impact in terms of convincing staff of the validity of carrying out such a broad-scale, thorough analysis. This gave momentum to the whole process and maintained enthusiasm within the group as well as providing conclusive evidence to inform the next step— choosing the school's strategic direction. This is encapsulated in the focus statement and list of long-term objectives.

Accommodation audit

Results of the accommodation audit were fed into a plan drawn up by the deputy head in liaison with the site manager. Immediate action on minor jobs boosted staff morale. Feedback on long-term objectives was equally important.

Culture survey

The open nature of the questions comprising the culture survey made it very difficult to quantify the results. Relevant aspects of culture which the results do manifest include:

1 the existence of sub-cultures

2 the existence of a 'role' culture

3 problems associated with consultation

223

Comments supporting these aspects confirmed my own observations of the culture of the school and were consonant with concerns expressed by several members of the group over the draft 'Organisation and Decision Making' document.

The way in which sub-cultures blend and relate to management's intended culture surfaced as an issue for our school which the strategic planning process itself started to address. The existence of conflicting cultures (as distinct from multiple cultures which can be complementary to a participative management style) is at times divisive and dysfunctional, particularly where sub-culture groups *perceive* a top-down line of authority and view of management. Likert's System 3 and Handy's 'Role Culture' (Handy and Aitken, 1986, p. 87) most closely matched the prevailing culture of our school, I believe. Communications, systems and procedures were formalised and impersonal (note cynicism to the new 'chatty' style of the newsletter); emphasising roles, not individuals. There were procedures, rules and handbooks to cover every eventuality so that routine tasks would be carried out effectively and fairly. Relationships were basically hierarchical.

This created a tension with what I perceived to be the head's preferred culture and his expressed wish to move towards a more participative management style. For example, faculty heads are given considerable delegated responsibility for their own areas—staff have participated in operations such as the drawing-up of policies.

The value of this culture survey lies in raising awareness of such tensions. These can then be taken into account in formulating the strategic plan and the process of strategic planning itself can effect a stronger culture with a greater degree of consistency. Alternatively, the task of management could be to gather together the varied strengths of the school's cultural mix, using each in its appropriate place.

In retrospect, it would have been more useful, knowing to some extent the culture of the school, to have redesigned this exercise in a less open format.

Dissemination of evidence

All those involved in providing evidence are entitled to receive feedback. This was linked with thanks for co-operation.

An analysis of findings in report form was issued in the first instance to the SPG, who collectively then assessed its significance. Since the findings relate to the work of all staff they were then summarised and communicated via the newsletter. Other groups providing evidence received summative feedback (e.g. parents through their newsletter). This also placed the particular results in context. Issues raised under 'further comments' were also addressed. Where possible, response to individual concerns, not central to the main thrust of the strategic plan, were dealt with, e.g. the options system was changed in response to parental dissatisfaction.

Utilisation

Data collected through analysis thus far were used to inform the strategic plan, the first part of which could now be written. Evidence was conclusive and the group unanimously agreed that our five-year strategic plan should concentrate on three broad issues. They are:

- improving our academic record and achieving consistency across the whole curriculum

- improving our physical environment

- improving our external relationships with groups and individuals beyond the school

The next step was to formulate a focus statement and associated long-term objectives. The rest of the staff would then become increasingly involved as we developed organisational and decision-making structures, the four sub-plans and faculty and guidance plans. In the meantime, we were conscious that our work was taking longer than we had envisaged and that we needed to maintain staff interest.

Focus statement and long-term objectives

The focus statement is a concise, compact, meaningful statement outlining the specific purpose of a school. 'It should be capable of being "unpacked" to yield the core values of a school and its vision of the future. The most basic feature of the statement is that it should be a guide to action' (Fidler *et al.*, 1991, p. 23). The mission statement embodies the values and mandates and stipulates the long-term purpose to be pursued whilst providing social justification for an organisation's existence. The focus statement is the school's strategy or major development for the next few years. The focus statement must not be a blanket promise to do everything. This was a pertinent point for our school and probably many other comprehensive schools.

After establishing the nature of a focus statement, initial SPG discussions sought to identify key terms for the three areas identified. These were:

Academic
consistency
raising standards
overcoming obstacles
responding to change

Environment
stewardship
promotion of well-being and care
promotion of positive attitudes to work
appropriate purpose
responsiveness to change

External relationships
responsiveness
partnership
contribution to the community
adaptability
proactivity

Improved planning and performance were seen to hinge upon responsiveness to change in these three areas. The head produced the first draft from these deliberations for SPG comment. Revision efforts were directed towards brevity and maximising impact. After several revisions, a final version went out to all staff to be discussed at faculty/departmental meetings. There was a 50 per cent response. Some positive changes were made. Other changes were made for political reasons. Clearly it would be good to be seen to use the results of consultation. Other nuances of meaning were jealously guarded, e.g. we spent a great deal of time before arriving at the word 'stewardship' for one of the objectives and, although some staff said that they found it awkward and suggested alternatives such as 'caring', we clung to the original because of its implied additional shades of meaning (management and maintenance.) The head explained our reasoning on this to staff.

Staff indicated their pleasure at being consulted on this document. Analysis and formulation of the focus statement and long-term objectives took some two months to complete with more detailed plans for operationalisation yet to be considered.

Planning implementation

Organisation structure and decision-making

The first level of operationalisation is concerned with determining how all the staff within a school will work together to achieve the school's purpose. This entails determining the structure of responsibilities and how decisions are made.

The document drawn up by the head to describe this was itself highly controversial. Discussion exemplified the dilemma of making such a document acceptable to the existing culture versus using it as an instrument for shaping and developing that culture, i.e. as part of its organic growth.

Some criticisms were easily dealt with, e.g. those concerning the tone. 'A teacher with no responsibilities above . . .' was reworded, a structure diagram of non-teaching staff was added, and 'autocracy' was re-ordered within a list of forms of involvement in decision-making in order to lower the profile of potentially the most contentious approach. More serious was the concern voiced by the two deputies who felt that the document would alienate staff because:

1 it read like an essay (quoting Hoy and Miskell was out!)

2 it was too long

3 the language was too sophisticated

The culture of the school was such that it was feared that staff would not read it.

Such a document does need to deal with complex concepts and cannot be too simplistic. It was with some regret that the above criticisms were conceded and a proffered simplified version accepted.

The four sub-plans

The priorities indicated in the focus statement have implications for the series of sub-plans. These represent the main areas of decision-making. Preparation for drawing up these detailed plans necessitated further research with a strong emphasis on the raising of awareness. A range of exercises from the *ELMS Workbook* were considered. A number of factors determined their selection and use:

1 The need for whole-school involvement.

2 The need to keep governors involved.

3 Access to relevant information required for decision-making and cross-referencing, e.g. M2. This suggested that at least one member of the SMT should be involved in the development of each sub-plan. Individual members of the SPG took overall responsibility for drafting a sub-plan. If such members were not also members of the SMT then a member of the SMT was assigned to act in an advisory capacity.

4 The in-service training potential of some exercises for this and subsequent stages, e.g. MIS7.

5 The need to gather further evidence specifically related to particular areas, e.g. marketing, which had been less systematically addressed in the past. The chair of governors had also spoken informally to myself and the head regarding our need to improve press relations.

The number of exercises originally agreed for completion by SMT and SPG was later reduced. The head felt that given the time-scale (we were still aiming to complete within the 'three-month' slot), this would impose too great a workload on these particular individuals. It was therefore suggested that both groups worked on both areas (M and MIS) with exercises assigned according to expertise (M1 and M8—SMT, M3 and MIS7—SPG, M4—both if possible). In addition, the whole staff were still invited to put forward their views on marketing (an area they had identified in S7S as needing improvement). MIS7 on performance indicators was also carried out by members of the curriculum and guidance committees as preparation for their plans.

The suggestion was that even aspects designated 'covered' should still be reviewed by persons responsible for particular plans.

A common format was accepted and followed in the final plans (see example below taken from the marketing sub-plan).

Analysis of evidence

Evidence gathered through the marketing exercises (M1, M3, M4) confirmed the results of earlier, more general research, whilst focusing attention on particular issues which needed to be addressed by the marketing plan. They were also a useful process tool for maintaining staff interest. Significant points to emerge are summarised below:

1. M1—collaboration or competition?

One member of the SMT reported that he found this a very difficult exercise to complete. There was very little response from the group to consideration of the position of neighbouring schools, other than highlighting the fact that two new neighbouring schools would have new heads in September. It is relevant that there are surplus places within the town's eight schools. Most heads would have been pleased if one school had been closed instead of being refurbished as this would have reduced the pressure on schools with falling numbers. This has tended to trigger more aggressive marketing in some quarters.

Collaboration with a school with whom one is not in competition, e.g. from another county, was highly valued.

Competition has historically been looked upon disfavourably by the school except insofar as it places the pupil at the centre of our efforts. Marketing has been seen basically as a communication process wherein the school's aims, objectives and achievements are related to the needs and wishes of the community. Whilst acknowledging the need for market research and a 'distinctiveness' which gives the school a differential advantage, crucial in promoting a competitive edge, an aggressive approach to marketing is alien to the culture of the school. Marketing is grounded in good public relations and a co-operative venture between interested parties (school and client). Responsive marketing is seen as achieving a balance between what the customer wants and educating the customer to appreciate the aims and quality of the school.

There was the need for a marketing plan. Further, in the light of our falling roll and local context, the school needed to question its effectiveness in this area. At the same time it needs to be ready to respond to any changes in approach adopted by competitors, particularly with the demise of TVEE which has been instrumental in maintaining a co-operative spirit within the town.

2. M3—stages of marketing

There was a 32 per cent return (nineteen out of sixty) for this exercise. Timing (end of term) and time allowed (four days) were not good. Four responses were incomplete, leaving only a 25 per cent useable return. In following up these four, all commented on the awkwardness of the instructions and the ambiguity of some statements, e.g. who are the professionals in item 4—teachers or others as well? Others suggested the questions were leading. These criticisms may be partially justified and could have been overcome by verbal introduction and clarification.

With regard to analysis, using the difference in score is only a reliable indicator for action if that item also has a high desired rating. Results were consistent with an implied need for an increase in marketing of a high quality, with particular attention being paid to our partnership with parents in a competitive climate. The results were interpreted as desire for stage 4, i.e. 'balanced needs'. Viewed thus, promotion and public relations must become important elements of the school's marketing strategy. These results are consistent with those for M4 and emphasise the need to establish a culture in which all members of the school community appreciate their role in relating the school to its clients. The marketing plan therefore operates as a critical lever in triggering faculty and guidance plans such that, when combined, they act as explicit vehicles of accountability.

3. M4—customer/client orientation

Comments from 75 per cent of the returns recognised the increasing importance attached to informing parents and suggested that the views of clients should be more rigorously and systematically sought. 'It is essential that the views of parents and children are considered. Perhaps we have not got this right yet' and 'more effort needed'. Senior staff and others recognise that parents and pupils are more empowered as a result of the 1988 Education Reform Act (through open enrolment and formula funding). Prior to the introduction of strategic planning the school's position could be described as being 'casually responsive' (encouraging customer enquiries, complaints, suggestions and opinions, making occasional studies of customer satisfaction). The results of this exercise, together with the commitment made in the focus statement, suggests that the school believes it should move towards a more 'fully responsive' position whereby 'customer mindedness' is uppermost and a collaborative partnership based on mutual accountability exists.

4. MIS8—service developments

This exercise was useful in preparing for the 'Organisational Structure and Decision-Making' document as well as the marketing plan. Only one member responded to the question, 'How does your school rate on these dimensions?' with the comment, 'Lots of room for improvement'.

5. MIS7—performance indicators

As previously stated, exercises such as this were valuable primarily as process exercises rather than for the information they gave.

The final sub-plans

Each of the sub-plans went through a series of checks before final production. A detailed discussion of all four plans would be lengthy and repetitive. This section will therefore focus on this process in relation to the marketing plan for the following reasons:

1 This plan was the first to be produced and was, to some extent, used as an example for the others.

2 To date, relatively little structured planning on marketing had taken place compared with the other three areas, hence the more extensive preparatory exercises.

3 It was the most contentious of the four areas.

4 Comments made through consultation illustrate a dilemma in that, against all evidence, there was a strong desire to simply maintain the *status quo* rather than admit that radical change was necessary.

We considered it vital that plans be of a high quality, consistent in their presentation, intelligible and should facilitate response from the heads of faculty and heads of guidance (HoF and HoG respectively).

Prior to strategic planning, the school's concept of marketing was somewhat restricted and tended not to extend beyond minimum obvious requirements such as production of a school prospectus or the occasional press report. Such 'jobs' were divided between the two deputies and itemised as part of a lengthy job description. There seemed to be the need for a wider view of marketing and, as a corollary to this, a conditional target—the appointment of a marketing co-ordinator, to be responsible for consistency and quality. This was accepted in principle by the head. However, the idea of a marketing co-ordinator was anathema to three other members of the group (one senior teacher plus two other non-SMT members) who, despite accepting the broader scope of this area such as the inclusion of systematic research and despite our falling roll alongside close neighbours who are oversubscribed, were adamant that, 'at present the job has been carried out very successfully by the two deputies'. This can be seen as a major setback insofar as it typified a fundamental reluctance to change. Such attitudes could render the strategic planning process little more than a sophisticated paper exercise.

Faculty and guidance plans

The SPG appreciated from the outset the importance of conveying how changes introduced through a strategic approach to planning would affect faculty and guidance plans (the latter being a new initiative for these people) both in terms of outcome and process. For this reason, a comprehensive set of 'Notes of Guidance for Completion', together with a separate proforma for each of the four areas of decision-making, was drawn up by the SPG and issued with the strategic plan thus far developed (see Figures 10.2 and 10.3). A joint meeting of the heads of faculty and of guidance was devoted to a discussion of the process of developing faculty and guidance plans. The necessity for these to consult fully and involve all team members in developing their plans needed reinforcement.

The support given by the HoF and HoG as change agents working collaboratively with their teams is crucial. Belief in people's ability to respond creatively and positively through group participation is a prerequisite to establishing trust, open communication and equality of status. This is difficult and proved to be very time-consuming, both in terms of formal and informal discussions with members of the various teams. Nonetheless it is critical to a successful outcome and ownership of the plan. This affects not only the efficiency of the group's performance but also morale. Thus middle managers have a vital part to play in operationalisation of the school's strategic plan.

The way forward

The impact of a strategic approach to planning on the whole school has not, as yet, been fully realised. Benefits cannot be properly quantified until the plan has completed its five-year cycle. At this stage it will be possible to assess such things as the distinctiveness of the school within the local community and the success of targets detailed within the plan, such as a rise in academic standards and roll. However, it is possible to make some general observations at this stage.

The introduction of strategic planning required a change of school culture. At the same time it was recognised that the process itself had the potential to contribute to such a change. The faculty curriculum model developed in 1990 had already laid the foundations for delegated responsibility and accountability. However, staff readiness and ability to participate in decision-making could not be assumed. Neither was there complete commitment and understanding of the need to start from a zero base. This was

School objective (No.)	Faculty objective	Long/short	Performance indicators	Activities	Staffing	Resources

Figure 10.2   Faculty proforma for marketing sub-plan

Against a background of accelerating change and increased competition, we will endeavour to achieve and maintain a high profile within the local community. Particular attention will be paid to our relationship with pupils and parents with whom we will seek to build a collaborative partnership which will afford maximum educational value for the child.

Objectives
Objectives will be initiated and developed in the areas of market research; promotion and marketing; selling and promotion.

	Long/short term	*Performance indicators*
Market research objective M1 To identify and evaluate client needs by regular and systematic gathering of information.	Long	Collated results of client response demonstrating over the years fewer negative responses to factors within our control.
	Staffing	*Resources* Admin. assistance. Photocopying costs. Non-contact time.
	SPG	
Activities Distribution and collection of questionnaires—20% sample of pupils and parents every two years.	Head of year and tutors	
Results are collated and fed back to relevant personnel for future action. Reappraising and upgrading questionnaires on an on-going basis. SPG is alert to position of competitors, drawing on a wide network to inform. Developing strategies which will enable the school to gain feedback on relevant contacts.		

Figure 10.3   Format for sub-plans: example taken from marketing sub-plan

apparent from one SMT member's over-reliance on past experience, i.e. management's 'recipes' in relation to the appointment of a marketing co-ordinator (even as a conditional target), despite evidence to the contrary. Combined with problems associated with the draft 'Organisational Structure and Decision-Making' document, this demonstrated that where new strategy requires a change in culture, this has to be thought through as a major change in itself.

In relation to the outcome, the resultant plan represents a significant move towards being more outward-looking, longer-term and concerned with the whole scope of the school's activities. This first plan should, perhaps, be seen as an embryonic stage in the development of more radical future plans. This will be possible as the lessons regarding the political and cultural context of rational decision-making are assimilated.

In relation to the process, the organisational structure and decision-making document has made explicit the ways in which decisions will be made and staff will work together to achieve the school's purpose. A participative view of human resource management would seem to be vital to the introduction of strategic planning. However, the management style of a particular school cannot be changed overnight. Staff participation is both a prerequisite and a measure of success for the strategic planning process. It is also extremely time-consuming, as is the sheer workload for a school undertaking strategic planning for the first time. The necessary climate for this new way of working has to be created as was exemplified, possibly, by the low response of volunteers at different stages. Persistence was needed to overcome initial resentment of a change of management style.

Finally, there must be a willingness to change fundamentally if the need for this is demonstrated. A negative attitude to change could render the strategic planning process little more than a sophisticated paper exercise. These issues will need on-going attention in the form of encouragement, support, training and opportunity if staff are to be ready and capable of accepting shared responsibility for implementation of this plan, thereby contributing to individual and organisational health.

11

Strategic planning: The way ahead

This chapter reflects on the strategic planning process illuminated by the case studies in Chapters 7, 8, 9 and 10 and considers ways in which strategic planning in schools can be encouraged.

Strategic planning in practice

Reasons for engaging in strategy

In three of the case studies there was an early indication of a fall in school roll, but this was coupled with a wish to become more proactive and less reactive to events. In the other case there was a general feeling of unease about sixth-form provision and decisions were required about vocational alternatives. In this case a holding decision was made whilst a more thorough analysis was carried out.

In the case of the first school in Chapter 7, the school had been working on its curriculum, and parents, when consulted, were reasonably happy with the curriculum but wanted a greater degree of involvement with the school and their child's education. Had parents not been consulted, and other sources of dissatisfaction discovered, the falling roll might have continued despite staff efforts to improve the curriculum.

Influence of previous development planning

In each of the schools there was a history of planning on a more restricted time-scale and with a more inward-looking approach than strategic planning. It would be easy to overlook the importance of this, in view of the dissimilarities with strategic planning, but undoubtedly the initiative to produce plans had been exercised in each school and staff had been involved in various ways in contributing to, and implementing, each school's plans. Although this had involved staff working together, other effects had not been entirely positive. The first school noted that development planning had been entirely concerned with implementing external requirements, whilst one of the secondary schools noted that the LEA forms, which had to be completed, introduced a mindset of incrementalism.

Strategy formation

In all the cases the headteacher or a senior member of staff played a leading role. A small group of staff carried out the role of a strategy steering group. This involved governors where they had appropriate expertise and a wish to be involved. The strategic planning group comprised a combination of volunteers and those with appropriate positional power. This combination needs a very sensitive way of working if it is to be effective. Initial use of the nominal group technique (Fidler *et al.*, 1991) can ensure that worthwhile contributions are made by all and establishes a way of working within the group which is non-hierarchical. A tension comes from trying to do this whilst the head exercises a leadership role and guides these discussions and subsequent actions. Although this small group may have steered the process, the whole teaching staff were regularly involved.

Using Inset days, where the whole staff could work together, was found to work well, but such days need to be earmarked in advance. There is a tension between programming events into a timetable and flexibility. In primary schools, getting the whole staff together on other occasions was also possible and a new meeting structure was trialled in one school to ensure a worthwhile pattern of meetings. Where such a pattern of meetings wasn't possible in secondary schools, briefing papers were circulated and a regular newsletter kept staff in touch. The full teaching staff were consulted at critical stages of the process at staff meetings. This ensured that all members of the teaching staff contributed, but it also meant that time was very restricted.

Collecting data

Involving staff in collecting data at the analysis stage ensured that they personally were exposed to some outside views about the school. Data were collected by a variety of means. There were formal questionnaires and, although the response rates were not high, these gave a more comprehensive base for parental views than any previous method used. Children and young people were consulted in various ways. In the first school this was accomplished by class teachers as part of the curriculum.

Data were collected both in systematic hard forms such as questionnaires and also by more anecdotal and softer forms. Potential clients were considered by asking a playgroup leader in the first school and parents collated the views of other parents for each class. In the primary school an evening workshop involving staff, governors and the PTA met in convivial surroundings to work in groups and exchange views. In addition to opinions, more factual data were collected, including a list of skills that parents would be willing to contribute and staff audits showing the extra skills which teachers were willing to volunteer.

Extensive data were collected to inform the analysis stage. In each case vital information emerged through this process—what other schools were doing, the wishes of children, parental preferences, and staff perceptions. Generally these pointed up clear issues to be addressed and, in the examples given here, there was broad general agreement about priorities.

Making the change

The pressure of falling rolls undoubtedly had an effect on staff attitudes when they were acquainted with the financial and other implications of a continuing fall in the school roll. Many heads wish to protect teachers from the external pressures on schools when teachers have so many other calls on their time. On occasions like these, however, it is very important for staff to see the constraints and recognise that these issues concern and have implications for everybody in the school. However, once staff are involved with the external context, they need to be kept in touch and not only told at times of crises.

Unfreezing was an issue in each of the schools. In the case of the sixth-form curriculum change the decision involved a calculation as to how far the change could go on this occasion, but with a clear recognition that in future it may have to go further and be more radical. In the other cases there were substantial efforts to involve teachers and to begin to change the culture. Collecting data from children or other groups made them aware of client and external views. The consequences of falling rolls were also made clear. Some improvements to accommodation produced an early positive reaction to change in one school. A previous change which involved working in teams was built upon to aid a climate in which the changes could be discussed freely. A staff handbook was produced in the primary school and policies were written in a collaborative way.

Teaching staff were involved in planning the detail of changes and setting up targets for their implementation. In the first school, job descriptions were altered as a formal and symbolic indication that the teacher's job had altered to include a greater involvement with parents.

Schools used various techniques for planned change, so that points of resistance could be identified and tackled before the process could continue. This meant the time-scale for the change was much slower than originally envisaged and a great sense of determination was required by the head and strategic planning group.

Leadership

In each case the headteacher and a small strategic planning group oversaw the process. This involved steering the process and collecting and collating information and making proposals to a larger group for consultation. A sense of impatience comes through in a number of the accounts, but this is balanced by a recognition that without the commitment of staff the strategy can't be made to work. This represents an acceptance of the fact that sometimes 'You can't get there from here' (Wilkins and Patterson, 1985). In other words, at this point in time, this change is too great and can only be accomplished in stages over a longer period of time and by using intermediate stages (if it can be achieved at all).

A particular conundrum is that strategic planning may need a change in the culture of the school, but engaging in the process may also be one of the means of bringing about the change in the culture. Where external data were collected and shared with staff, this led them to see the need for change. This, combined with purposeful leadership and some symbolic actions that demonstrated that the management and decision-making style in the school had begun to change, were powerful influences.

Time

In each case where the school produced a strategic plan the time involved was substantial. In 1991 Geoff Bowles and I anticipated a period of three months to formulate the plan. This relatively long period was to redress what seemed to be the prevailing assumption at that time that the essence of a school development plan could be formulated in an inservice day. From the experiences related here, it is clear that we underestimated the time required to collect data and carry out the 'unfreezing' process. In one secondary school the process took nine months and in the primary school low-key operations over two years were required to move to a position where some changes could be made, but only subsequently could larger changes to classroom practices be contemplated.

There is a tension between taking time over the analysis stage and becoming seemingly bogged down in the inevitable uncertainties which result from interpreting the data that have been collected. Time is needed to collect, analyse and assimilate the information from the data. Time is required for communication, discussion, formulation of alternatives and choice. People need time to assimilate the possible effects of the changes and to become comfortable with the prospects of the chosen changes. But there is also a momentum which needs to be kept up so that the whole process doesn't falter and stall. This is a matter of supreme judgement and leadership—maintaining a sense of purpose and action without it seeming a steam-rollered rush.

Benefits

Collecting data on the state of the school and the views of stakeholders was found to be invaluable. It made those in school more outward-looking and less insular. Information resulted which made a successful future direction of the school clearer. There was better communication with both those inside the school and those outside. There was an orientation to the longer term and a greater sense of being in control and knowing where the school should be heading.

Work on producing a specific mission statement that encapsulated the particular aims of each school gave a greater sense of purpose to the school. The statement had to be formulated very carefully with each word being carefully debated for its nuance, such as stewardship in one of the secondary schools. The first school was able to produce a priority list of developments which it intended to implement as finances allowed.

Encouraging strategic planning for school improvement

Our over-riding aim is to encourage and stimulate schools to take responsibility for their own future success through strategic planning. Ironically this has to come from school level and cannot be imposed from outside. Thus we suggest ways in which present schools and school leaders can be encouraged to begin the process or to formalise an informal process. In the future, school leaders will need to be better prepared to undertake the process.

In the UK there is a clear recognition that the main responsibility for school improvement lies with each school (DFE, 1995a) and that it is the 'key unit of improvement' (DFEE, 1995a). As we said in 1989, 'the Education Reform Act very much leaves the destiny of an individual school dependent upon its own actions . . . its expansion and greater success, will also be as a result of its own efforts' (Fidler and Bowles, 1989, p. 18). The ERA made the assumption that competition for pupils would lead to school improvement. It was clear at the time that competitive forces would leave many schools unaffected, particularly those in rural areas. We now know more about the basis of parents' choice of school and their calculus of competing priorities. Thus competition seems a somewhat inadequate engine for genuine school improvement.

Implicitly all hopes of school improvement rested on the professionalism of headteachers, teachers and other staff of schools, which would lead them to wish to improve the opportunities to learn of children and young people. Whilst ultimately this may be very powerful, those who wish to improve need to understand successful ways of going about it and it would be unwise to assume that, without stimuli, legitimation and encouragement, all those who work in schools will regard improvement as their highest priority. In some cases, pressure may also be required.

Three approaches to change

There are three general approaches to change (Chin and Benne, 1976) and, as we have remarked earlier, a combination of approaches has the best chance of being successful. A consideration of encouragements of strategic planning for school improvement under those three headings yields:

1 Power/coercive

Actions could include: DFEE placing a legal requirement on schools to produce a strategic plan; LEAs requiring their schools to engage in the process; reporting on strategic planning in OFSTED school inspections; and providing incentives. For GM schools the National Audit Office (1994) has already raised the need for more encompassing planning than school development planning. FAS/DFEE could directly require GM schools to incorporate strategic elements in their development planning.

Where schools are planning significant changes of character (DFE, 1994b) they could be required to demonstrate that they have carried out strategic planning processes and, for changes that are not regarded as significant, governors could be advised that it is good practice to plan the change as a strategy. Grants for specific curricular specialisms, e.g. technology, could similarly be made conditional on a strategic plan following a strategic analysis.

2 Empirical/rational

Management courses provide an obvious vehicle for providing knowledge and understanding. Books and other media can seek to provide knowledge and rational arguments about the value of strategic planning and its potential for school improvement. This approach undoubtedly has a part to play. Schools cannot engage in strategic planning if they don't know what it involves, but they should seek evidence that it is worthwhile and not just another passing fad.

Empirical research has a limited role to play until there is a nucleus of schools practising strategic management which can be studied. Until then, research and development projects, which provide schools with knowledge and understanding and provide training in the skills which are required, could have value. Dissemination of the findings from such projects could make a large contribution to increasing knowledge of how to go about strategic management in different types of schools in different contexts. Although there is a systematic framework for strategic planning, this has to be tailored and adapted to the context of the school. There is no 'one best way' or 'quick fix'.

3 Normative/re-educative

This approach involves influencing the culture of school management such that there is a general expectation that schools will engage in strategic planning to ensure their future survival and success, and that they will use the process to improve their schools. This has largely been the case with school development planning, although in some cases the requirements of LEAs have been counter-productive (Wallace, 1991).

Those on governing bodies with experience of the process in other types of organisation could reinforce the expectation that any autonomous organisation, particularly if it is exposed to competition and a changing environment, needs to plan for a successful long-term future through systematic processes.

Four areas

From this range of possibilities we shall discuss four areas in more detail, describing current developments and identifying gaps:

- management development
- OFSTED school inspections
- consultancy
- resources for school improvement

Management development

Existing headteachers need to be introduced to the concept of strategy and the process of strategic management. External courses, either as part of longer award-bearing courses or shorter specialist courses, could perform this function. As heads and others engage in strategic management, the process of learning by reflecting on experience can take place. As this learning takes place the process in schools will be carried out with greater skill and confidence.

As senior staff take courses involving strategic management and engage in strategic planning in schools they will be better prepared to lead such planning when they become headteachers. It will be for appointing committees of governors to ensure that the candidates they consider for a headship have the capacity to formulate and manage a successful strategy for their school.

There is a scheme for providing assistance to newly appointed headteachers (HEADLAMP) in England beginning in 1995 (TTA, 1995a). This could be used to ensure that all those who have no previous experience with the process of strategic management are required to include this in their development programme funded by HEADLAMP. Those who have previous experience and understanding of strategic management may need help in tailoring the process to their new context. In October 1995, TTA began consultations on a new professional qualification for headteachers prior to their appointment (TTA, 1995b). It is essential that knowledge and understanding is included in such a qualification, and also an assessment of whether potential candidates for headships have the necessary personal qualities and skills to undertake strategic leadership. However, attitudes and norms are built up much earlier in a professional career than at senior management level. It is therefore important that as part of continuing professional development (TTA, 1995c), middle managers and others play their part in strategic management and are introduced to the concepts.

As we suggest later, the use of consultants is a worthwhile aid to problem-solving and strategy in schools, but senior managers need to appreciate the full value of consultants and consultancy. Senior managers and their schools also need to engage in preparatory activities if they are to make good use of consultants. Courses for senior staff on how to work with consultants to gain maximum benefit will be needed.

General funds for staff development and other purposes are distributed through GEST for LEA schools and comparable grants for GM schools. These have a general allocation for all schools for school improvement (DFE, 1995a; 1995d).

OFSTED school inspections

Within the OFSTED inspection framework there are references to strategic planning. However, these need to be made more specific, since it is doubtful whether most inspectors are sufficiently familiar with the ideas in this book to be able to judge the extent to which schools are assessing the strategic standing of their institution, have a vision of the future and have credible long-term plans for moving their school in that direction.

With additions to the framework and greater familiarity by inspectors, schools could be assessed on how well they are carrying out strategic management. This could be reflected in the points for action and priorities for longer-term development that are required in response to inspection reports. Although this stops short of being mandatory it gives a clear and unambiguous expectation to schools and requires them to formulate a response and alerts governors to their full responsibilities. The crucial question concerns the degree to which the requirement should be prescriptive. Is a situation where a strategic thinking headteacher operates strategically but does not reflect this in formal planning processes acceptable? As we have indicated earlier, we believe that some degree of formality is necessary in order to involve others in the process and to ensure that important factors are not ignored.

The proposed changes to the inspection process (OFSTED, 1995a; 1995b) to operate from April 1996 will involve a greater scrutiny of the school's self-evaluation and planning processes. An opportunity will have been missed if the changes are seen as merely a return to school self-evaluation. The extent to which schools plan strategically could be assessed as part of these changes but will need much careful development of criteria to do this (Fidler *et al.*, 1995).

There has been a great deal of attention paid to the improvement of failing schools as a result of OFSTED school inspections. Whilst crises can be expected to command attention, it should be borne in mind that most children are not in failing schools, nor in schools with serious weaknesses. It has been recognised that the steps needed to improve more successful schools are not the same as those required to improve failing schools (DFEE, 1995a). Indeed there are particular dangers for organisations following a period of sustained success (Miller, 1994). It is important that all schools should be encouraged to engage in strategic planning for school improvement.

School inspections can play a number of roles in school improvement. They can emphasise and legitimate the importance of improvement. They can provide an assessment of the performance of each school and signal areas that need attention. They can be used by schools which are confident of their overall standards to probe specific areas that would be helpful to the school (Rose, 1995) and obtain data which the school itself would find difficulty in obtaining on such a scale and with such objectivity.

General funds for staff development and other purposes are being increasingly distributed to schools after OFSTED school inspections for implementing their action plans. In 1996–97 a grant will be available to inspected schools to claim after submitting their action plans (DFE, 1995a; 1995d).

Consultancy

Whilst it is clear that schools have to be 'in the driving seat' of school improvement, the use of disinterested consultants acting as critical friends to schools would be most beneficial. This is a tradition, however, which will have to be created for it is not part of the current culture of schools in the UK. This will require learning on the part of schools about how to manage consultants. Initially, this will have to begin with consultants taking rather more of the lead than might be desirable in the longer term, but as schools gather experience and confidence they will be in a position to take control. It would be a mistake to try to do this too quickly, since there is a danger that schools will only opt for comfortable actions and be reluctant to try something new from which valuable learning experiences may come. Ultimately consultants should see themselves as working *for* schools although they may initially have to see themselves as working *with* schools or even *on* schools.

If schools are to learn, what about the consultants? For consultancy on a scale such that all schools could have access, there will be problems of both quantity and quality in the availability of suitable consultants. Consultants need at least two sorts of skills and knowledge:

(a) understanding and experience of *process* skills of organisational change;

(b) *behavioural* skills to act as a consultant and interact with members of the school in a variety of different ways.

How far an individual consultant possesses those skills appropriate to the issue for which they are being engaged is the $64,000 question. Schools will only be in a position to judge after the event and even then their verdict may be dependent on their state of readiness. Thus reputation will be some guide, but a rather incomplete one. A Society of Education Consultants has been founded and produces a list of members and some indication of their self-declared expertise (SEC, 1995). Some improvement in quality assurance will probably be needed to ensure that consultants have the necessary general expertise identified above. Further information is also needed to provide the basis for schools to choose, from a list of those qualified, consultants who meet their particular needs.

DFEE has assembled a list of advisers and consultants willing to work with schools with serious weaknesses (DFE, 1995a). Whilst this recognises a need, the scale and quality assurance of what is required will be more difficult issues. A qualification for consultants will probably be required. This needs to provide an education in organisational change and training in the process skills which a consultant requires. Such a qualification should probably be in two parts—an academic course and workplace-demonstrated competences.

A further issue then is how to change the culture of schools to include a more widespread use of consultants. This provides yet another paradox. Consultants should not be imposed, for all except schools in crisis or in need of special measures. Schools need to take the initiative and see the use of consultants as an opportunity, but on schools' own terms. One expedient to raise the profile of consultancy and to increase its attractiveness would be either:

(a) to provide an earmarked sum of money for each school to spend only on consultancy (or return unspent); or

(b) to allow schools to bid for money for consultancy for particular projects.

The second proposal requires a bureaucracy to allocate money which may deter schools from applying and cost money to operate, but would provide some sort of check on what was happening. As we know, the provision of specific external additional finance or 'honeypot management' (Knight, 1987) has been found highly tempting (Ouston et al., 1992).

Resources

The resources element has three aspects:

(a) provision of information

(b) networks of support

(c) financial and material resources

(a) Provision of information

As the STRB has pointed out in a number of its reports, school managers have very little comparative information on the performance of other schools with which to compare their own performance. The term benchmarking (LGMB, 1994) has been used for this comparative process. DFEE is encouraging LEAs and groups of schools to collect comparable financial information (DFEE, 1995b) to help those in schools to compare their expenditure patterns with aggregate figures from other schools. Whilst such a process may have advantages, it also has its dangers. It is likely to encourage regression to the mean and may cause schools with advanced expenditure patterns to revert to more typical patterns. To be of value, examples of advanced expenditure patterns with the accompanying reasoning need to be circulated along with aggregate information.

For schools with sixth forms there is increasing comparative data on progress from GCSE to GCE A/AS level (DFE, 1995b; 1995c). Proformas are available to simplify the comparison of progress in an individual school with national norms. Trials are being carried out on similar progress comparisons between ages 7–11 and 14–16. The OFSTED database which is being built up as a result of school inspections could provide a source of further performance benchmarks to supplement the more easily obtained financial information. This database will have a great deal of information about classroom processes from which all teachers could benefit.

It is an irony of benchmarking that either schools must co-operate to pool information for their mutual benefit, or another agency needs to collect the information, process it and make it available to schools. However, merely making information known to schools does not of itself bring about improvement (Williamson and Fitz-Gibbon, 1990). The form in which the information is made available is important. Guidance on how to assess the information is necessary (Gray and Wilcox, 1995). But most important is for teachers to see this as an aid to school improvement, and not as further external criticism of schools.

(b) Networks of support

Although each school needs to formulate its own strategic plan for school improvement, there are many advantages to working in supportive networks. Such networks can be of a number of different kinds. There are designated school improvement projects with support and funding from LEAs, TECs and higher education institutions (Arnold, 1995; Barber and Dann, 1996). Such networks can provide expertise in the improvement process and can also provide confidence and reassurance by working alongside other schools with similar problems. The tension is to allow each school the flexibility to formulate its own strategic plan, meeting its own needs, whilst also providing group support and shared expertise. Networks of support for strategic planning could provide support for the strategic planning process whilst recognising that a strategic plan will be different in each school.

(c) Financial and material resources

This raises similar issues to the last section. Incentives are needed to encourage schools to engage in strategic planning for school improvement. For most schools, a positive approach involving incentives can be expected to be effective. Thus the promise of extra resources for approved strategic improvement projects could be highly influential. Some elements of bureaucracy would be required to assess the proposals and require amendments to those either failing to tackle appropriate issues for their school or not having a credible plan to deliver the improvements. The proposed scheme for GEST funding represents a move in this direction, but larger sums of money are probably required. This will be highly efficient if relatively small sums are used to leverage substantial improvement.

Problem-solving schools

One of the early hopes of Organisation Development was that, through the efforts of OD consultants, schools could become more autonomous and problem-solving. Although the early evidence from the USA (Fullan *et al.*, 1981) was less than encouraging, as a concept a problem-solving, learning organisation might be a useful one. But the most tangible evidence of an autonomous school is one which can successfully engage in strategic planning.

Each school needs to begin with improvements which are relevant to it and not simply part of someone else's, however well-meaning, external agenda. This means starting from each school's problems and beginning to solve (or circumvent) them. The problems may not initially be concerned with teaching and learning. They may be about falling rolls, children's behaviour, leaking roofs etc. These strategic problems have to be tackled first.

One of the greatest protections against being beguiled by fads and silver bullets is to start with problems and not with solutions. Changes should be made which solve identified problems, implement widely shared visions of the future, and command wide acceptance from stakeholders. Strategic management provides a systematic process for identifying problems and their immediate context, considering solutions in the longer term and taking account of future influences.

We hope that we have contributed to an understanding of strategic management in schools and provided conceptual frameworks to envisage how the process may be carried out in a school. Most of all, we hope that we have given confidence to headteachers and schools to engage in strategic planning by presenting the accounts of the four case-study schools and the benefits which they derived from strategic planning.

References

Acton, T.A. (1980) 'Educational criteria of success: some problems in the work of Rutter, Maughan, Mortimore and Ouston', *Educational Research*, 22(3), 163–169.

Argyris, C. and Schon, D.A. (1978) *Organizational Learning: A Theory of Action Perspective* (2nd edn.), Reading, MA: Addison-Wesley.

Arnold, R. (1995) *The Improvement of Schools through Partnership: School, LEA, and University*, Slough: Education Management Information Exchange.

Audit Commission (1986) *Towards Better Management of Secondary Education*, London: HMSO.

Audit Commission (1991a) *Management within Primary Schools*, London: HMSO.

Audit Commission (1991b) *Two Bs or Not . . .? Schools' and Colleges' A-level Performance*, London: Audit Commission.

Audit Commission (1993) *Unfinished Business: Full-time Education Courses for 16–19 Year Olds*, London: HMSO.

Barber, M. and Dann, R. (1996) *Raising Educational Standards in the Inner Cities: Practical Initiatives in Action*, London: Cassell.

Barry, B.W. (1986) *Strategic Planning Workbook for Nonprofit Organizations*, St Paul, MN: Amherst H. Wilder Foundation.

Beckhard, R. and Harris, R.T. (1987) *Organizational Transitions: Managing Complex Change* (2nd edn.), Reading, MA: Addison-Wesley.

Bell, J. (1993) *Doing Your Research Project* (2nd edn.), Buckingham: Open University Press.

Bennett, N. and Rutter, M. (1980) 'Review dialogue: fifteen thousand hours: secondary schools and their effects on children', *British Educational Research Journal*, 6(1), 97–102.

Bennett, N., Glatter, R. and Levacic, R. (eds.) (1994) *Improving Educational Management through Research and Consultancy*, London: Paul Chapman Publishing.

Bennis, W. (1984) 'Transformative power and leadership', in Sergiovanni, T.J. and Corbally, J.E. (eds.) *Leadership and Organizational Culture: New Perspectives on Administrative Theory and Practice*, Urbana, IL: University of Illinois Press.

Bliss, J.R. (1991) 'Strategic and holistic images of effective schools', in Bliss, J.R., Firestone, W.A. and Richards, C.E. (eds.) *Rethinking Effective Schools Research and Practice*, Englewood Cliffs, NJ: Prentice Hall.

Bolam, R. (1990) 'Recent developments in England and Wales', in Joyce, B. (ed.) *Changing School Culture through Staff Development: The 1990 ASCD Yearbook*, Alexandria, VI: Association for Supervision and Curriculum Development.

Bolman, L.G. and Deal, T.E. (1991) *Reframing Organizations: Artistry, Choice and Leadership*, San Francisco, CA: Jossey-Bass.

Bolman, L.G. and Deal, T.E. (1994) 'Looking for leadership: another search party's report', *Educational Administration Quarterly*, 30(1), 77–96.

Bower, M. (1966) *The Will to Manage*, New York: McGraw-Hill.

Bowles, G. (1989) 'Marketing and promotion: aspects of marketing in schools', in Fidler, B. and Bowles, G. (eds.) *Effective Local Management of Schools*, Harlow: Longman.

Boyatzsis, R. (1982) *The Competent Manager*, New York: Wiley.

Braund, C. (1989) 'Income generation: aspects of income generation', in Fidler, B. and Bowles, G. (eds.) *Effective Local Management of Schools*, Harlow: Longman.

Brown, M., Taylor, J. and Whittaker, R. (1996) 'Achieving school improvement through "Investors in People"', in Earley, P., Fidler, B. and Ouston, J. (eds.) *Improvement through Inspection? Complementary Approaches to School Development*, London: David Fulton.

Bryson, J.M. (1988) *Strategic Planning for Public and Nonprofit Organizations: A Guide to Strengthening and Sustaining Organizational Achievement*, San Francisco, CA: Jossey-Bass.

Bryson, J.M. and Roering, W.D. (1987) 'Applying private-sector strategic planning in the public sector', *American Planning Association Journal*, Winter, 9–22.

Burns, J.M. (1978) *Leadership*, New York: Harper & Row.

Burns, T. and Stalker, G.M. (1961) *The Management of Innovation*, London: Tavistock Publications.

Bush, T. (1995) *Theories of Educational Management* (2nd edn.), London: Paul Chapman Publishing.

Caldwell, B. and Spinks, J. (1988) *The Self-Managing School*, Lewes: Falmer Press.

Carlson, R.O. (1975) 'Environmental Constraints and Organisational Consequences in the Public School and its Clients', in Baldridge, J.V. and Deal, T. (eds.) *Managing Change in Educational Organizations*, Berkeley, CA: Jossey-Bass.

Carnall, C. (1990) *Managing Change*, London: Routledge.

Chin, R. and Benne, K.D. (1976) 'General strategies for effecting changes in human systems', in Bennis, W.G., Benne, K.D., Chin, R. and Corey, K.E. (eds.) *The Planning of Change* (3rd edn.), New York: Holt, Rinehart & Winston.

Cleland, G. (1996) 'Developing the effectiveness of senior management teams through the use of school management competencies', in Earley, P., Fidler, B. and Ouston, J. (eds.) *Improvement through Inspection? Complementary Approaches to School Development*, London: David Fulton.

Cohen, D.K., March, J.G. and Olsen, J.P. (1972) 'A garbage can model of organizational choice', *Administrative Science Quarterly*, 17(1), 1–25.

Coleman, J.S., Campbell, E.Q., Hobson, C.J., McPartland, J., Mood, A.M., Weinfeld, F.D. and York, R.L. (1966) *Equality of Educational Opportunity*, Washington, DC: US Department of Health, Education and Welfare, Office of Education, National Center for Educational Statistics.

Constable, H., Norton, J. and Abbott, I. (1991) *Case Studies in School Development Planning*, Sunderland: Sunderland Polytechnic School of Education.

Conway, J.A. (1984) 'The myth, mystery, and mastery of participative decision making in education', *Educational Administration Quarterly*, 20(3), 11–40.

Conway, K. (1992) A-level Analysis for Added Value—Good Value for . . . Students, Huddersfield: Greenhead College.

Cuban, L. (1984) 'Transforming the frog into a prince: effective schools research, policy, and practice at the district level', *Harvard Educational Review*, 54(2), 129–151.

Curtis, S.J. (1948) *History of Education in Great Britain*, Cambridge: University Tutorial Press.

Cyert, R.M. and March, J.G. (1963) *A Behavioral Theory of the Firm*, Englewood Cliffs, NJ: Prentice-Hall.

Davies, T.I. (1969) *School Organisation: A New Synthesis*, Oxford: Pergamon.

Deal, T.E. and Kennedy, A.A. (1988) *Corporate Cultures: The Rites and Rituals of Corporate Life*, London: Penguin Books.

DES (1987) *School Teachers' Pay and Conditions Document*, London: HMSO.

References

DES (1989) *Planning for School Development: Advice to Governors, Headteachers and Teachers*, London: DES.

DES (1991) *Development Planning: A Practical Guide: Advice to Governors, Headteachers and Teachers*, London: DES.

Devlin, T. and Knight, B. (1990) *Public Relations and Marketing for Schools*, Harlow: Longman.

DFE (1993) *Teachers' Qualifications and Deployment in Maintained Secondary Schools in England 1992 (Statistical Bulletin 24/93)*, London: DFE.

DFE (1994a) *Grants for Education Support and Training 1995–96 (Circular 18/94)*, London: DFE.

DFE (1994b) *Circular on the Supply of School Places (Circular 23/94)*, London: DFE.

DFE (1995a) *Improving Schools: Factsheets*, London: DFE.

DFE (1995b) *Value Added in Education: A Briefing Paper from the Department for Education*, London: DFE.

DFE (1995c) *GCSE to GCE A/AS Value Added: Briefing for Schools and Colleges*, London: DFE.

DFE (1995d) *Grants for Education Support and Training 1996–97 (Circular 8/95)*, London: DFE.

DFEE (1995a) *The Improvement of Failing Schools: UK Policy and Practice 1993–1995* (OECD UK Seminar November 1995), London: DFEE/OFSTED.

DFEE (1995b) *Benchmarking School Budgets: Sharing Good Practice*, London: DFEE.

DFEE (1995c) *Technology College Applications: A Guide for Schools*, London: DFEE.

DFEE (1996) *Language Colleges: A Guide for Schools*, London: DFEE.

Duignan, P.A. and Macpherson, R.J.S. (1992) 'A practical theory of educative leadership', in Duignan, P.A. and Macpherson, R.J.S. (eds.) *Educative Leadership: A Practical Theory for New Administrators and Managers*, London: Falmer Press.

Earley, P. (1992a) *School Management Competences Project: Final Report*, Crawley: School Management South.

Earley, P. (1992b) *School Management Competences Project: Standards for School Management* (3rd draft), Crawley: School Management South.

Earley, P. (1992c) *School Management Competences Project: A Guide to Evidence Collection and Assessment*, Crawley: School Management South.

Earley, P., Fidler, B. and Ouston, J. (eds.) (1996) *Improvement through Inspection? Complementary Approaches to School Development*, London: David Fulton.

Edmonds, R.R. (1979) 'Effective schools for the urban poor', *Educational Leadership*, 37(1), 15–24.

Eigerman, M.R. (1988) 'Who should be responsible for business strategy?', *Journal of Business Strategy*, November/December, 40–44.

Emmanuel, C. and Otley, D. (1985) *Accounting for Management Control*, Wokingham, Berks: Van Nostrand Reinhold.

Esp, D. (1992) *Competences for School Managers*, London: Kogan Page.

Everard, B. (1988) 'Training and consultancy: lessons from industry', in Gray, H.L. (ed.) *Management Consultancy in Schools*, London: Cassell.

Everard, K.B. (1986) *Developing Management in Schools*, Oxford: Basil Blackwell.

Everard, K.B. and Morris, G. (1990) *Effective School Management*, 2nd Edition, London: Paul Chapman Publishing.

Fidler, B. (1989) 'Strategic management in schools', in Fidler, B. and Bowles, G. (eds.) *Effective Local Management of Schools*, Harlow: Longman.

Fidler, B. (1992a) 'Handling poor performers', in Fidler, B. and Cooper, R. (eds.) *Staff Appraisal and Staff Management in Schools and Colleges: A Guide to Implementation*, Harlow: Longman.

Fidler, B. (1992b) 'Job descriptions and organisational structure', in Fidler, B. and Cooper, R. (eds.) *Staff Appraisal and Staff Management in Schools and Colleges: A Guide to Implementation*, Harlow: Longman.

Fidler, B. (1992c) 'How to get the top job', *Times Educational Supplement*, 21 February 1992, p. 17.

Fidler, B. (1994) 'Partnership in teacher education: partnership, integration and funding implications', in McCulloch, M. and Fidler, B. (eds.) *Improving Initial Teacher Training? New Roles for Teachers, Schools and Higher Education*, Harlow: Longman.

Fidler, B. (1996a) 'School development planning and strategic planning for school improvement', in Earley, P., Fidler, B. and Ouston, J. (eds.) *Improvement through Inspection? Complementary Approaches to School Development*, London: David Fulton.

Fidler, B. (1996b) 'The case for school leadership', in Watson, K. and Modgil, S. (eds.) *Educational Dilemmas: Debate and Diversity, Vol. 3: Power and Responsibility*, London: Cassell, forthcoming.

Fidler, B. and Bowles, G. (eds.) (1989) *Effective Local Management of Schools: A Strategic Approach*, Harlow: Longman.

Fidler, B. and Bowles, G. with Hart, J. (1991) *ELMS Workbook: Planning Your School's Strategy*, Harlow: Longman.

Fidler, B., Earley, P. and Ouston, J. (1995) 'OFSTED school inspections and their impact on school development', Paper presented at the ECER/BERA Annual Conference, Bath.

Fidler, B., Ouston, J. and Earley, P. (1994) 'OFSTED inspections and their contribution to school development', Paper presented at the BERA Annual Conference, Oxford.

Firestone, W.A. (1991a) 'Introduction', in Bliss, J.R., Firestone, W.A. and Richards, C.E. (eds.) *Rethinking Effective Schools Research and Practice*, Englewood Cliffs, NJ: Prentice Hall.

Firestone, W.A. (1991b) 'Educators, researchers, and the effective schools movement', in Bliss, J.R., Firestone, W.A. and Richards, C.E. (eds.) *Rethinking Effective Schools Research and Practice*, Englewood Cliffs, NJ: Prentice Hall.

Firestone, W.A. and Wilson, B.L. (1985) 'Using bureaucratic and cultural linkages to improve instruction: the principal's contribution', *Educational Administration Quarterly*, 21(2), 7–30.

Fletcher, J. (1994) 'Learning from business: core process re-engineering', Paper presented at the BEMAS Annual Conference, UMIST.

Fullan, M. (1989) 'Managing curriculum change', in Preedy, M. (ed.) *Approaches to Curriculum Management*, Milton Keynes: Open University Press.

Fullan, M.G. (1986) 'The management of change' in Hoyle, E. and McMahon, A. (eds.) *The Management of Schools: World Yearbook of Education 1986*, London: Kogan Page.

Fullan, M.G. (1991) *The New Meaning of Educational Change*, London: Cassell.

Fullan, M.G. (1992) *Successful School Improvement* (with a critical introduction by M. Huberman), Buckingham: Open University Press.

Fullan, M., Miles, M.B. and Taylor, G. (1981) *Organizational Development in Schools: The State of the Art*, Washington, DC: National Institute of Education.

Giles, C. (1995a) 'Marketing, parental choice and strategic planning; an opportunity or dilemma for UK schools?', *International Journal of Educational Reform*, 4(1), 25–28.

Giles, C. (1995b) 'School-based planning: are UK schools grasping the strategic initiative?', *International Journal of Educational Management*, 19(5).

Gleick, J. (1988) *Chaos: Making a New Science*, London: William Heinemann.

Glogg, M. and Fidler, B. (1990) 'Using examination results as performance indicators', *Education Management and Administration*, 18(4), 38–48.

References

Glover, D., Levacic, R., Bennett, N. and Earley, P. (1996) 'Leadership, planning and resource management in four very effective schools', *School Organisation*, 16)2), forthcoming.

Gray, H.L. (1988) 'Management consultancy in education: an introduction to practice', in Gray, H.L. (ed.) *Management Consultancy in Schools*, London: Cassell.

Gray, H. (1993) 'OD revisited', *Educational Change and Development*, 14(1), 49–56.

Gray, J. and Wilcox, B. (1995) *'Good Schools, Bad Schools': Evaluating Performance and Encouraging Improvement*, Buckingham: Open University Press.

Griffiths, A. (1995) 'The management of the National Curriculum in a small secondary school with special reference to science as a core subject and modern foreign languages as a foundation subject', unpublished MSc dissertation, University of Reading.

Grundy, T. (1993) *Implementing Strategic Change*, London: Kogan Page.

Hales, C.P. (1986) 'What do managers do? a critical review of the evidence', *Journal of Management Studies*, 23(1), 88–115.

Hallinger and Murphy (1985) 'Instructional leadership and socioeconomic status: a preliminary investigation', *Administrator's Notebook*, 31(5), 1–4.

Hammer, M. and Champy, J. (1993) *Reengineering the Corporation: A Manifesto for Business Revolution*, London: Nicholas Brealey.

Handy, C.B. (1985) *Understanding Organisations*, 3rd Edition, Harmondsworth, Middx: Penguin Books.

Handy, C. and Aitken, R. (1986) *Understanding Schools as Organisations*, Harmondsworth, Middx: Penguin Books.

Hargreaves, D.H. (1995) 'Self-managing schools and development planning—chaos or control?', *School Organisation*, 15(3), 215–227.

Hargreaves, D.H. and Hopkins, D. (1991) *The Empowered School: The Management and Practice of Development Planning*, London: Cassell.

Harvey-Jones, J. (1988) *Making It Happen: Reflections on Leadership*, Glasgow: Fontana/Collins.

Hatten, M.L. (1982) 'Strategic management in not-for-profit organizations', *Strategic Management Journal*, 3, 89–104.

Healy, M. (1994) 'BS 5750 and beyond in a secondary school: a chance for the best', in Parsons, C. (ed.) *Quality Improvement in Education: Case Studies in Schools, Colleges and Universities*, London: David Fulton.

Heath, A. and Clifford, P. (1980) 'The seventy thousand hours that Rutter left out', *Oxford Review of Education*, 6(1), 3–19.

Hersey, P. and Blanchard, K. (1988) *Management of Organizational Behavior: Utilizing Human Resources* (5th edn.), Englewood Cliffs, NJ: Prentice-Hall.

Hinkley, T. and Seddon, J. (1996) 'The Deming approach to school improvement', in Earley, P., Fidler, B. and Ouston, J. (eds.), *Improvement through Inspection? Complementary Approaches to School Development*, London: David Fulton.

Hopkins, D., Ainscow, M. and West, M. (1994) *School Improvement in an ERA of Change*, London: Cassell.

Horine, J.E. and Lingren, C.E. (1995) 'Educational improvement using Deming's profound knowledge', *New Era in Education*, 76(1), 6–11.

House of Commons (1992) *Choice and Diversity: A New Framework for Schools*, Cm 2021, London: HMSO.

House of Commons (1994) *Education Committee Session 1993–94: Disparity in Funding Between Primary and Secondary Schools*, London: HMSO.

Hoy, W.K. and Miskel, C.G. (1978) *Educational Administration: Theory, Research and Practice*, New York: Random House.

Hoy, W.K. and Miskel, C.G. (1991) *Education Administration: Theory, Research and Practice* (4th edn.), New York: McGraw-Hill.

Hoyle, E. (1986) *The Politics of School Management*, London: Hodder & Stoughton.

Huberman, M. (1992) 'Critical introduction' to Fullan, M.G. *Successful School Improvement*, Buckingham: Open University Press.

Huberman, A.M. and Miles, M.B. (1984) *Innovation up Close: How School Improvement Works*, New York: Plenum.

Hughes, M. (1985) 'Theory and practice in educational management', in Hughes, M., Ribbins, P. and Thomas, H. (eds.) *Managing Education: The System and the Institution*, London: Cassell.

Hugill, B. (1995) '25 private schools bid to rejoin state fold', *Observer*, 2 April 1995.

Hutchinson, P. (1993) 'The coupling of financial and curriculum decision making in two comprehensive schools', unpublished MSc dissertation, University of Reading.

ILEA (1977) *Keeping The School Under Review—A Method of Self Assessment*, London: ILEA.

Ireland, R.D., Hitt, M.A., Bettis, R.A. and De Porras, D.A. (1987) 'Strategy formulation processes: differences in perceptions of strength and weaknesses indicators and environmental uncertainties by managerial level', *Strategic Management Journal*, 8, 469–485.

Ishikawa, K. (1990) *Introduction to Quality Control*, London: Chapman and Hall.

Jamieson, I. (1988) 'Consultancy in the management of curriculum development', in Gray, H.L. (ed.) *Management Consultancy in Schools*, London: Cassell.

Jencks, C., Smith, M., Ackland, H., Bane, M., Cohen, D., Gintis, H., Heyns, B. and Michelson, S. (1972) *Inequality: A Reassessment of the Effect of Family and Schooling in America*, New York: Basic Books.

Jenkins, H.O. (1985) 'Job perceptions of senior managers in schools and manufacturing industry', *Educational Management and Administration*, 13(1), 1–11.

Jirasinghe, D. and Lyons, G. (1995) 'Management competencies in action: a practical framework', *School Organisation*, 15(3), 267–281.

Johnson, G. (1987) *Strategic Change and the Management Process*, Oxford: Basil Blackwell.

Johnson, G. and Scholes, K. (1984) *Exploring Corporate Strategy*, Hemel Hempstead, Herts: Prentice Hall.

Johnson, G. and Scholes, K. (1988) *Exploring Corporate Strategy* (2nd edn.), Hemel Hempstead, Herts: Prentice Hall.

Johnson, G. and Scholes, K. (1993) *Exploring Corporate Strategy* (3rd edn.), Hemel Hempstead, Herts: Prentice Hall.

Jones, A. (1987) *Leadership for Tomorrow's Schools*, Oxford: Basil Blackwell.

Joyce, B. (1991) 'The doors to school improvement', *School Leadership*, 48(8), 59–62.

Joyce, B. and Showers, B. (1988) *Student Achievement through Staff Development*, New York: Longman.

Kanter, R.M. (1989) *When Giants Learn to Dance: Mastering the Challenge of Strategic Management and Careers in the 1990s*, Englewood Cliffs, NJ: Simon & Schuster.

Kast, F.E. and Rosenzweig, J.E. (1970) *Organization and Management: A Systems Approach*, New York: McGraw-Hill.

Kaufman, R. (1995) *Mapping Educational Success: Strategic Thinking and Planning for School Administrators*, Thousand Oaks, CA: Corwin.

Kaufman, R. and Herman, J. (1991) *Strategic Planning in Education*, Lancaster, PA: Technomic.

References

Knight, B. (1987) 'Managing the honeypots', in Thomas, H. and Simkins, T. (eds) *Economics and the Management of Education: Emerging Themes*, Lewes: Falmer Press.

Knight, B. (1989) *Managing School Time*, Harlow: Longman.

Knight, B. (1993) *Financial Management for School: The Thinking Manager's Guide*, London: Heinemann.

Leithwood, K. (1990) 'The principal's role in teacher development', in Joyce, B. (ed.) *Changing School Culture Through Staff Development: The 1990 ASCD Yearbook*, Alexandria, VA: Association for Supervision and Curriculum Development.

Leithwood, K., Begley, P.T. and Cousins, J.B. (1994) *Developing Expert Leadership for Future Schools*, London: Falmer Press.

Leithwood, K., Jantzi, D. and Steinbach, R. (1995) 'An organisational learning perspective on school response to central policy initiatives', *School Organisation*, 15(3), 229–252.

Levine, D.U. and Lezotte, L.W. (1990) *Unusually Effective Schools: A Review and Analysis of Research and Practice*, Madison, WI: The National Centre for Effective Schools Research and Development.

Lewin, K. (1947) 'Frontiers in group dynamics: concept, method and reality in social science; social equilibria and social change', *Human Relations*, 1(1), 5–41.

LGMB (1994) *Performance Benchmarking for Schools: Commentary by the National Employers' Organisation for School Teachers*, London: Local Government Management Board.

Lippitt, G. and Lippitt, R. (1978) *The Consulting Process in Action* (2nd edn.), San Diego, CA: University Associates.

Loucks-Horsley, S. and Mundry, S. (1991) 'Assisting change from without: the technical assistance function', in Bliss, J.R., Firestone, W.A. and Richards, C.E. (eds.) *Rethinking Effective Schools Research and Practice*, Englewood Cliffs, NJ: Prentice Hall.

Louis, K.S. (1981) 'External agents and knowledge utilization: dimensions for analysis and action', in Lehming, R. and Kane, M. (eds.) *Improving Schools: Using What We Know*, Beverly Hills, CA: Sage.

Louis, K.S. and Miles, M.B. (1991) 'Towards effective urban high schools: the importance of planning and coping', in Bliss, J.R., Firestone, W.A. and Richards, C.E. (eds.) *Rethinking Effective Schools Research and Practice*, Englewood Cliffs, NJ: Prentice Hall.

Louis, K.S. and Miles, M.B. (1992) *Improving the Urban High School: What Works and Why*, London: Cassell.

Macdonald, J. (1995) *Understanding Business Process Re-engineering in a Week*, Corby: Institute of Management.

MacGilchrist, B., Mortimore, P., Savage, J. and Beresford, C. (1995) *Planning Matters: The Impact of Development Planning in Primary Schools*, London: Paul Chapman Publishing.

Matthews, P. and Smith, G. (1995) 'OFSTED: inspecting schools and improvement through inspection', *Cambridge Journal of Education*, 25(1), 23–34.

Maughan, B., Mortimore, P., Ouston, J. and Rutter, M. (1980) 'Fifteen thousand hours: a reply to Heath and Clifford', *Oxford Review of Education*, 6(3), 289–303.

McCane, S.D. (1986) *Guide to Strategic Planning for Educators*, Alexandria, VA: Association for Supervision and Curriculum Development.

MCI (1995) *Senior Management Standards*, London: Management Charter Initiative.

McMahon, A., Bolam, R., Abbott, R. and Holly, P. (1984) *Guidelines for Review and Internal Development in Schools (GRIDS): Primary and Secondary Handbooks*, York: Longman for Schools Council.

McPherson, A. (1992) *Measuring Added Value in Schools: NCE Briefing Paper No. 1*, London: National Commission on Education.

Mendelow, A. (1981) 'Environmental scanning: the impact of stockholder concept', *Proceedings of 2nd International Conference on Information Systems*, Cambridge, MA.

Miles, M.B. and Ekholm, M. (1985) 'What is School Improvement?' in Van Velzen, W.G., Miles, M.B., Ekholm, M., Hameyer, U. and Robin, D. (eds.) *Making School Improvement Work: A Conceptual Guide to Practice*, Leuven, Belgium: ACCO.

Miller, D. (1990) *The Icarus Paradox*, New York: Harper Business.

Miller, D. (1994) 'What happens after success: the perils of excellence', *Journal of Management Studies*, 31(3), 325–358.

Mintzberg, H. (1978) 'Patterns in strategy formation', *Management Science*, 24(9), 934–948.

Mintzberg, H. (1990) 'Strategy formation: schools of thought', in Frederickson, J. (ed.) *Perspectives on Strategic Management*, Boston, MA: Ballinger.

Mintzberg, H. (1994) *The Rise and Fall of Strategic Planning*, Hemel Hempstead: Prentice Hall.

Montanari, J.R., Morgan, C.P. and Bracker, J.S. (1990) *Strategic Management: A Choice Approach*, Chicago: The Dryden Press.

Morris, G. (1988) 'Applying business consultancy approaches to schools', in Gray, H.L. (ed.) *Management Consultancy in Schools*, London: Cassell.

Morris, R. (1995) *School Choice in England and Wales: An Exploration of the Legal and Administrative Background*, Slough: NFER/EMIE.

Mort, P.R. and Ross, D.H. (1957) *Principles of School Administration: A Synthesis of Basic Concepts* (2nd edn.), New York: McGraw-Hill.

Mortimore, P. (1991) 'The nature and findings of research on school effectiveness in the primary sector', in Riddell, S. and Brown, S. (eds.) *School Effectiveness Research: Its Messages for School Improvement*, Edinburgh: HMSO.

Mortimore, P., Sammons, P., Stoll, L., Lewis, D. and Ecob, R. (1988) *School Matters: The Junior Years*, Wells, Somerset: Open Books.

Murgatroyd, S. (1988) 'Consulting as counselling: the theory and practice of structural consulting', in Gray, H.L. (ed.) *Management Consultancy in Schools*, London: Cassell.

Murgatroyd, S. (1993) 'Implementing total quality management in the school: challenges and opportunity', *School Organisation*, 13(3), 269–281.

Murgatroyd, S. and Morgan, C. (1992) *Total Quality Management and the School*, Buckingham: Open University Press.

National Audit Office (1994) *Value for Money at Grant-Maintained Schools: A Review of Performance, Appendix 3: Strategic Planning and Budgeting in Grant-Maintained Schools*, London: HMSO.

Newton, M. (1986) *The Management of Teacher Substitution in Secondary Schools*, Sheffied: Sheffield City Polytechnic.

Noble, T. and Pym, B. (1970) 'Collegial authority and the receding locus of power', *British Journal of Sociology*, 21, 431–445.

Oakland, J.S. (1993) *Total Quality Management: The Route to Improving Performance*, Oxford: Butterworth Heinemann.

OFSTED (1992) *The Handbook for the Inspection of Schools*, London: HMSO.

OFSTED (1994a) *The Handbook for the Inspection of Schools*, London: HMSO.

OFSTED (1994b) *Improving Schools*, London: HMSO.

OFSTED (1995a) *The OFSTED Framework: Framework for the Inspections of Nursery, Primary, Secondary and Special Schools*, London: HMSO.

OFSTED (1995b) *Update: Fifteenth Issue*, London: OFSTED.

References

OFSTED (1995c) *Planning Improvement: Schools' Post-inspection Plans*, London: HMSO.

O'Looney, J. (1993) 'Redesigning the work of education', *Phi Delta Kappan*, 74(5), January, 375–381.

Olsen, J.B. and Eadie, D.C. (1982) *The Game Plan: Governance with Foresight*, Washington, DC: Council of State Planning Agencies.

Ouston, J., Earley, P. and Fidler, B. (eds.) (1996) *OFSTED Inspections: The Early Experience*, London: David Fulton.

Ouston, J., McMeeking, S. and Haddow, P. (1992) 'Schools and honeypot management: the impact of project funding mechanisms on the implementation of educational innovations', *Educational Management and Administration*, 20(3), 170–178.

Owens, R.G. (1991) *Organizational Behavior in Education* (4th edn.), Boston, MA: Allyn & Bacon.

Pascale, R. (1991) *Managing on the Edge: How Successful Companies Use Conflict to Stay Ahead*, London: Penguin Books.

Paterson, L. (1991) 'Socio-economic status and educational attainment: a multi-dimensional and multi-level study', *Evaluation and Research in Education*, 5(3), 97–121.

Patterson, J.L., Purkey, S.C. and Parker, J.V. (1986) *Productive School Systems for a Nonrational World*, Alexandria, VA: Association for Supervision and Curriculum.

Peters, T.J. and Waterman, R.H. (1982) *In Search of Excellence: Lessons from America's Best-Run Companies*, New York: Harper & Row.

Pocklington, K. and Weindling, D. (1996) 'Improving schools through organisational development', in Earley, P., Fidler, B. and Ouston, J. (eds.) *Improvement through Inspection? Complementary Approaches to School Development*, London: David Fulton.

Porter, M.E. (1985) *Competitive Advantage: Creating and Sustaining Superior Performance*, New York: The Free Press.

Quinn, J.B. (1980) *Strategies for Change: Logical Incrementalism*, Homewood, IL: Irwin.

Quinn, J.B., Mintzberg, H. and James, R.M. (1988) *The Strategy Process: Concepts, Contexts and Cases*, Englewood Cliffs, NJ: Prentice Hall.

Reynolds, D. (1992) 'School effectiveness and school improvement: an updated review of the British literature', in Reynolds, D. and Cuttance, P. (eds.) *School Effectiveness: Research, Policy and Practice*, London: Cassell.

Ribbins, P. (1985) 'Organisation theory and the study of educational institutions', in Hughes, M., Ribbins, P. and Thomas, H. (eds.) *Managing Education: The System and the Institution*, London: Cassell.

Richards, C.E. (1991) 'The meaning and measure of school effectiveness', in Bliss, J.R., Firestone, W.A. and Richards, C.E. (eds.) *Rethinking Effective Schools Research and Practice*, Englewood Cliffs, NJ: Prentice Hall.

Rose, J. (1995) 'OFSTED inspection—who is it for?', *Education Review*, 9(1), 63–66.

Rutter, M., Maughan, B., Mortimore, P. and Ouston, J. (1979) *Fifteen Thousand Hours: Secondary Schools and their Effects on Children*, London: Open Books.

Sallis, E. (1993) *Total Quality Management in Education*, London: Kogan Page.

Sallis, E. and Hingley, P. (1991) *College Quality Assurance Systems*, Blagdon, Bristol: The Staff College.

Sammons, P., Hillman, J. and Mortimore, P. (1995) *Key Characteristics of Effective Schools: A Review of School Effectiveness Research*, London: OFSTED.

Sapienza, A.M. (1985) 'Believing is seeing: how culture influences the decisions top managers make', in Kilmann, R.H., Saxton, M.J., Serpa, R. and Associates, *Gaining Control of the Corporate Culture*, San Francisco, CA: Jossey-Bass.

SCAA (1993) *The National Curriculum and its Assessment: Final Report* (Chairman Sir Ron Dearing), London: Schools Curriculum and Assessment Authority.

SCAA (1994) *Value-Added Performance Indicators for Schools*, London: SCAA.

Schein, E.H. (1985) *Organizational Culture and Leadership: A Dynamic View*, San Francisco, CA: Jossey-Bass.

Schein, E.H. (1992) *Organizational Culture and Leadership* (2nd edn.), San Francisco, CA: Jossey-Bass.

Schmuck, R.A. and Runkel, P.J. (1985) *The Handbook of Organization Development in Schools* (3rd edn.), Prospect Heights, IL: Waveland Press.

Schmuck, R.A., Runkel, P.J., Saturen, S.L., Martell, R.T. and Derr, C.B. (1972) *Handbook of Organization Development in Schools*, Palo Alto, CA: Mayfield Publishing Company.

Schon, D.A. (1983) *The Reflective Practitioner: How Professionals Think in Action*, London: Maurice Temple Smith.

Schon, D.A. (1984) 'Leadership as reflection-in-action', in Sergiovanni, T.J. and Corbally, J.E. (eds.) *Leadership and Organizational Culture: New Perspectives on Administrative Theory and Practice*, Urbana, IL: University of Illinois Press.

Schon, D.A. (1987) *Educating the Reflective Practitioner: Towards a New Design for Teaching and Learning in the Professions*, San Francisco, CA: Jossey-Bass.

Scott-Clark, C. and Hymas, C. (1995) 'Primary aim for secondaries', *Sunday Times*, 2 April 1995, p. 11.

SEC (1995) *Membership Directory 1995/96*, Coventry: Society of Education Consultants.

Sergiovanni, T.J. (1990) *Value Added Leadership: How to Get Extraordinary Performance in Schools*, New York: Harcourt Brace Jovanovich.

Sergiovanni, T.J. (1991) *The Principalship: A Reflective Practice Perspective* (2nd edn.), Boston, MA: Allyn and Bacon.

Simkins, T. (1981) *Economics and the Management of Resources in Education*, Sheffield: Sheffield City Polytechnic.

Simkins, T. and Lancaster, D. (1987) *Budgeting and Resource Allocation in Educational Institutions*, Sheffield: Sheffield City Polytechnic.

Slavin, R.E. (1989) 'PET and the pendulum: faddism in education and how to stop it', *Phi Delta Kappan*, June, 752–758.

Stacey, R.D. (1993) *Strategic Management and Organisational Dynamics*, London: Pitman.

Steiner, G.A. (1979) *Strategic Planning: What Every Manager Must Know*, New York: The Free Press.

Stevenson, H.H. (1976) 'Defining corporate strengths and weaknesses', *Sloan Management Review*, Spring, 51–68.

Stewart, R. (1976) *Contrasts in Management*, Maidenhead: McGraw-Hill.

Stewart, R. (1982) *Choices for Managers*, Maidenhead: McGraw-Hill.

Stewart, R. (1989) 'Studies of managerial jobs and behaviour: the ways forward', *Journal of Management Studies*, 26(1), 1–10.

Straker, A. (1988) *School Development Planning*, Reading: Berkshire County Council.

Swieringa, J. and Wierdsma, A. (1992) *Becoming a Learning Organization: Beyond the Learning Curve*, Wokingham: Addison-Wesley.

Thomas, P. (1996) 'The experience of working towards "Investors In People" in a comprehensive school', in Earley, P., Fidler, B. and Ouston, J. (eds.) *Improvement through Inspection? Complementary Approaches to School Development*, London: David Fulton.

References

Toft, G.S. (1989) 'Synoptic (one best way) approaches to strategic management', in Rabin, J., Miller, G.J. and Hildreth, W.B. (eds.) *Handbook of Strategic Management*, New York: Marcel Dekker.

Torrington, D. and Weightman, J. (1989) *The Reality of School Management*, Oxford: Blackwell Educational.

Tovey, P. (1994) *Quality Assurance in Continuing Professional Education: An Analysis*, London: Routledge.

TTA (1995a) *Headteachers' Leadership and Management Programme (HEADLAMP)*, London: Teacher Training Agency.

TTA (1995b) *National Professional Qualification for Headteachers*, London: Teacher Training Agency.

TTA (1995c) *Teacher Training Agency Announces National Strategy for Continuing Professional Development* (TTA17/95), London: Teacher Training Agency.

Wallace, M. (1991) 'Contradictory interests in policy implementation: the case of LEA development plans for schools', *Journal of Education Policy*, 6(4), 385–399.

Warner, M. (1994) 'Towards clarification in determining school strategy', *School Organisation*, 14(2), 219–233.

Watson, T. (1994) *In Search of Management*, London: Routledge.

Weindling, D. and Earley, P. (1987) *Secondary Headship: The First Years*, Windsor: NFER-Nelson.

West-Burnham, J. (1992a) 'Total Quality Management in education', in Bennett, N., Crawford, M. and Riches, C. (eds.) *Managing Change in Education: Individual and Organizational Perspectives*, London: Paul Chapman Publishing.

West-Burnham, J. (1992b) *Managing Quality in Schools: A TQM Approach*, Harlow: Longman.

Wheelan, T.L. and Hunger, J.D. (1990) *Strategic Management* (3rd edn.), Reading, MA: Addison-Wesley.

Whittington, R. (1993) *What Is Strategy and Does It Matter?*, London: Routledge.

Wilkins, A.L. and Patterson, K.J. (1985) 'You can't get there from here: what will make culture-change projects fail', in Kilmann, R.H., Saxton, M.J., Serpa, R. and Associates, *Gaining Control of the Corporate Culture*, San Francisco, CA: Jossey-Bass.

Williamson, J. and Fitz-Gibbon, C.T. (1990) 'The lack of impact of information: performance indicators for A levels', *Educational Management and Administration*, 18(1), 37–45.

Willmott, H. (1993) 'Strength is ignorance; slavery is freedom: managing culture in modern organizations', *Journal of Management Studies*, 30(4), 515–552.

Willms, J.D. (1992) *Monitoring School Performance: A Guide for Educators*, Lewes: Falmer Press.

Zienau, N. (1996) '"Investors In People": the consultant's view', in Earley, P., Fidler, B. and Ouston, J. (eds.), *Improvement through Inspection? Complementary Approaches to School Development*, London: David Fulton.

Index

Index